Java Closures and Lambda

Robert Fischer

Apress®

Java Closures and Lambda

Copyright © 2015 by Robert Fischer

This work is subject to copyright. All rights are reserved by the Publisher, whether the whole or part of the material is concerned, specifically the rights of translation, reprinting, reuse of illustrations, recitation, broadcasting, reproduction on microfilms or in any other physical way, and transmission or information storage and retrieval, electronic adaptation, computer software, or by similar or dissimilar methodology now known or hereafter developed. Exempted from this legal reservation are brief excerpts in connection with reviews or scholarly analysis or material supplied specifically for the purpose of being entered and executed on a computer system, for exclusive use by the purchaser of the work. Duplication of this publication or parts thereof is permitted only under the provisions of the Copyright Law of the Publisher's location, in its current version, and permission for use must always be obtained from Springer. Permissions for use may be obtained through RightsLink at the Copyright Clearance Center. Violations are liable to prosecution under the respective Copyright Law.

ISBN-13 (pbk): 978-1-4302-5998-5

ISBN-13 (electronic): 978-1-4302-5999-2

Trademarked names, logos, and images may appear in this book. Rather than use a trademark symbol with every occurrence of a trademarked name, logo, or image we use the names, logos, and images only in an editorial fashion and to the benefit of the trademark owner, with no intention of infringement of the trademark.

The use in this publication of trade names, trademarks, service marks, and similar terms, even if they are not identified as such, is not to be taken as an expression of opinion as to whether or not they are subject to proprietary rights.

While the advice and information in this book are believed to be true and accurate at the date of publication, neither the authors nor the editors nor the publisher can accept any legal responsibility for any errors or omissions that may be made. The publisher makes no warranty, express or implied, with respect to the material contained herein.

Managing Director: Welmoed Spahr
Lead Editor: Steve Anglin
Development Editor: Deidre Miller
Technical Reviewer: John Zukowski
Editorial Board: Steve Anglin, Gary Cornell, Louise Corrigan, Jonathan Gennick, Robert Hutchinson, Michelle Lowman, James Markham, Matthew Moodie, Jeff Olson, Jeffrey Pepper, Douglas Pundick, Ben Renow-Clarke, Gwenan Spearing, Matt Wade, Steve Weiss
Coordinating Editor: Mark Powers
Copy Editor: Karen Jameson
Compositor: SPi Global
Indexer: SPi Global
Artist: SPi Global
Cover Designer: Anna Ishchenko

Distributed to the book trade worldwide by Springer Science+Business Media New York, 233 Spring Street, 6th Floor, New York, NY 10013. Phone 1-800-SPRINGER, fax (201) 348-4505, e-mail orders-ny@springer-sbm.com, or visit www.springeronline.com. Apress Media, LLC is a California LLC and the sole member (owner) is Springer Science + Business Media Finance Inc (SSBM Finance Inc). SSBM Finance Inc is a Delaware corporation.

For information on translations, please e-mail rights@apress.com, or visit www.apress.com.

Apress and friends of ED books may be purchased in bulk for academic, corporate, or promotional use. eBook versions and licenses are also available for most titles. For more information, reference our Special Bulk Sales–eBook Licensing web page at www.apress.com/bulk-sales.

Any source code or other supplementary material referenced by the author in this text is available to readers at www.apress.com/9781430259985. For detailed information about how to locate your book's source code, go to www.apress.com/source-code/.

Contents at a Glance

Contents

About the Author

Robert Fischer is a software developer, open source software contributor, technical commentator, and engineering manager. He has consulted, written, and spoken broadly on technical topics including concurrency, JVM bytecode, Groovy, Grails and Gradle, and functional programming. Robert has a Masters of Divinity degree from Duke University; works as the VP of Engineering at Webonise Lab; and lives in Durham, North Carolina, with his wife, dog, and baby girl.

About the Technical Reviewer

John Zukowski is currently a software engineer with TripAdivsor, the world's largest travel site (www.tripadvisor.com). He has been playing with Java technologies for twenty years now and is the author of ten Java-related books. His books cover Java 6, Java Swing, Java Collections, and JBuilder from Apress, Java AWT from O'Reilly, and introductory Java from Sybex. He lives outside Boston, Massachusetts, and has a master's degree in software engineering from The Johns Hopkins University. You can follow him on Twitter at http://twitter.com/javajohnz.

Acknowledgments

It's hard for non-writers to appreciate the sheer amount of work that goes into writing a text. From the long-suffering publisher, to the family members who see you only by ghastly screenlight, to friends who get tired of hearing you talk it through, writing is truly a corporate event. The author's name may be on the cover, but it is the community of people behind the author who truly allowed the book to come into being.

For this book, the team at Apress is made up of Steve Anglin, Anamika Panchoo, Mark Powers, and their group of editors. Thanks to them for giving me the opportunity to write this book, and for patience throughout the process. They made this book look and read better than I could have done on my own, and you are seeing it because of their work.

Thanks to my friend, mentor, and co-blogger, Brian Hurt, who had the wisdom in the late twentieth century to recognize functional programming as the transformative technology of the early twenty-first. This was one time, of many others, where he has set me on the right course early on.

Thanks also to the JRuby guru, Charlie Nutter (aka: Headius), who well-tolerated a young, starry-eyed developer with no love for Ruby but a deep interest in the JVM technology underlying JRuby.

More broadly, thanks to the various tech communities who made programming seem cool, and to the friends that I made there. Thanks to Object Technology Users Group (OTUG), Ruby.MN, Groovy.MN, NFJS, and TriJug. Thanks specifically to Hamlet d'Arcy, Ted Naleid, Shaun Jurgemeyer, Ben Edwards, Jesse O'Neill-Oine, Scott Vlamnick, Ryan Applegate, Brian Sletten, and David Hussman.

Thanks to my Other Mother, who did well reminding me that there was more to life than programming. If there is any charm, grace, and wit in this book, it's because she demonstrated that one can both be a geek and have social skills.

Thanks to my parents, whose Apple Macintosh was the first computer I broke, and who kicked me off the computer late at night more times than I care to remember. They banned me from the computer just enough to make it overwhelmingly enticing. The magical world constructed by computers in software has never lost its glamour.

Thanks to my wife, Ashley, who gave me the time to write the book even as our child was growing through her first year. I could not have done it without her support.

Introduction

This book is the culmination of many brash years and hard lessons. The story starts all the way back when I migrated from C++ into perl. The perl programming language was amazingly powerful compared to the low-level manipulations and bookkeeping of C++. (The fact that it was "slow" never bothered me – I would rather write powerful, effective slow code than weak, buggy fast code.) In the world of perl, there was the idea of an "anonymous subroutine" that could be passed around and manipulated. You could also directly manipulate the symbol table. The symbol table is the collection of function names available to the program. Between these two things, I realized that I could code at a higher level: I could write subroutines that returned subroutines and store those into the symbol table, effectively having my code write code at runtime. In perl, these subroutine factories are called "template functions." I proceeded to write some truly unreadable – but truly powerful – perl.

I shared this revelation with my friend and mentor, Brian Hurt. He was the grizzled veteran developer who seemed to have seen it all. Brian told me that what I was doing was this thing called "functional programming," and encouraged me to look into proper functional languages, specifically OCaml, and its derivative, JoCaml. I was immediately hooked. By 2008, I presented "Why Rubyists Should Learn OCaml" to the Ruby Users Group of Minnesota (Ruby.MN).[1] There was a power in functional programming that was truly incredible compared to the then-standard way of writing code. Moreover, my mathematical background played very nicely with functional programming: the fact that state did not change meant that I could employ the same kind of reasoning to my programs that I employed with mathematical equations. I presumed at the time that a functional programming language would rise and fundamentally transform what it means to program, much as Java ascended and made Object Oriented Programming ubiquitous. So far, this hasn't happened.

The next chapter came with the rise of the Groovy programming language. Groovy's MetaClass functionality provided a way for me to perform the same tricks as in perl, but in a way that leveraged all that existing Java code. This was having my cake and eating it, too. All that open source software that existed for Java, and all that technical expertise that had been built up on the JVM could finally mix with these "functional stunts." It wasn't functional programming – and I got in quite a bit of trouble on the Internet for saying as much – but it was certainly borrowing some powerful tricks from functional programming. We get into what was happening in chapter 1.

When Java 7 rolled out, it introduced the invokedynamic keyword (which we cover in chapter 8). The keyword was touted as being support for dynamic languages, but I recognized it for what it was: JVM support for those same functional stunts. There was no longer any technical reason why you could not perform the same functional stunts in Java itself. The Java language's syntax, however, simply could not keep up with its underlying implementation. We had to wait until Java 8. With Java 8, we finally got lambdas into the Java language itself, along with basic support for some of the most powerful functional stunts.

This is a truly exciting language change. I think it is as transformative to the Java language as the introduction of object oriented programming in the first place, and it shows that the functional stunts, which were esoteric yet impressive back in perl, are truly primed to become industry standard practices. That is why this book is so critical: it is no exaggeration to say that learning the content in this book will help you program throughout the remainder of your career. Sooner or later, you are going to have to learn to harness the power of lambdas. Might as well start now.

---

[1]http://www.youtube.com/watch?v=2T5syww4Nn4.

CHAPTER 1

■ ■ ■

Java 8: It's a Whole New Java

This book is about lambdas (closures) in Java 8. More than that, though, it's about the new language that Java has become. The revolution was not televised, and it was met with little fanfare, but it has happened. It is possible for you to continue to write the same old Java code in our new Java 8 world, but unless you get onboard with the revolution, you will increasingly discover code that is called "Java," but which has language, syntax, and customs that are foreign to you.

This book is here to help you enter into this exciting new world. You should be eager to join this brave new Java 8 world, because it will actually enable you to write code that is more succinct, more readable, and more performant: it's rare that you get all three of these wins together, but lambdas in Java 8 bring all this to the table.

To understand exactly where the new Java is coming from, let me go back into history. A long time ago in an old version of Java, a member of my team wrote a piece of code that would clone a list, but without including any of the null elements that may have been in the original list. That team member's implementation looked something like Listing 1-1. The tech lead saw that code and was not impressed, and so he rewrote it into Listing 1-2, which was longer, but both more readable and more efficient.

Listing 1-1. Original Implementation of cloneWithoutNulls(List)

```
public static <A> List<A> cloneWithoutNulls(final List<A> list) {
        List<A> out = new ArrayList<A>(list);
        while(out.remove(null)) {}
        return out;
}
```

Listing 1-2. Refined Implementation of cloneWithoutNulls(List)

```
public static <A> List<A> cloneWithoutNulls(final List<A> list) {
        List<A> out = new ArrayList<A>(list.size());
        for(A elt : list) {
                if(elt != null) out.add(e);
        }
        return out;
}
```

This is when I became responsible for that code. I reimplemented the method as something more readable to my eyes. I did so by leveraging Apache's Commons-Collections library. This creates the implementation given in Listing 1-3. The additional readability is because Commons-Collections has a way of saying, "Give me all of the collection's elements where some predicate is true."[1] Because they had this predicate infrastructure, you can express that idea succinctly. I thought that I had really made some progress in clarifying and simplifying the code. Plus, if we ever needed to add another criterion to filter on, it's easy to extend the Predicate to make that happen.

Listing 1-3. Apache Commons-Collections Implementation of cloneWithoutNulls(List)

```
public static <A> List<A> cloneWithoutNulls(final List<A> list) {
    Collection<A> nonNulls = CollectionUtils.select(list, PredicateUtils.
notNullPredicate());
    return new ArrayList<>(nonNulls);
}
```

Unfortunately, the time came when the new hot library, Google's Guava, replaced Apache Commons-Collections on this project. Guava also contains a Predicate infrastructure, but it has an entirely different package name, inheritance tree, and API than the Commons-Collections Predicate infrastructure. Because of that, we had to change the method to the new code in Listing 1-4.

Listing 1-4. Google Guava Implementation of cloneWithoutNulls(List)

```
public static <A> List<A> cloneWithoutNulls(final List<A> list) {
    Collection<A> nonNulls = Collections2.filter(list, Predicates.notNull());
    return new ArrayList<>(nonNulls);
}
```

The problem is that the Predicate infrastructure was useful, but Java didn't have it in its core, and so extensions to the standard library such as Guava and Apache Commons each ended up building their own implementations. Of course, none of these implementations are compatible with the others. The alternative JVM languages also started shipping their own (universally mutually incompatible) implementations. With Java 8, we finally have a canonical implementation of that infrastructure and a lot more with it. The directly converted Java 8 version of this code looks like Listing 1-5.

Listing 1-5. Java 8 Predicate Implementation of cloneWithoutNulls(List)

```
public static <A> List<A> cloneWithoutNulls(final List<A> list) {
    List<A> toReturn = new ArrayList<>(list);
    toReturn.removeIf(Predicate.isEqual(null));
    return toReturn;
}
```

But these predicates are not the extent of what Java 8 introduces. There's a whole new syntax to succinctly express this idea: see Listing 1-6. That right arrow? That's an example of the most exciting new feature of Java 8: it's a lambda. But it goes even further. You will increasingly see Java code that looks like Listing 1-7. In this example, we have an interface (Comparator) with static and instance methods, and some real strangeness happening involving two colons. What is going on? That's the Java 8 revolution, and that's what this book is all about.

---

[1]Unfortunately, they don't have the same capability with Lists specifically, so I had to do some work to get to the right type.

Listing 1-6. Java 8 Lambda Implementation of cloneWithoutNulls(List)

```java
public static <A> List<A> cloneWithoutNulls(final List<A> list) {
    List<A> toReturn = new ArrayList<>(list);
    toReturn.removeIf(it -> it == null);
    return toReturn;
}
```

Listing 1-7. Example of Defining a Comparator of Java 8

```java
Comparator c =
    Comparator
        .comparing(User::getLastName)
        .thenComparing(User::getFirstName);
```

Java 8 Returns Java to the Forefront

Software development is exciting because its core problems have not been solved yet: the practices, processes, and tools that go into software development are in a state of constant evolution and development. We can see this in the way that the dominant programming paradigm has changed: in the late '80s and through the '90s, the answer to every question was objects; now, programmers expect a wider palette with which to express code.

Over the course of the last decade, programmers have begun borrowing more from a paradigm called "functional programming." Whereas an object-oriented paradigm thinks about objects, and objects have behaviors, functional programming thinks in terms of verbs (functions), which act on nouns (arguments). Whereas object-oriented programming builds up a mechanism of interacting objects, functional programming builds up a function that is resolved through composite functions.

An object-oriented program can be thought of as a corporate environment. You have a CEO (the "Main Class"), who issues high-level orders. Subordinates take up these orders. Although these subordinates each have some of their own data (their own files on their computer and their own stickie notes on their desk), these subordinates mostly delegate to their own subordinates. As you get farther down this chain, the subordinates become more technical (implementation-specific), with the end of the chain performing the last precise bit of work. Then the result of the action (either an exception or a return value) is communicated back up through the chain of subordinates to the CEO, who may then issue another command.

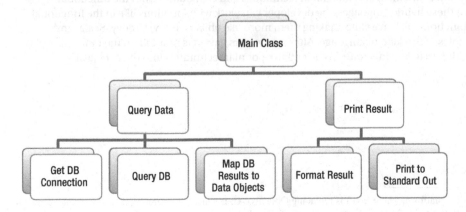

A functional program, however, is modeled on mathematics. The idea is that the inputs to the application are the arguments to a function, and the outputs of the application are the value that the function returns. Whereas the object-oriented subordinates may contain their own state, mathematical functions are stateless: they will always return the same value and have no side effects. A mathematical function is not so much a behavior as a statement of eternal truth: "f(2)" does not mean "apply 2 to f", but rather "the value when f's argument is bound to 2". In functional programming, the goal is to have all the functions in the application behave like these mathematical functions. This function may be defined in terms of other functions, but the program is ultimately a single function application, not a series of executive commands.

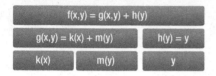

Although functional programming and object-oriented programming are theoretically equivalent, some solutions are more naturally expressed in one paradigm versus the other: for a given problem, the intuitive solution within each paradigm can be quite different. In the example I gave at the start of this chapter, object oriented required us to create a "Predicate" object with the behavior of returning true if the argument is not null. In functional programming, we simply provide a function that returns true if the argument is not null: there's no need for an object to hold onto that behavior. In this case, functional programming was the more intuitive solution to the problem because there was no state, nothing to encapsulate, and inheritance was nonsensical.

Throughout the early 21st century, many forward-looking developers saw the value in the functional programming style. That style melds especially well with many development techniques that were then becoming popularized, such as test-driven development, and it was especially useful in highly distributed or highly concurrent environments. Many of the problems people were encountering—such as how to send not just data but also commands over a line—have natural solutions within functional programming style. Some technology pundits, including your humble author, predicted that a new functional programming language would arise that would render Java obsolete in much the way that Java has rendered C++ obsolete. Obviously, this did not happen on the Java Virtual Machine.[2]

What happened was actually stranger than we expected. Instead of a pure functional programming language arising, new object-oriented languages populated the development environment. These languages, although undoubtedly object oriented, also integrated techniques and capabilities from the functional programming styles. In these hybrid languages, the developer can work with functions like in the functional languages, but those functions can have state, making them more like objects. Ruby, Groovy, Scala, and JavaScript are all examples of this kind of language. After many years, Java has now joined the ranks with Java 8. Starting with Java 8, Java integrates some of these popular techniques into the core Java language itself.

---

[2]It has happened on Apple's platform, where Swift is replacing Objective-C. It's also worth noting that Clojure has made a valiant effort on the JVM front. Some of my peers will defend themselves by pointing to the relative success of Scala, but Scala is not actually a functional programming language: http://blog.enfranchisedmind.com/2009/05/scala-not-functional/.

Within the functional programming paradigm, one of the most popular techniques is lambdas, which are more informally called closures.[3] A lambda is a set of instructions that can be saved as a variable, passed about through the program, and executed at a later time (possibly multiple times). To understand what this means, consider a simple for loop, such as in Listing 1-8: when the program execution encounters this loop, it executes the loop immediately and then moves on. Imagine, instead, that you could store the loop into a variable, and then pass it around, executing it later at some faraway location, such as in the made-up code in Listing 1-9. That is what lambdas allow you to do; Java 8's version of this code is in Listing 1-10.

Listing 1-8. Simple Loop

```
for(Object it : list) {
    System.out.println(it);
}
```

Listing 1-9. Storing a Simple Loop (Not Real Code)

```
// This is not Java code
Loop printObjects = for(Object it : list) {
    System.out.println(it);
}
```

Listing 1-10. Storing a Simple Loop in Java 8

```
Consumer<Iterable> printObjects = list -> {
  for(Object it : list) {
    System.out.println(it);
  }
};
// For the record, this is the same result in more idiomatic Java 8 code:
Consumer<Iterable> printObjects = list -> list.forEach(System.out::println);
```

This may seem like a relatively minor language feature, but the impact of introducing lambdas was so significant that the lambdas were too big to be a part of Java 7's Project Coin,[4] and instead became the driving feature of Java 8. This language feature is so significant because it enables a new way of interacting with the objects that make up a Java program: now, we can have behaviors without needing to reference an object; and we can define verbs without first having to define a noun.

The rest of this book will explore the implications of this new language feature, and how we can change the way that we write Java code to take advantage of this change. The result will be more functional code in both respects: both more function-oriented code, and also code that works better. The reason is because we can now express more directly and succinctly our intent in certain very common cases, and we have a powerful new tool for decomposing our code into more maintainable pieces. To understand how this works, let's turn to a very specific and likely familiar situation in Java.

---

[3]We will get into the language of "closure" vs. "lambda" later on. In general, a developer can get along just fine treating them as synonyms. Java prefers "lambda," whereas most other languages on the Java Virtual Machine prefer "closure." Ruby, notably, has seven variations on "lambda" and "closure," leading to this quite entertaining exploration of the programming language: http://innig.net/software/ruby/closures-in-ruby.

[4]Project Coin was a project for small change. (Get it?) Introducing lambdas was initially proposed as a bit of syntactic sugar, but it quickly became clear that the implications of having lambdas would have wide-reaching ramifications for the Java SDK's API.

Java Has Had Functional Programming All Along

If you ask around about Java 8 and lambdas, you may hear someone say that Java 8 makes it possible to "do functional programming" in Java. Yet the reality is that Java has always been capable of functional programming: it's just been disguised and awkward. What lambdas do is remove the disguise and make it easier to work with functions directly. Although I could (and many do) try to explain this fact through abstract arguments, this is best demonstrated through an example of practical Java code and how it changes with the introduction of lambdas.

We will draw our example from the world of database access, since it is a place near to my heart. Before the rise and fall of Object-Relational Mapping (ORM) frameworks[5] and the innovation of other data access tools such as JOOQ,[6] there was the venerable JdbcTemplate from Spring's JDBC support library.[7] This class—with help from a broad family of interfaces and supporting classes—allows developers to avoid the coding overhead of interacting with a database, and keeping both developers and the code focused on the relevant and interesting bits of code.

JdbcTemplate does this through a pattern called "Inversion of Control." The basic idea is that you can get rid of boilerplate by having some library execute the boilerplate, and then calling back to client code with the relevant pieces of context. The "control" is "inverted" because calling into a library normally gives control to that library, but in this case the library is giving control back to the caller.[8]

A standard example of using JdbcTemplate this way (before Java 8) is given in Listing 1-11. The boilerplate creation of the statement, execution of the statement, iteration over the result set, closing of objects, and handling of errors is all managed by JdbcTemplate. The arguments to the JdbcTemplate call fill in the gaps: the SQL given as the first argument is used to prepare a statement; the interface implementation passed as the second argument is used to assign the parameters; and the interface implementation passed as the third argument is used to consume each row of the result set.

The lambdas introduced in Java 8 make this kind of code much easier to write, much more succinct, and much more expressive. The Java 8 example is given in Listing 1-12. Using lambdas drops the code from 16 lines to 4. How? Why did Java once require this overhead, and how does the introduction of lambdas enable shorter code?

Listing 1-11. Example of JdbcTemplate usage before lambdas

```
jdbcTemplate.query("SELECT bar FROM Foo WHERE baz = ?",
               new PreparedStatementSetter() {
                 @Override
                 public void setValues(PreparedStatement ps)
                   throws SQLException
                 {
                   ps.setString(1, "some value for baz");
                 }
               },
               new RowMapper<SomeModel>() {
                 @Override
                 public SomeModel mapRow(ResultSet rs, int rowNum)
```

---

[5]E.g., Hibernate.
[6]http://www.jooq.org/.
[7]API at http://bit.ly/jdbcTemplate.
[8]The more generalized version of the "Inversion of Control" pattern is the "Hole in the Middle" pattern. http://blog.enfranchisedmind.com/2007/07/the-hole-in-the-middle-pattern/.

```
            throws SQLException
        {
            return new SomeModel(rs.getInt(1));
        }
    }
);
```

Listing 1-12. Example of JdbcTemplate usage with lambdas

```
jdbcTemplate.query("SELECT bar FROM Foo WHERE baz = ?",
                   ps -> ps.setString(1, "some value for baz"),
                   (rs, rowNum) -> new SomeModel(rs.getInt(1))
);
```

With Java 8, Java has opened up its syntactic purview. When Java started, it was a cutting-edge implementation of a cutting-edge programming paradigm: object-oriented programming. Java went solidly into object-oriented programming, which meant that you were to no longer think of "implementing functions," but of "defining behavior." Conceptually, all activity within a program was the behavior of an object,[9] with similar objects implementing interfaces. The theory is that this encourages reuse and testability: a good object-oriented programming team would define discrete, extensible, well-exercised, and well-tested implementations of these interfaces. Anonymous inner classes, like the ones we used above, are not reusable and aren't discrete at all. They are therefore fighting against the object-oriented paradigm and sacrificing its major advantages.[10]

But if anonymous inner classes are so bad, why does everyone use them in this circumstance? The reason is because the logic is extremely contextual and therefore not much eligible for reuse. Furthermore, defining an additional type would be more obfuscating than clarifying by creating "spaghetti code"; the call stack would wander into and out of a variety of source files, which makes it hard for the developer to understand the program flow. These anonymous inner classes are therefore the best solution within the object-oriented paradigm, but they are obviously not great.

The fundamental problem is that within the object-oriented paradigm, it is not possible to directly express, "Give me a way to assign the parameters on the JDBC Statement instance I will create." That is what the JdbcTemplate wants, but that isn't an object-oriented kind of question. What the JdbcTemplate has to do is define an interface, and the user has to define a function that fulfills that interface. This means that the JdbcTemplate is asking, "Give me an object fulfilling a certain API contract that I can trigger to assign the parameters on the JDBC Statement that I will create." Since requiring an object requires a type, requiring an object therefore requires the syntactic overhead of the anonymous inner class.

The lambdas in Java 8 actually step out of the object-oriented paradigm, and therefore allow the syntax to express precisely what the JdbcTemplate is asking for. The functional paradigm does not create the rich and descriptive API that the object-oriented program has,[11] but the trade-off is that the code itself becomes much more succinct and self-expressive. This is the same trade-off used by many of the alternative languages on Java's virtual machine, and now Java has joined that club.[12]

---

[9]Static methods are the obvious exception to this rule, although you can think of the static members of a class as implementing a singleton object. This way of thinking is demonstrated best by Scala's "object" keyword.

[10]It's worth noting at this point that inner classes—including anonymous inner classes—were not part of the Java 1.0 specification. They arrived in Java 1.1.

[11]Is there any question what an implementation of the PreparedStatementSetter interface is supposed to do?

[12]Because of Java's adamant object-oriented roots, the language itself is still a bit awkward with this trade-off: for instance, the java.util.function documentation specifies that it's okay to refer to a lambda as "this function" instead of "the function represented by this object." Nonetheless, lambdas are a powerful feature borrowed from the functional programming paradigm, and integrated well into Java 8.

There is a neat feature snuck into this example, though, which makes Java's take on functional programming very interesting. Did you see it? Note that the JdbcTemplate code that we called in both Figures 1-11 and 1-12 was the same, and it is code that predates Java 8 and was written before lambdas were a part of the Java spec. In one case, we had to specify the types that we were passing in through anonymous inner classes; in the other case, we specified no types at all, but the compiler still figured out what types we meant. The compiler not only figured out what interfaces we implemented, but also figured out the types of the parameters that we were passing in, saving us substantially on code noise.

This capability is called *type inference*, and it's an extremely powerful programming language feature. Historically, Java has done very little type inference. Generics introduced some very limited type inference. Java 7's Project Coin gave us the empty generic (<>), such as in `"List<Integer> ints = new ArrayList<>();"`, which is also an example of limited type inference. Java 8 introduces substantially expanded type inference capabilities, especially when it comes to the Java's lambdas. In Java 8, any time that you could pass an interface with a single method, you can pass in a function that is an implementation of that method, and the compiler will infer what type you are talking about.[13]

This type inference allows the API authors to use the rich, object-oriented style of API. The API can provide hints to both the developer and the developer's tools through meaningful interfaces with useful documentation and informative method names. The consumer of the API, meanwhile, can simply pass in the functional implementations of these interfaces, just as we passed in a `PreparedStatementSetter` as `"ps -> ps.setString(1, "some value for baz")"`. This means that Java gives us the best of both worlds. We get our descriptive object-oriented API and leave the door open for reusable implementations; we also enable users with strongly contextual logic to pass in succinct inline implementations. It's a very clever, very useful, and very much underestimated feature of Java's functional programming capabilities.

The fact that legacy APIs are automatically promoted to support functional-style calls demonstrates well that Java has always had functional programming capabilities. Before now, though, those capabilities required messy syntactic glue; the dominant object-oriented paradigm got in the way of the functional programming capabilities that exist within Java. With Java 8, the effective functional programming techniques that existed beneath Java's object-oriented crust can finally come out.

Java 8 Is Not Just Syntactic Sugar

As far as we have seen, lambdas are just a more succinct way to express an anonymous inner class. While this is both powerful and useful, it is hardly sufficient grounds for an entire book. Where is this revolution that was advertised at the beginning of the chapter?

The revolution happens when these functions meet the new APIs scattered throughout the SDK. Most of the changes are integrated into existing classes or packages, but there is one very striking addition. One the new APIs is the introduction of the concept of a "stream," which is kind of like an Iterator and kind of like a grown-up Reader. Streams provide a huge stage for the functional syntax changes to perform their magic.

To tackle streams, let's return to the JdbcTemplate example. In that case, the second argument is a RowMapper interface implementation, which is responsible for translating the results coming from the database into a collection of the resulting objects. It is not possible at this point to filter out certain results; attempts to do so involve hacks such as returning null and then filtering out the nulls at the end. It is also not simple to partition the results or to calculate statistics from them. It's not easy to work with the elements as a whole, and working with any given element requires loading the entire result set into memory. When you think about it, both result sets and collections of models are really a rather awkward way to deal with database results.

---

[13]There are, of course, corner cases to this claim, especially when you're calling a method overloaded with similar interface type structures. We will get into these boundary cases later.

Streams provide a reinvention of the standard Java processing model. Instead of working directly on data, your program builds up a set of instructions about how to work the stream. These instructions can range from simple filtering and conversion rules to complex map/reduce structures and everything in between. They work by passing functions onto the methods of the Stream object.

For instance, in the FunJava library,[14] there is a JdbcTemplate-like class that provides the results as a stream of ResultMap objects. These objects are the raw JDBC object types that come out of the database, indexed by column name and by column index. Whatever you want to do with the data is up to you. The great news is that the JVM will automatically optimize the stream processing in order to keep your memory load down and your concurrent processes up: this means that the JVM is getting efficiency out of your code for free!

Say that you queried the database, and for some reason you couldn't do reasonable SQL work in the database, but had to do it programmatically instead. (I wish this were as hypothetical as it sounds.) Perhaps you wanted to find the salary statistics for people whose first name was "Robert." The stream code for this using the FunJava library is given in Listing 1-13. This example demonstrates how lambdas and streams work together to make expressive code. The JVM has a lot of freedom to implement that code, as well, which enables it to make significant optimizations on our behalf. In Chapter 3, we will explore the power of streams further and look into exactly what those optimizations are.

Listing 1-13. Using streams for processing database results

```
funConnection.queryToStream("/* SQL HERE */")
  .filter(it -> it.get("firstName").equals("Robert"))
  .collectors(Collectors.summarizingInt(it -> it.getSalary()));
```

Is Java 8 a Functional Programming Language?

Now that Java is borrowing such a powerful feature from functional programming, does that make Java a functional programming language? Many developers that I talk to have "Learn a functional programming language" on their bucket list,[15] so does learning to code in idiomatic Java 8 count as learning a functional programming language?

Martin Odersky, the creator of Scala, weighed in on what made a "functional programming language."[16] With the introduction of Java 8, Java now has all those features in an obvious way. Yet, just as Martin pointed out about Scala, idiomatic Java 8 still does not strongly resemble idiomatic code in the functional programming languages.[17] The term Martin coined to describe this kind of language is "postfunctional," which works well enough: Java 8 brings Java into the ranks of the postfunctional languages.

Part of the difficulty when talking about "functional programming" is that it's a strategy for programming. Some languages more naturally express this strategy than others, but it is possible to do functional programming in any language, just as it is possible to do object-oriented programming in any language.[18] This means that we have been able to do functional programming in Java all along.

In fact, many of the innovations that have entered the Java ecosystem are actually functional programming maneuvers in an object-oriented guise. This is exactly what we are seeing with our inversion-of-control example: those interface implementations providing callbacks to JdbcTemplate are actually just an object-oriented way of passing in a function. All JdbcTemplate wants is that function. In the object-oriented world, we needed to create a structure to support it; in the functional world, we can just pass the function in. What lambdas enable us to do is to express these programming strategies using a more natural language.

---

[14]http://github.com/webonise/funjava.
[15]The author does grant that this could be selection bias.
[16]http://www.scala-lang.org/old/node/4960.
[17]E.g., Haskell, OCaml, Lisp.
[18]If you would like to see object-oriented programming done in C, for instance, see the GMP library's C API.

Since Java 8 code does not look like idiomatic code in more functional programming languages, however, there is still much to be gained by learning those other functional programming languages. So if learning a functional programming language is on your to-do list, stick with it.[19] When you do learn that language, you will be introduced into its new ideas, and you will develop a new sense of what is natural. What Java 8 allows you to do is to bring those new ideas and that new sensibility back into the Java world without feeling constrained, or feeling like the language is getting in your way of doing what you want.

Java 8 does not make Java a "functional programming language." It does allow you to more naturally do functional programming in Java, however. Java 8 is a huge evolution of Java, making it a flexible and multi-paradigm language, and it makes Java competitive with the other JVM programming language forerunners such as Groovy, Scala, Ruby, and Clojure.

Enough with the Theory; onto the Implementation!

It is impressive just how naturally Java 8's lambdas fit into the Java syntax, and how easy they are to read. This chapter took advantage of this fact to introduce lambdas informally and indirectly; we learned the basics of lambdas gradually by comparing them to imaginary Java code and to legacy Java code. We also spent a lot of time examining what lambdas are at a high level, and how they impact what kind of language Java is.

In the next chapter, we will look into what lambdas are from a technical standpoint, both from the standpoint of computer science theory, and from the standpoint of Java's implementation. We will expand on our examples to see how we can perform even cooler stunts, and we will begin to interact with streams at the most basic level in order to discover how they really work. In short, things are about to get real.

---

[19]Might I suggest picking up OCaml over the course of an evening or two?

CHAPTER 2

■ ■ ■

Understanding Lambdas in Java 8

The core new functionality in Java 8 is the introduction of lambdas. However, most introductions will show a couple of examples of lambdas, and then they leave it to the developer to figure out the rest. If you are going to be developing modern Java programs, however, you are going to need to be well versed in how lambdas can be used. Throughout this chapter, we will dig into the particularities of the syntax and semantics of lambdas, including how to create more complex lambdas, how to work with method calls and lambdas, and what this all looks like under the hood. We will also look at some classic ways to manipulate lambdas, and how they are implemented within Java. By the end of this chapter, you should be fluent in how to create the lambdas that you want.

While I promise that this chapter is very concrete, its purpose is to present the syntax and semantics of lambdas. In order to maintain the clarity and precision of the examples, we will present them without creating a context for their application. If your inner schoolchild begins saying, "Yeah, but when are you ever going to use this?" then please feel free to peruse the practical examples throughout every other chapter of this book. Here, the goal is to become a technical expert on lambdas, method references, and the functional interfaces that support them. With that grounding, we can move into the more interesting and complex cases in the rest of the book.

Java 8's Lambda Syntax

The simplest lambda is one that takes a single argument and returns that argument, and we have a method that generates that lambda in Listing 2-1. It is easiest to understand that method if we work from the outside in. Let's start with the signature: the method is named identityFunction, and it will return a Function. The Function type is a new interface in Java 8, part of the java.util.function package, and that interface represents a single-argument lambda with a return value. Our returned Function takes an object of variable type V and provides an object of the same type, so the type is <V, V>. A different function might take one type and return another; a function might take any object and return a String, for instance. In that case, its type would be <Object,String>. But the types are the same here: the return value is the same as the argument. Moving into the body of the method itself, we have a return statement. That return statement returns a lambda, and that lambda is the implementation for our Function interface. The lambda takes a single argument named value on the left side of the arrow, and it returns value on the right side of the arrow.

Listing 2-1. Identity Function Implemented Using a Lambda

```
public static <V> Function<V, V> identityFunction() {
  return value -> value;
}
```

Listing 2-2. Identity Function Implemented Using an Anonymous Inner Class

```java
public static <V> Function<V, V> identityFunctionAIC() {
  return new Function<V, V>() {
    @Override
    public V apply(V value) {
      return value;
    }
  };
}
```

Since `Function` is an interface, it is entirely possible to reimplement `identityFunction()` using an anonymous inner class. The equivalent anonymous inner class implementation is given in Listing 2-2. If you compare the two implementations, there are a few interesting things to note. First, the new format is much more succinct. Second, the `return` found inside the anonymous inner class is implicit with the lambda: the lambda is made up of a single statement, and so that statement's value is implicitly returned. Third, the lambda version has no explicit declaration of `value`'s type: the compiler infers out the type of `value` based on the context in which the value is used. This is a capability called "type inference," and it is one of the nicest things to come out of functional programming languages.

The type inference is why Listing 2-1 had to be wrapped in a method: you need to provide a way for the compiler to know the argument and return type of the function. It is possible to assign a lambda directly to a variable, but things get a bit tricky here: after all, what's the type? Truly old school Java developers might be tempted to assign it to `Object` and circumvent the type of system completely, as in Listing 2-3. If you do that, however, you will get a compiler error: the compiler needs to know what type you are trying to implement. More modern Java developers would want to use generics to solve this purpose, as in Listing 2-4. This will compile and work just fine. Unfortunately, that loses type information: the compiler no longer knows the argument and return type are the same type. The method allows us to keep that information by communicating all the type information that we have while remaining as generic as possible. If, however, you knew that it was always going to be a `Number`, then you could define it as in Listing 2-5, and you'd get all the succinct inline definition along with the type information. (The repetition of <Number,Number> in Listing 2-5 is because both the argument and the return value are a Number: the first Number denotes the argument's type, the second Number denotes the return value's type.) As a general rule, define lambdas inline to the variable assignment if you know the concrete types, and define lambdas within methods to capture more complex type information. Now that the Java compiler has type inference, that type information is worth its weight in gold: don't lose it!

Listing 2-3. Identity Function Assigned to an Object Variable

```java
// This code does not compile
Object funObject = it -> it;
```

Listing 2-4. Identity Function Assigned to a Generic Function Variable

```java
Function<?,?> function = it -> it;
```

Listing 2-5. Identity Function for Number Instances Assigned to a Function Variable

```java
Function<Number,Number> function = it -> it;
```

Lambdas as Closures

Java 8's lambdas act as closures. Although the term "lambda" and "closure" are effectively interchangeable in most programming conversations, there is a technical difference. The good news is that Java 8's lambdas are also closures, so you can call them either and be technically correct. Understanding the distinction, however, helps you be clear about what you are saying.

The term *lambda* comes from a branch of mathematics exploring what can and cannot be computed, specifically from a structure called the *lambda calculus*. The lambda calculus explores function application as the primary action in computation, and so it works with functions in the most abstract sense, without any consideration of what the function itself might represent or calculate. Functions themselves are the relevant values in the lambda calculus. When programming languages borrow the term *lambda* from the lambda calculus, they mean functions that can be treated as values. A lambda can be assigned to a variable (or multiple variables), passed around as method arguments, and generally manipulated like one might manipulate the values 2, true, or "foo".

The term *closure*, however, refers to a later innovation of the lambda. For Java developers, it is easiest to think of the term *closure* as meaning *encapsulating function*. In the same way that an object can encapsulate state and expose it through a particular API (such as properties exposing fields), a closure can also encapsulate some state and then act on that state wherever and whenever the closure is invoked. The "close" part of *closure* refers to "open" versus "closed" variables. This idea comes directly from mathematics: a variable that does not have a value bound to it is said to be "open," while a variable that does have a value bound to it is said to be "closed." A closure is a lambda that closes certain variables, and it does this by enclosing a variable environment.

This may sound like a strange and technical concept, but it is actually quite familiar in practice. Before Java 8 introduced lambdas, Java arguably already had closures in the form of anonymous inner classes.[1] Anonymous inner classes could capture variable state in one context and execute on it in another: see Listing 2-6 as an example. In that case, the anonymous inner class implementing Greeter closes the variable greeting. You knew you were creating a closure in Java whenever the compiler would insist that you add final to your variable or parameter declaration.

Java 8's lambdas also act as closures, meaning that they will capture variables that are in scope. This is just like how the anonymous inner classes did it, and an equivalent example of a lambda as a closure is given in Listing 2-7. As a bit of syntactic sugar, though, you no longer have to explicitly declare your variables as final: the compiler implicitly makes enclosed variables final, and will raise a compiler error if they are not treated as final.[2]

Listing 2-6. Anonymous Inner Classes as a Closure

```java
public interface Greeter {
  String createGreeting(String whom);
}

public static void main(String[] args) {
  // Create variable in this scope
  final String greeting = "Hello, ";
```

---

[1]This strange fact provides the opportunity for a rather annoying and pedantic yet useful interview question: "Please write a closure in valid Java 7 syntax."

[2]We will address why the final variables are necessary in the section below named "Lambdas Should Always Be Threadsafe."

```
  Greeter greeter = new Greeter() {
    @Override
    public String createGreeting(String whom) {
      // Close (ie: capture) the variable here
      return greeting + whom + "!";
    }
  };
  greetWorld(greeter);
}

public static void greetWorld(Greeter greeter) {
  // Have the greeter use the closed variable here
  // Note that the "greeting" variable is out of scope
  System.out.println(greeter.createGreeting("World"));
}
```

Listing 2-7. Lava 8's Lambda as a Closure

```
public static void main(String[] args) {
  String greeting = "Hello, ";
  Function<String, String> greeter = whom -> greeting + whom + "!";
  greetWorld(greeter);
}

public static void greetWorld(Function<String, String> greeter) {
  System.out.println(greeter.apply("World"));
}
```

No-Argument and Multi-Argument Lambdas

The basic lambda is one that takes a single argument, but Java does not limit you to that case: you can have zero-argument lambdas, and you can have many-argument lambdas.[3] The syntax for each of these cases is slightly different and more complicated than the simple case.

The syntax for a lambda with zero arguments is strange: how do you represent the absence of any arguments? Simply using the right arrow without any arguments would lead to many ambiguous cases in the Java syntax, so that is not an option. Instead, they introduced a placeholder for zero-argument functions, just like numbers have a placeholder symbol for zero. That placeholder is a left parenthesis immediately followed by a right parenthesis, which even looks like zero: (). An example of using it is in Listing 2-8; in that listing, we create a lambda that takes no arguments and always returns 1 as a Number.

Listing 2-8. Constant Supplier of Number Instances

```
Supplier<Number> function = () -> 1;
```

---

[3]The upper limit of arguments to a lambda function is de facto unlimited. If you discover that upper bound in the course of normal development, you are doing something really wrong.

Note that we have a different type: the method signature that we want is no arguments and returning Number, but Function is an interface whose only method has a signature with a single argument, and so we need a different interface to represent this different signature.[4] For lambdas without arguments, the functional interface is Supplier: the name was picked because they are used to supply values without needing any input.

It is also possible to have multi-argument lambdas. At this point, the syntax should be predictable: we will again use parentheses to demarcate the argument list, and we will again use type inference to specify our types. An example of a two-argument function (called a *bifunction*) is given in Listing 2-9. The functional type for these kinds of methods is BiFunction. Java's SDK does not contain support for lambdas with more than two arguments, because you really shouldn't be using lambdas for that kind of complex case. If you really want to have a lambda with lots of arguments, see "Lambdas as Interface Implementations" below for how to handle that case. It is also worth noting that you cannot use varargs (e.g., String... strings) as a lambda argument type: you have to treat the varargs parameter as an array. This sad fact is due to an unfortunate limitation in Java's type system.[5] The good news is that there are limited cases when you need to have three or more arguments or varargs: zero-, one-, and two-argument functions handle most of your cases. Streams (covered in the next chapter) and currying (covered in the next subsection) provide for almost all these cases.

Listing 2-9. String Concatenation Bifunction

```
BiFunction<String, String, String> concat = (a, b) -> a + b;
```

Partial Function Application and Mr. Curry's Verb

Every culture and subculture has its own language that identifies members of the tribe. One of the weird tribal codewords in the functional programming tribe is "currying," which is a verb coined after the logician Haskell Curry. To understand what it means to curry a function and why one might want to do it, let's start in another place: partial function application.

Partial function application is exactly what it says it is: the application of part of a function. Consider, for instance, the string concatenation bifunction given in Listing 2-9. What if you wanted to concatenate the same thing to the front of a number of strings? Repeating yourself is one of the cardinal sins of programming ("DRY"), and passing the same argument in over and over and over again is certainly repeating yourself. What you want is a version of the bifunction with the first argument fixed to a certain value. Fixing that first argument is called "applying" the argument, and since you're only fixing the first of two possible arguments, the application is "partial." In Listing 2-10, we demonstrate what we are doing when we do partial function application: we are creating a Function that applies a fixed first argument to a BiFunction. The resulting Function can then be applied over and over again to multiple arguments. In Listing 2-11, we see how this is implemented: although Java does not provide a built-in partial function application method, it is simple to write one. We simply accept the bifunction that we want to apply along with the first argument, and then return a function that calls back to that bifunction with the first argument already set.

---

[4]This is one of the places where Java is decidedly not a functional language: function types are still communicated via interfaces, instead of being intrinsic within the language itself.

[5]Some people claim that vargargs in lambdas are unnecessary, and that attempting to use them is a sign that you are doing something wrong. If you want to see both the good and the bad of vararg lambdas, see JavaScript's arguments object and the places where it is directly used.

Listing 2-10. Implicit Partial Function Application of String Concatenation

```java
public static void main(String[] args) {
  BiFunction<String, String, String> concat = (a,b) -> a + b;
  greetFolks(whom -> concat.apply("Hello, ", whom));
}

public static void greetFolks(Function<String, String> greeter) {
  for(String name : Arrays.asList("Alice", "Bob", "Cathy")) {
    System.out.println(greeter.apply(name));
  }
}
```

Listing 2-11. Explicit Partial Function Application of String Concatenation

```java
public static void main(String[] args) {
  BiFunction<String, String, String> concat = (a,b) -> a + b;
  greetFolks(applyPartial(concat, "Hello, "));
}

public static <T,U,V> Function<U,V> applyPartial(
  BiFunction<T,U,V> bif, T firstArgument
) {
  return u -> bif.apply(firstArgument, u);
}

public static void greetFolks(Function<String, String> greeter) {
  for(String name : Arrays.asList("Alice", "Bob", "Cathy")) {
    System.out.println(greeter.apply(name));
  }
}
```

Mr. Curry's Verb and Functional Shape

Partial function application acts on one function and takes another. Programming at the level of functions like this is where "functional programming" got its name, and functional programming languages encourage you to think at this level instead of at the level of data and instructions. Think of functional arguments as voids in a jigsaw puzzle. Only a specific shape will fill that void. Every method you have access to is a piece of that jigsaw puzzle, and they each have a shape. The shape of those methods is defined by the arguments that they take and the arguments that they return. Like jigsaw puzzle pieces, you can also connect the shapes together to make new shapes. Functional programming is the art of connecting the appropriate method shapes together to fit the functional void.

For instance, the greetFolks method in Listing 2-10 and 2-11 provides a void with the shape of String ➤ String: to call that method, we need to provide a function that takes a string and returns a string. Unfortunately, we only had (String ➤ String) ➤ String: we only had a function that takes two strings as arguments and returns a string. That shape does not quite fit. So what we did was partially apply the first argument, which shaved that first argument off the shape of the method. This left us with a function with the required shape of String ➤ String.

You could think of the applyPartial method in Listing 2-11 as fixing the first argument. However, the applyPartial method is really changing a function of the form (x,y)->z into a function of the form x->(y->z). The method takes a function with two arguments that returns a value, and it produces a function with one argument that returns a function. That returned function takes another argument and returns a value. Conceptually, the applyPartial method then applies x to that new function and returns y->z. There are two distinct steps here: first, the change of the shape of the function to x->(y->z); second, the application of the first argument, x.

Let's say that you wanted to create a lot of different greeter functions. Perhaps you want to do internationalization, so now you have many different ways of saying "Hello." You could partially apply each different "Hello" each time, but then you are performing the shape-changing first step of applyPartial over and over again. If you wanted to save that repeated effort, you would get your hands on the intermediate function that applyPartial creates. That would allow you to generate greeter functions yourself. Creating the function shaped x->(y->z) from the function shaped (x,y)->z is called *currying*. The more you work with functional shapes, the more common this maneuver will become. We demonstrate currying to create intermediate greeter functions in Listing 2-12.

This may seem like a strange stunt at this point, but we will see this in use later in the book. It is such a useful stunt, in fact, that functional programming languages usually ship their functions pre-curried: in OCaml, for instance, defining a function using the expression "let add x y = x + y" will create a function named add with type x->y->z[6], which can be used either as a bifunction producing z or as function producing y->z. The reason functional programming languages have this implicit currying is because the shape of functions matters more than their content in functional programming. The shape of (x,y)->z is a bifunction: it takes two arguments to produce a value. Bifunctions appear very rarely, and they are hard to fit into the program. The shape of x->y->z, however, is still a function: you can think of it as x->w, where w is the y->z function. While bifunctions are rare, functions crop up everywhere. Therefore, you can often use currying to make a bifunction fit into a function's slot.

Listing 2-12. Explicit Currying of String Concatenation Bifunction

```java
public static void main(String[] args) {
  BiFunction<String, String, String> concat = (a, b) -> a + b;
  Function<String, Function<String, String>> curriedConcat = curry(concat);
  for (String greetings : Arrays.asList("Hello", "Guten Tag", "Bonjour")) {
    greetFolks(curriedConcat.apply(greetings + ", "));
  }
}

public static <T,U,V> Function<T,Function<U,V>> curry(BiFunction<T,U,V> bif) {
  return t -> (u -> bif.apply(t,u));
}

public static void greetFolks(Function<String, String> greeter) {
  for (String name : Arrays.asList("Alice", "Bob", "Cathy")) {
    System.out.println(greeter.apply(name));
  }
}
```

---

[6]If you are the kind of person who knows OCaml, you are the kind of person who probably just caught me in a pedagogical lie. For the rest of you, discovering how I lied to you is left as an exercise to the reader.

Lambdas with No Return Value

So far, we have been addressing lambdas that always return a value. A very common type of lambda, however, returns no value at all: these are terminal lambdas. You see them, for instance, when consuming every element of a collection or when terminating a stream of values. They are the opposite of suppliers; they take a value and produce nothing as a result. Predictably, the functional interface for these consuming lambdas is Consumer. An example of a consumer is given in Listing 2-13: there, we use a consumer to represent how we print out the greeting. A more idiomatic Java 8 way of writing this code will be given when we get to collections in Chapter 3.

Listing 2-13. Example of a Consumer and BiConsumer

```
public static void greetFolks() {
  Consumer<String> doGreet = name -> System.out.println("Hello, " + name);
  for (String name : Arrays.asList("Alice", "Bob", "Cathy")) {
    doGreet.accept(name);
  }
}

public static void concat() {
  BiConsumer<String,String> printConcat = (left,right) ->
    System.out.println(left + right);
  for (String name : Arrays.asList("Alice", "Bob", "Cathy")) {
    printConcat.accept("Goodbye, ", name);
  }
}
```

Lambdas with Complex Bodies

Usually, lambdas are simple, single-element affairs. Occasionally, however, you need to do something a bit more involved. This is especially common when you are writing code that interfaces with a pre-lambda API, such as working with an Autocloseable. If you need to create a complex body on a lambda, you can specify the body within brackets. When you do so, however, you take on responsibility for explicitly calling a return. An example of a lambda wrapping an Autocloseable is given in Listing 2-14. As you can see there, this approach makes your lambda look a lot more like a method, and you may be better off defining a method and referring to it explicitly. There's even a nice syntax for turning a method back into a lambda if you need to: see "Making Methods into Lambdas" below.

Listing 2-14. Lambda with a Complex Body That Wraps an Autocloseable

```
Function<File, Byte> firstByte = file -> {
  try (InputStream is = new FileInputStream(file)) {
    return (byte) is.read();
  } catch (IOException ioe) {
    throw new RuntimeException("Could not read " + file, ioe);
  }
};
for (String filename : args) {
  File file = new File(filename);
  int byte1 = firstByte.apply(file);
  System.out.println(filename + "\t=>\t" + byte1);
}
```

18

Lambdas with Explicit Typing

Some Java developers just can't bear to part with explicit typing, some code analysis tools (such as IDEs) need a little extra help from time to time, and sometimes you may even manage to confuse the compiler.[7] In these cases, you need to provide the compiler with explicit types to help it out. When you get to these cases, it is a sign that something is probably wrong with your API, and you might be best off fixing whatever ambiguity it is that caused the problem. If you really want to specify your types explicitly, though, you can do so by using the parenthesized argument list. If you put parentheses around your arguments (even if there is only one), then you can add explicit types. In Listing 2-15, we see a case that raises some confusion, and how we can add explicit types to solve it.

Listing 2-15. Using Explicit Typing to Resolve Overloaded Method Ambiguity

```java
public static void main(String[] args) {
  // .toUpperCase() exists in String, but not on CharSequence
  transform(args[0], (String str) -> str.toUpperCase());
}

public static String transform(
  String str,
  Function<String, String> transformer
) {
  return transformer.apply(str);
}

public static CharSequence transform(
  CharSequence str,
  Function<CharSequence, CharSequence> transformer
) {
  return transformer.apply(str);
}
```

Lambdas as Operators

Java 8 provides a bit of shorthand for the common case when the types of the arguments and return values are the same. In this case, you can save repeating yourself by using the "operator functional interfaces."[8] There are two of these that work on objects: BinaryOperator and UnaryOperator. BinaryOperator is a BiFunction whose arguments and return types are all the same type; UnaryOperator is a Function whose arguments and return types are all the same type. Aside from the much more succinct type signature, there's no difference between these operators and their corresponding functional interfaces. Listing 2-16 demonstrates using the operator types to capture the uppercase and string concatenation lambdas that we have seen throughout this chapter.

---

[7]As we will see in Listing 2-15, the best way to confuse the compiler is with overloaded methods, especially if you combine overloaded methods and inheritance. Aside from that, the type inference in the Oracle SDK is actually quite good.

[8]If you are looking for Java to allow you to override operators like + and -, you are going to be sorely disappointed. It's just not something that will make it through the Java Community Process as things stand. You may want to look at the Java-OO javac plugin, however: http://amelentev.github.io/java-oo/

Listing 2-16. Using Operator Types to Capture Familiar Lambdas

```
UnaryOperator<String> upperCase = str -> str.toUpperCase();
BinaryOperator<String> concat = (left,right) -> left + right;
```

Lambdas as Predicates

This book opened up with a story about the usefulness of predicate types. Java has implemented predicates as a special case of the Function functional interface: specifically, one that takes any type and returns a boolean. This is an extremely common functional type that simply returns true or false and that is used any time your functional program has a conditional branch, a filter, or a guard. We demonstrate a basic "not null or empty" check for a String in Listing 2-17.

Listing 2-17. Predicate Lambda Checking if a String Is Null or Empty

```
Predicate<String> notNullOrEmpty = s -> s != null && s.length() > 0;
```

Lambdas with Primitive Arguments

In Listing 2-8, we saw a Supplier that returned a given integer value, 1. However, that value was returned as an object extending Number, not as the primitive value. This is an example of a "boxed integer," and the implicit conversion that just happened is called "autoboxing." Many developers have an allergy to boxing primitive values, even though the real performance impact of boxing is largely negated through compiler optimizations, standard library performance tricks, and Java's excellent garbage collector. However, there are still cases when the performance cost of autoboxing is significant; and if you are dealing with a lot of integer values, you might as well avoid the autoboxing. For those cases, you can create lambdas that use primitives.

There are primitive functional interfaces for the double, int, and long primitive types. There are also functional interfaces that take one of those primitive types and produce another of those primitive types, such as DoubleToIntFunction. Java provides primitive versions of most of the functional interfaces. The most notable missing entry in this list is ObjIntBifunction: I don't know why Java didn't provide this interface.

While we only take a look at the int interfaces in Listing 2-18, rest assured, there are corresponding versions of each of these interfaces for the double and long primitive types, too. Just replace "Int" with "Double" in the class name, and you have the corresponding functional type for the double type.

Listing 2-18. Predicate Lambda Checking if a String Is Null or Empty

```
IntFunction<String> intToString = i -> Integer.toString(i);
ToIntFunction<String> parseInt = str -> Integer.valueOf(str);
IntPredicate isEven = i -> i % 2 == 0;
ToIntBiFunction<String,String> maxLength =
  (left,right) -> Math.max(left.length(), right.length());
IntConsumer printInt = i -> System.out.println(Integer.toString(i));
ObjIntConsumer<String> printParsedIntWithRadix =
  (str,radix) -> System.out.println(Integer.parseInt(str,radix));
IntSupplier randomInt = () -> new Random().nextInt();
IntUnaryOperator negateInt = i -> -1 * i;
IntBinaryOperator multiplyInt = (x,y) -> x*y;
IntToDoubleFunction intAsDouble = i -> Integer.valueOf(i).doubleValue();
DoubleToIntFunction doubleAsInt = d -> Double.valueOf(d).intValue();
IntToLongFunction intAsLong = i -> Integer.valueOf(i).longValue();
LongToIntFunction longAsInt = x -> Long.valueOf(x).intValue();
```

Note that there is now a new way to have ambiguity in methods: you can have an overloaded method that accepts both a Function<Integer,X> and an IntFunction<X>, such as in Figure 2-19. If you do this, the compiler's error message will almost certainly confuse you. There are two error messages you could get at this point, and which one depends on details of the lambda implementation.[9] Both of these messages compete for least helpful error messages in Java 8, and they are "Cannot resolve method" and "Argument cannot be applied to <lambda parameter>." In this case, you will need to provide explicit typing, as we discussed in "Lambdas with Explicit Typing." If your explicit typing references the primitive type, you will get the IntFunction variant; if your explicit typing references the boxed type, you will get the Function variant.

Listing 2-19. Ambiguous Method Types When Using Primitive Functional Interfaces

```
static void methodBeingCalled(Function<Integer, String> function) {}
static void methodBeingCalled(IntFunction<String> function) {}

public static void main(String[] args) {
  // This will throw an exception
  methodBeingCalled(i -> Integer.toString(i));

  // This will not
  methodBeingCalled((int i) -> Integer.toString(i));
}
```

Making Methods into Lambdas

Throughout this chapter, we have been constructing all of our lambdas explicitly: we have been constructing our lambdas as anonymous functions. You can, however, also take any method call and turn it into a lambda. When I say "any method call," I mean it: static methods, instance methods, and constructors are all fair game. This tiny little bit of syntactic glue makes transitioning from object-oriented code into functional code very easy, and really provides a powerful way to get the best of both paradigms.

The structure that creates a lambda from a method is called a "method reference." You create a method reference much like you call a method, but use double colons (::) instead of a period (.). I like to think of the period as a single dot meaning, "let me call this method once," whereas the colons are lots of dots meaning, "let me call this method many times." Once you create the method reference using the double colons, you can work with the method reference just as you would work with an explicit lambda. The details of making methods into lambda calls are handled in each of the subsections below.

Making Static Methods into Lambdas

The simplest case is turning a static method into a lambda. To do this, you will simply follow the formula we laid out above: take the method call, and replace the period with a colon. The compiler will look into the signature of that method and perform type inference, constructing the appropriate interface implementation for you. Listing 2-20 shows static alternatives to a couple of the lambdas that we saw in 2-18: note that the compiler successfully discovers that we want an IntFunction<String>, not a Function<Integer,String>, and provides the appropriate type. If the target type signature is ambiguous, such as in Listing 2-19, then you have to get an explicit type signature in place. There are two ways to do this: either use an explicit lambda with explicit typing to resolve it, or assign the method reference to a variable with the desired type and then pass the variable in. As of Java 8, there is no way to do an inline cast operation on a method reference.

---

[9]Namely, an explicit lambda versus a method reference. For information on method references, see the next section.

Listing 2-20. Lambdas Made from Static Methods

```
IntFunction<String> intToString = Integer::toString;
ToIntFunction<String> parseInt = Integer::valueOf;
```

Making Constructors into Lambdas

Constructors live in that weird realm between static methods and instance methods: they are static methods whose implementation acts on an instance. Depending on where you are looking, they could be called "new," "<init>," or share their name with the class. Getting a method reference to a constructor is the same as getting a method reference to a static method: just use "new" as the name of the method. From the user's standpoint, it's really that simple. However, many classes have multiple constructors, so type inference does a lot of heavy lifting here. See Listing 2-22 for an example of BigInteger's String constructor as a Function.

Listing 2-21. Lambdas Made from a Constructor

```
Function<String,BigInteger> newBigInt = BigInteger::new;
```

Making Instance Methods into Lambdas

The most interesting and clever method reference is the instance method reference: you can literally package up any object and pass its method call around. That object can then fall out of scope, but its method is still available for use by way of this lambda. In Listing 2-22, we show a variety of different kinds of instance method references. In print, we use a static field reference to construct the method reference. For makeGreeting, we are using a String constant value. Both lookup and randomInt demonstrate a clever way to have a variable that is only accessible through the lambda: in the case of lookup, it is the return value of a method; in the case of randomIt, the object is constructed inline; resolvePath works off the base field value; the compareAgainst method uses the argument to generate a method reference. In all these cases, the instance is captured when the lambda is created. This means that if base is reassigned, for instance, resolvePath will still resolve against the previous base. Also, randomInt always acts on the exact same Random instances, no matter how many times it is called. Using instance methods this way allows you to configure an object, and then use a key piece of functionality provided by that object without worrying that someone will mess with the configuration.

Listing 2-22. Lambdas Made from an Instance Method

```
Consumer<String> print = System.out::println;
UnaryOperator<String> makeGreeting = "Hello, "::concat;
IntFunction<String> lookup = Arrays.asList("a","b","c")::get;
IntSupplier randomInt = new Random()::nextInt;

Path base = Paths.get(".");
Function<String,Path> resolvePath = base::resolve;

public IntUnaryOperator compareAgainst(Integer compareLeft) {
  return compareLeft::compareTo;
}
```

Specifying a Method to Be Used Later

The final way to use method references is perhaps the strangest in Java's object-oriented world: you can specify a method to be executed later on some arbitrary instance. The idea here is that you specify the name of an instance method, and that becomes a function whose first argument is the one that is implemented.

So this:

```
UnaryOperator<String> stringOp = String::concat
```

Is equivalent to:

```
UnaryOperator<String> stringOp = (x,y) -> x.concat(y);
```

As you can see, the method reference is constructed exactly the same way as the static method. Java recognizes it as an instance method, and therefore constructs the appropriate kind of lambda. Again, type inference is doing a lot of heavy lifting for us in order to maintain a nice syntax.

This use of a method reference is very common as an alternative to iteration: you can pass in a method that is executed for each element of a collection. Most developers familiar with this kind of stunt are used to seeing it in dynamically typed languages: for instance, this is the "star-dot operator" in Groovy. In Java 8, you can now pull off a similar stunt while retaining type safety.

Lambdas as Interface Implementations

If you are following along at home, you may have noticed the error when we attempted to assign a lambda to an `Object` way back in Listing 2-3. That error read, "Target type of a lambda conversion must be an interface." That is some highly precise jargon, so let's unpack it. When the compiler encounters a lambda, it attempts to make that lambda into a type that is sensical within Java's type system. That process is called "lambda conversion," and the destination for the lambda's conversion is called the "target type." The compiler only knows how to convert lambdas into interfaces—it cannot convert into primitive types, abstract types, or concrete types. So far, we have been exclusively using Java's functional interfaces, but lambdas can also be used to implement other interfaces, including interfaces that you define. This is very powerful, especially when combined with the ability to make any method call into a lambda. We already saw this at work in the previous chapter, in Listing 1-11 and 1-12. Here, we will get into the details and limitations.

The basic idea is that if you have an interface with a single abstract method, you can use a lambda to provide an implementation of that interface. This means that it is easy to provide a lambda as an implementation of `Comparable`, `Iterable`, and `Autocloseable`, but not `Iterator` or `Collection`. In Listing 2-23, we see a few useful and common tricks.

Listing 2-23. Various Examples of Useful Interfaces Implemented by Lambdas

```
/**
 * Given a {@link java.sql.Connection} in transactional mode, automatically
 * commit a transaction using Java's {@code try-with-resources}.
 */
public static AutoCloseable autoCommit(Connection c) throws SQLException {
  if (c == null) return () -> {};
  return c::commit;
}
```

```
// Create concurrency interfaces from lambdas
Runnable runMe = () -> System.out.println("Ran!");
Callable<Long> callMe = System::currentTimeMillis;
ThreadFactory t = Thread::new;

// Implement listener interfaces
ExceptionListener listener = Exception::printStackTrace;
```

Default Methods

The ability to define an interface inline makes interfaces much more succinct and pleasant to use. Yet Java 8 makes things even easier by allowing an interface to define a default implementation for its methods. This begins to seriously blur the lines between an interface and an abstract class: the java.util. AbstractCollection abstract class, for instance, could now be implemented purely as an interface.

As an example, let's create an Iterator type that can be defined inline by providing a lambda. The lambda is responsible for providing a "next element," perhaps consuming that element. A special value is used to signal when the elements have all been consumed. The user just provides that lambda; all the other Iterator methods are provided as default methods. The code for this class is given in Listing 2-24. As you can see there, default methods are provided using the default keyword. Just like any other member of an interface, all default methods are public. And just like any other member of an interface, you can specify public if you would like, although it is redundant and doing so has no effect.

Default methods are a major change to the Java ecosystem, and it seems like you would never use an abstract class again. However, there are a few caveats with default methods. First of all, there is no way to inherit a default method implementation: if you override the method, you have to implement it yourself. (Although, see the next section for a potential workaround.) Second, if you have a class with two interfaces that provided conflicting default methods, you will have to override the method and implement it yourself.

Default methods play a major part in Java 8 code, and have been retrofitted onto a number of standard Java interfaces. We will look into where they appear as we address each of these areas in later chapters.

Listing 2-24. The FunIterator Class, Demonstrating Default Methods

```
/**
 * An implementation of {@link java.util.Iterator} that can be implemented
 * as a lambda. You can also use this class as a simpler way to implement
 * an {@code Iterator}.
 * <p>
 * This interface does not support {@link #remove()} out of the box.
 */
public interface FunIterator<E> extends Iterator<E> {

  /**
   * Provides the next element, optionally consuming it. This is the abstract
   * method to implement as a lambda.
   * If {@code false} is passed in as an argument, this method should always
   * return the same value, and should never exhaust the iterator. If
   * {@code true} is passed in as an argument, the iterator should advance to
   * the next element after returning the value. At any point in time, if there
   * are no more elements, the iterator should return
   * {@link java.util.Optional#empty()}. This method should never throw an
   * exception or return {@code null}.
   *
```

```
 * @param consume  Whether the element should be consumed after being
 *                 returned.
 * @return {@link java.util.Optional#empty()} if there are no other elements;
 *         otherwise, an {@link java.util.Optional} containing the next
 *         element. Never {@code null}.
 */
Optional<E> nextElement(boolean consume);

@Override
default boolean hasNext() {
  return nextElement(false).isPresent();
}

@Override
default E next() {
  return nextElement(true).orElseThrow(
    () -> new NoSuchElementException("Iterator is exhausted")
  );
}

}
```

Static Methods

It's not directly related to lambdas, but now is a good time to mention it: as of Java 8, interfaces can also now provide static methods, just as any concrete or abstract class could provide static methods. If you want to provide a default method implementation to the outside world, you can use a static method to do so: simply have the default method call the static method.

Now that interfaces can have static methods, some Java interfaces have been extended to provide utility methods. The most notable to my mind is Comparator, which has picked up a large number of utility methods. For instance, in Listing 2-25, we define a Comparator that puts null File instances last and sorts the rest by file name. By allowing static methods, Java 8 has outdated the "utility class" convention, where an interface Foo would have utility class Foos or FooUtils. Now those utility methods reside directly on the interface itself.

Listing 2-25. Using Comparator Static Methods to Generate a Comparator

```
Comparator<File> fileComparator =
    Comparator.nullsLast(
      Comparator.comparing(File::getName)
    );
```

Functional Interface Helper Methods

The functional interfaces themselves carry a number of static and default methods to help you build the functions that you are looking for. Through this section, we will look at those methods, and get a sense as to when and why you want to use them.

Function.identity() and UnaryOperator.identity()

Perhaps the simplest to understand is `Function.identity()`. This provides a function that simply returns its argument. It is very useful in testing, when you want to test something that takes a function and acts on it. This can also be useful as a placeholder function: say that you have five types, and with four of them, you want to perform some transformation; with the fifth, you don't want to perform a transformation. In that case, you can maintain the symmetry of your codebase and avoid using `null` (and `NullPointerExceptions`) by using this method.[10] This method is also available under the `UnaryOperator` type, so that you can keep using that `Function` subclass and save yourself some typing.

Function.compose and Function.andThen

These two default methods provide the ability to take on functionality before and after a given function. The methods allow you to create a pipeline effect in a rather fluent API, and are especially useful for converting the types of a function to what you want them to be; you can prepend or append conversion functions inline.

If you want to change the result type, use `andThen`. Given the function `X->Y`, `andThen` allows you to create `X->Z` by specifying a function that takes the result, `Y`, and produces a `Z`. The argument, `X`, will be fed to the instance function, and then the results of the instance function, `Y`, are fed into the argument function. As an example, consider this series of method calls:

```
Function<Integer,String> f = Integer::toString;
f = f.andThen("10"::concat).andThen(Integer::parseInt);
```

These will create a function that will turn an `int` into a `String`, and then prepend "10," and then parse the value back out into an `int`. What started as an `int->String` type is now an `int(->String->String)->int`, returned in Java types as an `int->int`.

If you want to change the argument type, use `compose`. This method should have been called `butFirst`, because it works just like `andThen`, but on the front end instead of the back end. Given the function `X->Y`, `butFirst` allows you to create `W->Y` by specifying a function that takes some `W` and produces an `X`. The result of the specified function is fed as the argument to the instance function. We can specify the previous example "backwards" by doing this:

```
Function<String,Integer> f = Integer::parseInt;
f = f.compose("10"::concat).compose(Integer::toString);
```

Consumer.andThen

The Java SDK does not provide a `Consumer.compose` to modify the accepted type,[11] but there is a `Consumer.andThen`. Since the consumer takes in an argument but produces no result, all that `andThen` does is add additional processing; given two consumers of the same type, it provides a single consumer that executes both the given consumers. This lets you add additional processing to the end of your stream of processing. It is particularly useful for adding logging or other notifications into your consumer.

---

[10]See "Don't Use Null" below.
[11]See the FunJava project's `Functions` class: it provides a `compose` method that takes a `Function` and a `Consumer` and provides a `Consumer`.

Predicate.and and Predicate.or

Predicates are responsible for supplying Boolean checks, and those are usually composite kinds of structures. Although we opened the book talking about a simple case (a "not null" predicate), you are rarely so lucky as to have a simple predicate logic. Usually, you have complex chains of logic. In fact, one of the major advantages of using the predicate class is that you can construct this complex chain at a high level, and then execute it upon objects later. To join two predicates, you have to decide if you are joining them using an &&-style join or a ||-style join. The former case is handled by Predicate. and the latter case by Predicate.or.

In both these cases, the predicate is short circuiting: a predicate won't be executed if we already know the answer. If you have foo.and(bar).test(baz), and foo.test(bar) evaluates to false, then bar.test(baz) is never executed. Similarly, if you have foo.or(bar).test(baz), and foo.test(bar) evaluates to true, then bar.test(baz) is never executed. This is exactly how Java works with its Boolean operators.

Predicate.isEqual

If you have some specific value, and you want a test that will tell you if other values are equivalent to it, then use Predicate.isEqual. It uses Java's own Objects.equals(left,right) method, which first performs null checks and then returns left.equals(right), and so Predicate.isEqual can safely be used with null.

Predicate.negate

If you want the logical opposite of a given predicate, you can use Predicate.negate to get one. Combining Predicate.negate with Predicate.isEqual gives you the not-null check that started off Chapter 1: Predicate.isEqual(null).negate().

BinaryOperator.minBy and BinaryOperator.maxBy

These are two very useful methods, but many people do not realize they are there, since these methods are hidden out of the way among the functional interface types. Both of these methods provide a BinaryOperator, which is a BiFunction whose arguments and return value are all the same. Since BinaryOperator extends BiFunction, you can pass in these BinaryOperators any time your BiFunction type signature matches. The BinaryOperator that is supplied takes in two arguments of the same type, and returns the argument that is largest (maxBy) or smallest (minBy).

This may not seem like a big deal, but it very much is. In the next chapter, we will see how this works with collections and streams of objects, and how these methods fit naturally in. Even better, since these methods both take a Comparator as an argument, we can hook into all the useful utility methods provided on Comparator, which will also be covered in the next chapter.

The obvious use case is finding the smallest and largest element among many. However, you can use that Comparator to pick out the element that is closest to the value you want. You can also use the Comparator to provide a scoring algorithm, and then use this BinaryOperator to grab elements with the largest or smallest score. Any time that you have a proper ordering or a concept of "distance from a target," BinaryOperator.minBy and BinaryOperator.maxBy will probably help you out.

Lambda Best Practices

When people are first picking up object-oriented programming, there is a tendency to go nuts with inheritance. The language feature is so cool that you end up with layers upon layers of inheritance, and as a result, code becomes extremely difficult to follow and maintain. A similar thing happens with lambdas. At this point, you know enough about lambdas to be dangerous, and you will probably be overexcited to apply this newfound knowledge and use functional interfaces everywhere. That enthusiasm is great, but before you go out and lamdify all your code, let me give you some words of caution.

Use Interfaces

The most common misstep taken by an over-eager functional programmer is the use of functional interfaces in type signatures. In general, you should avoid using the functional interface types directly and instead provide single-method interfaces as arguments to your methods. These interfaces become a way to create self-documenting code and to provide meaningful type information, as well as leaving open the opportunity for your user to provide an actual Java type. If they want to implement your interface using lambdas and method references, they can still do that, but don't force them to.

Consider the two method signatures: `processFile(LineHandler handler)` and `processFile(Consumer<String> handler)`. In the latter case, it's not obvious what the `String` provides, or what the consumer is expected to do. Even more than that, though, if you later want to provide a `processFile(FileHandler handler)` method, then you can, whereas you would end up with conflicting types in the other case.

Use Method References

As much as possible, use a method reference instead of a lambda. Method references are not only shorter and easier to read, but using method references will get you thinking directly about the methods as values. This is the code you need to excise from your codebase and your brain:

```
x -> it.do(x)
```

If you are naturally writing that code, then you still have not made the leap to thinking at the higher level of functional programming. Once you make that leap, it will become much easier to communicate and work with complex functions, because you will be thinking in types, not in values.

Define Lambdas Inline

When you do use lambdas, define them inline. Unless you are doing some kind of fancy manipulation of your lambda, there is no reason to be assigning them to a variable. The reason that you want to define your lambdas inline is that it will allow your code to be more flexible when types change: you are letting type inference do more heavy lifting for you, and adapting your code to changing contexts. If you start assigning your lambdas to variables, you will have to start being explicit with types, and that is needlessly solidifying your types.

Lambdas Should Always Be Threadsafe

As we go through the rest of this book, we will see many places where lambdas make concurrent programming much easier. Many of the structures built off of lambdas will perform concurrent executions, sometimes without much warning. Because of this, your lambdas always need to be threadsafe. Pay particular attention to this with instance method handles, since thread-dangerous state can often be hiding within those instances.

Don't Use Null

The null keyword should never be used in your code. Now that Java has the Optional type, there is simply no need for it. Whenever you have a method, you should be explicit about whether or not you accept null, and you generally shouldn't accept it. This will save you from NullPointerException cropping up in obnoxious places, far from the site of the actual error. This is an especially painful problem when you start working with streams and lambdas, because the stack trace may not be very useful for you when you go to debug. The solution is to never accept null and to aggressively check for it, exploding loudly as soon as it occurs. Some developers are concerned that this is adding overhead to their code and hindering performance, but that concern is the height of premature optimizations. On the one hand, not guarding against null can lead your code to break badly, and so it is important to ensure correctness: I can give you the wrong answer infinitely fast. At the same time, adding in these guards will remove a lot of null from your code, and so those null checks will become cold branches and Java's highly optimized runtime will make them effectively costless. So these null checks are both high value and low cost.

Don't Release Zalgo

It's popular wisdom that programmers should learn multiple programming languages. The reasons for this are numerous, but one is often overlooked: programming languages form ecosystems with different people and different cultures, and you can often learn things in those cultures that enrich how you think about programming in general.

The JavaScript community, for instance, has discovered a monstrous entity named "Zalgo." Zalgo is an incomprehensible horror that seeks to consume and destroy you. Programmers are at risk, because Zalgo lurks beneath your code, waiting to be released by unwary programmers who write code that is impossible to reason about. Every programmer of functional code must be vigilant against the threat of Zalgo.

When you are passing around lambdas, it is easy to release Zalgo if you mix synchronous and asynchronous styles. When your code executes a user's lambda, it needs to be clear about whether the lambda will execute before the method resolves ("synchronous"), or at some point in the future ("asynchronous"). You must never mix the two approaches.

Consider, for instance, the following code:

```
List<Number> numbers = Arrays.asList(1, 2, 3);
numbers.forEach(i -> System.out.println(i));
System.out.println("Done");
```

What will print first in that code, "3," or "Done?" If you look up the API for Iterable.forEach, it tells you that it executes the lambda "until all elements have been processed or an exception is thrown," which tells you that it is synchronous. Therefore, you know that "Done" will come before "3."

On the other hand, consider this code:

```
Files.lines(Paths.get("build.gradle")).forEach(
  s -> System.out.println(s)
);
System.out.println("Done");
```

In this case, there is no guarantee about whether "Done" will come before the contents of build.gradle — the API for the Stream.forEach method explicitly states, "For any given element, the action may be performed at whatever time and in whatever thread the library choses," which tells you that it is asynchronous.

It may seem obvious enough at this point to avoid Zalgo, but the path to Zalgo is easy to tread for the unwary.

The story often goes something like this. Let's say you have a method that is going to do some expensive work, such as going to the database. Instead of having your code block for the trip, you have the user pass you a callback that executes when the data returns. The code looks something like this:

```java
public void readData(String key, ResultsHandler handler) {
    threadPool.submit(() -> {
        SomeModel resultingModel = null;
        /* Do expensive query setting "resultingModel"... */
        handler.accept(resultingModel);
    }
    );
}
```

Later on, you decide to add a caching layer in front of this method, because that is even more efficient, and some slightly stale data is just fine. So you update your code to read something like this:

```java
public void readData(String key, ResultsHandler handler) {
    SomeModel cachedModel = cache.get(key);
    if (cachedModel != null) {
        handler.accept(cachedModel);
    } else {
        threadPool.submit(() -> {
            SomeModel resultingModel = null;
            /* Do expensive query setting "resultingModel"... */
            cache.put(key, resultingModel);
            handler.accept(resultingModel);
        }
        );
    }
}
```

Now we're mixing asynchronous and synchronous styles: the handler may be executed either in the current thread (before we return) or in another thread (at some arbitrary point). Zalgo has been released. I have told you that it's horrifically evil, but it seems innocuous enough. If it is going to block the thread for a long time, it executes the code in another thread. If it won't block, it executes in this thread. Seems helpful. What's the problem with that?

That, my child, is how Zalgo will consume you.

The problem is that you don't know how the callback code will behave. The handler can do whatever it wants, including doing very expensive blocking computations. If the method resolves asynchronously — as it did before — then that is fine, since the primary execution thread of your application will continue along. Now that you changed the method to *sometimes* resolve asynchronously but *sometimes* resolve synchronously, that means that it will now *sometimes* block your primary execution thread with very expensive blocking computations. Sometimes it won't, of course. This is going to make for an infuriating debugging experience.

When the developer reasons about this code, mixing asynchronous and synchronous execution creates a branch with two very different but equally possible realities: one where the code executes synchronously and one where the code executes asynchronously. The way the application behaves in these two cases can vary wildly, so the developer has to hold both possibilities in mind. Each time the developer encounters this code, it creates another fork, doubling the complexity of the application. In some cases, both these branches are pretty much the same, but mark my words: the differences in those branches will crop up in surprising, unfortunate, and hard-to-debug circumstances.

If you are going to execute asynchronously, *always* execute asynchronously. If you are going to execute synchronously, *always* execute synchronously. Don't mix synchronous and asynchronous styles. Don't release Zalgo!

Build Complexity from Simple Parts

When we looked at `Function.compose` and `Function.andThen`, we built a function in one line that will give you the integer whose value in decimal is "10" concatenated with the given value. So if you give it "0," you get "100." If you give it "10," you get "1010." That's a nontrivial piece of logic, but we built it up by gluing together three method references, and then we got a handle on a single function that performed that behavior.

In the same way that we build up methods by delegating to other methods, we can build up functions by delegating to and wrapping other functions: find some way to perform the core logic, then prepend the function with type conversions and argument manipulation, and then append the function with result conversions.

This approach lets us do what aspect-oriented programming was aiming at: you can wrap your simple pieces of logic in handlers that perform additional processing without muddying up the core implementation with ancillary details. This approach allows us to continue to write focused, limited, type-specific methods that do one thing and do it well. These methods are easier to write and provide fewer nasty corners where bugs can reside.

Most importantly, these simple parts are more apt to be reused. Code reuse is the second derivative of code:[12] it is through code reuse that we not only accelerate our development, but accelerate the acceleration of our development. The old acronym is "KISS": "Keep It Simple, Silly," and as developers, we KISS for speed.

Use Types and the Compiler to Your Advantage

The major advantage that languages such as Scala and Java have over all other postfunctional languages is their type system. The type system will catch many of your errors. In our "Don't Release Zalgo" example, for instance, we could have returned a `Future` type instead of delegating to the callback. That type would denote that we execute asynchronously and would have given us pause when we went to execute synchronously. Similarly, if you drive `null` out of your codebase, the `Optional` type denotes when a value may or may not exist, ensuring that you handle the "may not exist" case more explicitly. It is easier for us to build up simple types from complex ones when the compiler tells us if our types mismatch: it is easy to get lost in a chain of andThen instances without compiler assistance.

There are other ways in which the compiler can help you out. For instance, if you declare a variable `final`, the compiler will ensure that you have it assigned before you use it. This is useful for ensuring that a variable is assigned once (and only once) when you enter into an `if/else` block. Here is an example of that code:

```
final Function<String,Integer> converter;
if(str == null || str.isEmpty()) {
  converter = s -> 0;
} else if(str.matches("\\d+")) {
  converter = Integer::parseInt;
} else {
  Function<String,String> eliminateNondigits = s -> {
    return s.replaceAll("[^\\d]", "");
  };
```

---

[12]See http://blog.enfranchisedmind.com/2007/09/use-vrs-reuse-or-the-second-derivitive-of-programming/ and http://blog.enfranchisedmind.com/2007/09/development-acceleration-the-second-derivative-of-functionality/ for more on this.

```java
Function<String,String> defaultString = s -> {
  if(s.isEmpty()) {
    return "0";
  } else {
    return s;
  }
};
converter = eliminateNondigits
  .andThen(defaultString);
  .andThen(Integer::parseInt);
}
```

In that example, the compiler ensures us that converter is set before we leave the if/else chain. No matter how many cases we have, and no matter how complex the code may get in each case, we know that each and every case will set a converter.

The type system is a powerful tool in the hands of a functional programmer because it allows you to enforce the constraints of the system and reason about how they are applied. Use the type system to the best advantage that you can, and avoid circumventing it.

CHAPTER 3

■ ■ ■

Lambda's Domain: Collections, Maps, and Streams

In the last chapter, we saw how lambdas themselves work, but we explicitly focused on lambdas without creating a context for their use. We extracted lambdas from their natural environment in order to analyze them under a microscope. In this chapter, we will begin to see lambdas in the wild.

Specifically, we will see how lambdas can be used with the familiar structures of collections and maps. However, collections and maps actually limit the power of lambdas. To get at their true power, Java introduced a new concept using an old word: streams. This chapter will close with an analysis of Java 8's streams, and how these functional streams allow for new forms of code reuse and expressiveness.

This chapter will be more concrete than the last, and we will stay tied to a particular example. This particular example will have specific use cases where lambdas will help us out. However, to understand all of this, we first have to understand where Java 8's lambdas are coming from. This requires us to make a quick return trip back into the strange world of functional programming languages.

Lambdas and Functional Programming

Java 8's lambdas come out of the world of functional programming. Functional programming models computer programs based on mathematical functions. In functional programming, lambdas represent the functions themselves. But, every mathematical function acts over a particular set of possible inputs, and produces a particular set of possible outputs. The inputs are called the "domain of the function," and the outputs are called the "range of the function."

Abstractly, the types of the lambda represent the function's domain and range. The Java type of the Function interface is Function<T,U>: T is its domain, and U is its range. This is why types are so useful in the world of functional programming: types allow you to clearly communicate the definition of the function. For the developers reading the API, types allow them to succinctly describe what you expect to receive and what you will return. The compiler also reads these types, and it reasons about your code using those types, providing optimizations not otherwise available.

However, abstractions only take you so far. Sooner or later, you have to execute your code against real data. You might build up the most beautiful chain of function applications ever conceived, but they won't accomplish anything for you until you apply them to something. In the functional programming approach, the goal of your application is simple: collect up all the domain objects that you care about and feed them through the function. So what kind of thing provides those domain objects for the functions to operate upon?

If you talk to your average Java developer about collecting up objects, he will reach to the Collection class and its related APIs. Historically, this has been how functional Java code has been written: you take a collection, apply a function to each element, and return the resulting collection. A function that acts on a collection this way is called a "comprehension." Java 8 makes comprehensions possible, and we will go through the APIs enabling comprehensions in this chapter. This approach works very well for relatively small collections of known items, and it is a very natural evolution for a Java developer.

There are, however, some serious limitations. The most obvious limitation is that the Collection API presumes to have all the data in memory, or at least readily at hand. This may not be the case if you are acting on all the rows in a database or all the words in a file. A more subtle consequence is that chaining together a series of these operations creates a series of intermediary collections, each of roughly the same size, and that is simply wasteful. Finally, most of the Collection API is not thread safe, or has only limited thread safety characteristics, which hamstrings the concurrent capabilities of lambdas.

To solve this, Java 8 introduced a concept of "functional streams." The term "stream" already has an established usage in Java, and functional streams are a new application of this old concept. Traditionally, the term "stream" refers to Java's I/O world, where we have an I/O stream representing a sequence of bytes. Most Java developers are used to working with these streams, and know how their bytes can be wrapped and contorted and manipulated through the decorator pattern, all while staying within the InputStream API. This is a powerful way to gain significant code reuse.

Functional streams are like these I/O streams, but they act on a sequence of objects instead of a sequence of bytes. Objects can be wrapped and contorted and manipulated as they pass through the stream, and we can gain the same kind of reuse. Thanks to the introduction of lambdas, we don't need the decorator pattern anymore: we can simply pass our implementations into the Stream object itself and get a new Stream back.

Functional streams work better than the collection approach because you don't need all the data in a collection up front, and the Java runtime is free to automatically leverage opportunities for concurrent execution when it can. The resulting API is extremely powerful, although it can be somewhat intimidating for Java developers: it is coming from a different world, so it may be unintuitive at the start. The rest of this chapter is about making streams make sense; by the time we are finished, they should be as intuitive for you to use as the Collection and Iterator classes.

To get there, let's start back with the Collection interface that is already familiar. Unlike the previous chapter, where we discussed things in the abstract, let's set a more concrete example. Let's say that we have a Library class. Instances of this class store Book objects in an arbitrary but significant order; the user of the class sets the order of the books, and we don't want to mess with that. Based on that requirement, we store a List<Book> instance in each Library instance. In addition, the Library has to provide functionality for "featured books." Some books are specially featured optionally with a particular feature message. To provide that functionality, we store a Map<Book,String> instance in each Library instance.

The starting code for Library and Book is given in Listing 3-1. Throughout the rest of this chapter, we will build out functionality for our Library class using the new functional tools provided in Java 8.

Listing 3-1. The Library and Book classes

```
Import java.util.Objects;
/**
 * Class representing an element of a {@link Library}.
 */
public class Book {

  /**
   * Represents the allowed genres of a book.
   */
  public static enum Genre {
    HORROR, COMEDY, TECHNICAL;
  }
```

```java
  private final String title;
  private final String author;
  private final Genre genre;

  /**
   * Constructor.
   *
   * @param title  The title of the book; may not be {@code null}.
   * @param author The author of the book; may not be {@code null}.
   * @param genre  The genre of the book; may not be {@code null}.
   */
  public Book(final String title, final String author, final Genre genre) {
    Objects.requireNonNull(title, "title of the book");
    this.title = title;
    Objects.requireNonNull(author, "author of the book");
    this.author = author;
    Objects.requireNonNull(genre, "genre of the book");
    this.genre = genre;
  }

  @Override
  public String toString() {
    return "\"" + title + "\" by " + author +
      " (" + genre.toString().toLowerCase() + ")";
  }

  @Override
  public int hashCode() {
    int result = title.hashCode();
    result = 17 * result + author.hashCode();
    result = 31 * result + genre.hashCode();
    return result;
  }

  @Override
  public boolean equals(final Object o) {
    if (o == null) return false;
    if (this == o) return true;
    if (!(o instanceof Book)) return false;

    final Book book = (Book) o;

    if (!author.equals(book.author)) return false;
    if (genre != book.genre) return false;
    if (!title.equals(book.title)) return false;

    return true;
  }

}
```

```java
import java.util.List;
import java.util.Map;
import java.util.Objects;
import java.util.ArrayList;
import java.util.HashMap;
/**
 * Class representing a collection of {@link Book} objects. The {@code Book}
 * objects are stored in a user-defined order, which defaults to insertion
 * order. A given {@code Book} can also be specified by the user as
 * <i>featured</i>, optionally with a <i>featured message</i>.
 */
public class Library {

  private final List<Book> books = new ArrayList<>();
  private final Map<Book, String> featuredBooks = new HashMap<>();

  /**
   * Adds a book to the end of the books list.
   *
   * @param book The book to add; may not be {@code null}.
   */
  public void addBook(Book book) {
    Objects.requireNonNull(book, "book to add");
    this.books.add(book);
  }

  /**
   * Adds a book to the end of the books list, and adds it as a featured book
   * with the given message.
   *
   * @param book    The book to add; may not be {@code null}.
   * @param message The featured message, which may be {@code null}.
   */
  public void addFeaturedBook(Book book, String message) {
    this.addBook(book);
    this.featuredBooks.put(book, message);
  }
  /**
   * Provides direct access to the listing of books. Modifying the returned|
   * collection will modify the books in the library.
   *
   * @return The books in this library; never {@code null}.
   */
  public List<Book> getBooks() {
    return this.books;
  }

  /**
   * Provides direct access to the listing of featured books. Modifying the
   * returned map will modify the featured books and their messages.
   *
```

```
 * @return The featured books in this library mapped to their
 *         (possibly {@code null}) message; never {@code null}.
 */
public Map<Book, String> getFeaturedBooks() {
  return this.featuredBooks;
}

}
```

Functional Iteration

One of the marks of pride in post-functional language communities is that nobody uses a for loop anymore. The abandonment of the for keyword has become a minimally acceptable criteria for code, enforced with righteous zeal. Instead, these languages provide an iterator method. Java 8 joins the ranks of these post-functional languages with the forEach and forEachRemaining methods.

The Iterable interface now provides a forEach method. Some Java developers still don't know about the Iterable interface, which was introduced in Java 5. It is the base class underlying all the Java SDK classes that can provide an Iterator, and it is the class that enabled the enhanced for loop introduced in Java 5. Since the new forEach method is on this widely implemented interface, all those implementing classes now have a forEach method, as well.

Semantically, the forEach method is the same thing as a for loop: it takes a Consumer and executes it for each element in the loop. Practically, however, it's an inside-out for loop. Instead of creating a structure where you iterate over the collection and then execute a series of steps for each iteration, the forEach method provides the series of steps to the collection, and the collection applies it to each element in order. This allows the collection implementation to perform the iteration in the most efficient way possible. Even better, the code is much more succinct and readable, as Listing 3-2 shows.

Listing 3-2. Printing out each of the books using an enhanced for loop and forEach

```
for (Book book : library.getBooks()) {
  System.out.println(book);
}

library.getBooks().forEach(System.out::println);
```

If you do have some legacy code where you are provided an Iterator, however, you can still use a functional alternative to the loop. In this case, the method is forEachRemaining, which applies the lambda to all the remaining elements of the iterator and exhausts it in the process.

The situation is slightly different for Map.forEach. Historically, Java has wanted you to think of a Map as providing access to a Collection of Map.Entry objects. With Java 8 lambdas, they are breaking away from that: the Map.forEach method does not take a Consumer of Map.Entry objects, but a rather BiConsumer of the key and value pairs. On the one hand, this makes for reasonably nice-looking inline implementations, such as in Listing 3-3: there is no more having to call entry.getKey() and entry.getValue(). On the other hand, BiConsumer is an exotic functional type, and very few lambda manipulations or existing method definitions play nicely with it.

Listing 3-3. Printing out each of the featured books using the Map version of forEach

```
library.getFeaturedBooks().forEach(
  (book, msg) -> System.out.println(book + ": " + msg)
);
```

With knowledge of those methods, you can now write Java code that never again uses the for loop, making your code post-functional programmer compliant. The ironic part of this zeal for the iterator method is that you almost never use the iterator method in functional programming. The reason is the return value: it is void in Java and is equally useless in almost all languages. This means that it is a hard stop on function building: for the functional programmer, there is nowhere to go from the iterator method. Its usefulness is therefore dependent entirely on side effects, which is antithetical to the entire functional programming paradigm. In Listing 3-3, for instance, a functional programmer would map the Book to a String, then pipe that into String concatenation, then pipe the result into System.out.println. Unfortunately, the Consumer type prevents that kind of chaining, because it is depending on the side effect of the Consumer implementation to accomplish anything interesting.

This is one of the places where post-functional languages and functional languages part ways most strongly. Post-functional languages accept side effects as a reasonable way to accomplish the programmer's goals, whereas functional languages punish the programmer for trying to code with side effects. While post-functional languages provide significantly more flexibility to the programmer, they also make it harder to read the code, reason about the code, or provide guarantees about its behavior (such as thread safety). It's the classic case of great power bringing great responsibility.

The takeaway lesson for the Java 8 developer is that it is fine to use the forEach/forEachRemaining methods. However, any time you reach for these methods, consider carefully whether you really want one of the other comprehensions. Using the right method for the job will improve your code's readability, give power to the runtime and library developers to optimize it appropriately, and exercise your habit of programming in a more powerfully functional way.

It is also worth noting that if you want to manipulate the collection, such as adding and removing members, this is not the way to do it. Attempting to modify the collection from within the forEach method may result in a ConcurrentModificationException occurring. Since the contract for forEach just says that the exception *may* occur, it is safe to assume that the exception will wait to occur until the worst possible circumstance, and only then bring your code down. If you want to manipulate the collection or map by passing in a lambda, you will have to use special methods for that.

Manipulating Collections and Maps with Lambdas

Within mathematics, there is no mutability: something that is true is always true; something that is false is always false. Functional programming follows mathematics' lead on this, and presumes that the domain cannot be changed. When you use a collection or a map as the domain of a lambda, the result will be a new collection, map, or object. In this section, we will explore the particular kinds of operations that are available.

Filtering Collections and Maps

When you are working with collections, the most common manipulation that you will want to do is to remove certain elements. In other post-functional languages (and in Java's Stream API), this is referred to as "filter." When you want to modify the collection by removing the elements directly, the method to use is Collection.removeIf. The removeIf method takes a Predicate and will remove from the collection all those elements for which the Predicate tests true. Java does not provide any Map equivalent, but you can use removeIf on the collections returned by Map.entrySet(), Map.values(), and Map.keySet() in order to change the underlying Map. The method returns true if there was a change made to the collection but false if the collection remained unchanged.

In Listing 3-4, we use the removeIf functionality to extend our Library class, providing the ability to remove all the books of the given genre. Since we want to perform a test on the result of some processing, we define a utility method here: mapThenTest. This provides us a predicate that performs some mapping and tests the result of the mapping: in our case, we want to get the genre and then perform a test of the genre. With that predicate defined, we then pass it into removeIf for the books set and the featured books set.

There are a few key things to notice in Listing 3-4. Note that using the functional interfaces allows us to ensure we are using the same code for both the books list and the featured books set: any change to the predicate would be reliably applied in both cases. Also notice that the removeIf call entirely removes the iteration code in both places, leaving us with much cleaner and descriptive code. Since the featured books set is a strict subset of the books list, we can use the return value of the first call as an optimization to short-circuit our removal: if we found no books matching the genre, then there is no reason to check the featured books list. The use of functional code here saves us a lot of boilerplate and noise, and the variable names become labels describing what the function does. When you have behavior as variables, it is a lot easier to produce self-documenting code.

Listing 3-4. A Library instance method to remove genres using removeIf

```
/**
 * Maps an element to a value and then tests that mapped value.
 *
 * @param map The function that defines the map; never {@code null}
 * @param test The function that defines the test; never {@code null}
 * @return A predicate that tests the result of the mapping of its argument.
 */
private static <T,U> Predicate<T> mapThenTest(
  Function<T,U> map, Predicate<U> test
) {
  Objects.requireNonNull(map, "the map implementation");
  Objects.requireNonNull(test, "the test implementation");
  return t -> test.test(map.apply(t));
}


/**
 * Removes all books of the given genre from both the library collection
 * and the featured collection.
 *
 * @param genre The genre to compare against; never {@code null}.
 */
public void removeGenre(Book.Genre genre) {
  Objects.requireNonNull(genre, "the genre to compare against");
  Predicate<Book> hasGenre = mapThenTest(Book::getGenre, genre::equals);
  if (this.getBooks().removeIf(hasGenre)) {
    this.getFeaturedBooks().keySet().removeIf(hasGenre);
  }
}
```

Mapping Collections and Maps

If you have embraced a more functional style of development, you are probably using a lot of immutable objects. In this chapter, we are taking that approach with our Book class. However, this leads to a problem when we want to manipulate the objects: for instance, say that we want to add a star after the title if it is featured. Since the Book instances are immutable, we will need to replace the old instances with our new instances. To do this, we can use the List.replaceAll method. The method is attached to List and not to Collection because replacing elements in some kinds of collections raises awkward situations for their API, such as in the case of SortedSet. (If you transform the sorted elements of a SortedSet, what sorting do you apply to the result?)

If we want to add a star after the title if the book is featured, we will start by needing to define what it means to "add a star after the title." Given our available API for the Book class, we will have to define an inline lambda to do this. (This is a sign that our Book API is probably missing something useful, but that is another conversation.) Thinking functionally, we want to apply a transformation when certain criterion is true. This calls for another utility function: applyIf. That will take a predicate and a function, and apply the function only when the predicate is true. Since we are only working with a single data type, we can use the UnaryOperator shorthand to save some typing and some type variables. With that utility method available to us, we then need to get a handle on a Predicate to determine if the book is featured, as well as the function to perform the transformation. The resulting UnaryOperator does exactly what we are looking for: if the Predicate test returns true, we will execute our "add a star after the title" function; if the test returns false, we will return the Book instance we were provided. The code for this approach is given in Listing 3-5.

Listing 3-5. A Library instance method to star featured books using List.replaceAll

```
/**
 * Applies a mapping operation to the argument only when {@code test}
 * returns {@code true} for that argument.
 *
 * @param test Test determining if mapping is applied; never {@code null}
 * @param ifTrue Mapping to apply when the test is true; never {@code null}
 * @return Operator appling {@code ifTrue} when {@code test} is true
 *         and otherwise returning the argument.
 */
private static <T> UnaryOperator<T> applyIf(
  Predicate<T> test, UnaryOperator<T> ifTrue
) {
  Objects.requireNonNull(test, "the predicate to test");
  Objects.requireNonNull(ifTrue, "the method to apply if true");
  return t -> {
    if(test.test(t)) {
      return ifTrue.apply(t);
    } else {
      return t;
    }
  };
}


/**
 * Updates the library, replacing each book that is featured with a book
 * with the same title plus {@code *}.
 */
public void starFeatureBooks() {
  UnaryOperator<Book> starBook = book ->
    new Book(book.getTitle() + "*", book.getAuthor(), book.getGenre());
  Predicate<Book> isFeatured = getFeaturedBooks().keySet()::contains;
  UnaryOperator<Book> starIfFeatured = applyIf(isFeatured, starBook);
  getBooks().replaceAll(starIfFeatured);
}
```

There is also a way to perform this kind of manipulation on a Map instance, although you can only change the value: the keys cannot be changed through these manipulation calls for the same reason that replaceAll is hard for Set to implement. The method is still quite useful: consider, for instance, that we want to execute a hygiene method on the featured book messages: we would like to clean up the messages by providing a default message and remove trailing periods. We can do this by executing the replaceAll method and returning the updated value, which we do in Listing 3-6. The complexity of this body does not lend itself particularly nicely to a functional solution, so we went ahead with an inline function definition.

Listing 3-6. A Library instance method to clean up featured book messages using Map.replaceAll

```
/**
 * Performs various clean-up tasks on all the features messages.
 */
public void cleanUpFeaturedMessages() {
  this.getFeaturedBooks().replaceAll((book, msg) -> {
      // Set a default message
      if (msg == null || msg.isEmpty()) {
        msg = "Featured " + book.getGenre().toString().toLowerCase() +
              " book by " + book.getAuthor();
      }

      // Remove trailing periods unless they are an elipsis
      if (msg.endsWith(".") && !msg.endsWith("...")) {
        msg = msg.substring(0, msg.length() - 1);
      }

      return msg;
    }
  );
}
```

Map Computations

The Map class itself has been extended with some functional-style manipulations that allow you to work with particular keys. These methods are not directly inspired by functional programming techniques, but rather are shorthand for common code such as the following:

```
// Default values
String value = map.get(key);
if(value == null) {
  value = computeValue(key);
  map.put(key, value);
}

// Increment values
Integer value = map.get(key);
if(value != null) {
  value += 1;
  map.put(key, value);
}
```

This code is really four lines to accomplish a single piece of logic: get the value for the key, setting the value if it is missing. Aside from being lengthy, this code is also unclear; it's not clear that value is still effectively in the process of being generated after the get. Even more, this code is inefficient: it does a get followed by a put, requiring a duplicate lookup of the key.

Instead, the Map class now provides you with a way to access the map and implement this special handling in a single method call, which ensures that the returned value is fully configured when you receive it and saves you the overhead of the repeated lookup. This is a perfect case of how lambdas let developers write code that is more efficient and more expressive and safer – all at the same time.

The most common use case that I have encountered is for defaulted values. For instance, let's create a method that will get the featured book message, providing the default value if it is not set. We'll follow the same default message created in Listing 3-7, but provide the default value on key lookup. We will do this using the computeIfAbsent method, which is the easy way of calculating defaults. Note that the computeIfAbsent method is also a convenient way to implement multimaps or canonicalized mappings, which are simply special cases of defaulted values.

```
map.computeIfAbsent(key, k -> new HashMap<>()); // Multimap
map.computeIfAbsent(key, Function.identity()); // Canonicalized mapping
```

Listing 3-7. A Library instance method to provide featured book messages using Map.computeIfAbsent

```
/**
 * Provides a featured book message for the given book. If the book was not
 * previously a featured book, it will be after this method resolves. If it
 * did not previously have a featured book message, it will have one after
 * this method resolves.
 *
 * @param featuredBook The book whose message is desired; never {@code null}
 * @return The message for the featured book; never {@code null}
 */
public String getFeaturedBookMessage(Book featuredBook) {
  Objects.requireNonNull(featuredBook, "featured book");
  return this.getFeaturedBooks().computeIfAbsent(featuredBook, book ->
    "Featured " + book.getGenre().toString().toLowerCase() + " book by "
    + book.getAuthor()
  );
}
```

Another common task with maps is to keep track of instance counts. For instance, consider if we wanted to generate genre counts for certain user-specified genres. For this, we can specify computeIfPresent. This method is the complement to computeIfAbsent: it only executes its lambda if the value already exists. This functionality is very useful for updating certain existing values without creating additional values in the map. To provide these genre counts, we will first initialize the desired keys to zero, and then we will iterate over all the books, incrementing the count if it already exists. We do this in Listing 3-8. The computeIfPresent method is also useful for providing any kind of initialization or wrapping code on the values of the method while sidestepping the null check.

Listing 3-8. A Library instance method to provided featured book messages using Map.computeIfAbsent

```
public Map<Book.Genre, Integer> getGenreCounts(Book.Genre... genres) {
  Map<Book.Genre, Integer> toReturn = new HashMap<>();
  Arrays.asList(genres).forEach(genre -> toReturn.put(genre, 0));
  getBooks().forEach(book ->
    toReturn.computeIfPresent(book.getGenre(), (key, count) -> count + 1 )
  );
  return toReturn;
}
```

It is also possible to use a single manipulator method to handle both missing and existing values. This method is simply called compute, and the lambda is applied with the current value for that key: if the key was not in the map before the method was called, the lambda is passed null as the value. If the lambda passed in does not return null, then the compute method is effectively the same as this:

```
map.put(key, f(key, map.get(key)));
```

Obviously, this adds some complexity to the code, because you have to handle both the case when the key is already defined and the case when it is not. In exchange for handling this complexity, however, you get maximum flexibility. If we wanted to extend our code in Listing 3-6 to provide all the default message functionality that we implemented back in Listing 3-5, then we could use the compute method, and it would look like Listing 3-9.

Listing 3-9. A Library instance method to provide featured book messages using Map.compute

```
public String getFeaturedBookMessage(final Book featuredBook) {
  return getFeaturedBooks().compute(featuredBook, (book, msg) -> {
      // Set a default message
      if (msg == null || msg.isEmpty()) {
        msg = "Featured " + book.getGenre().toString().toLowerCase()
            + " book by " + book.getAuthor();
      }

      // Remove trailing periods unless they are a bad elipsis
      if (msg.endsWith(".") && !msg.endsWith("...")) {
        msg = msg.substring(0, msg.length() - 1);
      }

      return msg;
    }
  );
}
```

The final manipulation API in the Map is merge. This method has an implementation that seems strange at first: it takes a key, a value, and a "remapping function." If the key is not already assigned, it uses the value; if the key is assigned, it passes the argument value and the current value in the map into the remapping function and assigns that to the key. After all that, the method returns the new value mapped to the given key. As arcane as it may seem, this strange dance is exactly what you want for tracking counts in the map: you pass in the key, and pass in the count as the value, and then pass in addition as your lambda. It also works for tracking bitmasks, concatenating lists, and any other time that you are merging together values based on a key. In Listing 3-10, we provide a general genre count method based on this approach.

Listing 3-10. A Library instance method to count Map.merge

```
public Map<Book.Genre, Integer> getGenreCounts() {
  Map<Book.Genre, Integer> counts = new HashMap<>();
  getBooks().forEach(book ->
   counts.merge(book.getGenre(), 1, (i, j) -> i + j)
  );
  return counts;
}
```

When deciding between Map.compute and Map.merge, the important question is whether your new value cares about the key, or about the old value. If the new value is based on the key, use Map.compute (or one of its variants); if the new value cares about the old value, use Map.merge. However, if you forget the distinction, the type signatures are there to help you out.

Streams

So far, everything we have discussed has been about editing an existing Collection or Map in place. Throughout the rest of the book, however, we will focus on the true power of lambdas: functional streams (hereafter just "streams"). The classes for supporting streams are primarily collected in the new java.util.stream package, but there are little gems of stream APIs sprinked throughout the rest of the Java SDK API. The next few chapters will all circle around how those APIs (or their unfortunate lack) will change the way that you write code with Java 8. Before we can do that, though, we need to get a handle on what a stream is and how it works.

Streams are like iterators but have explicitly broader capabilities. There was always an assumption with an interator that you were only iterating through it once, and always on the same thread, and that there was always an underlying collection that was being iterated over. There were a few attempts to build iterators off of things other than collections (such as the lines of a file), and even a few attempts to make iterators act like lazy lists or suppliers. Making that desired functionality fit into the Iterator API always felt like attempting to shove a square peg into a round hole. Even more, you were always rather limited with what you could do with an iterator. Unlike I/O streams, for instance, there never developed significant and widely adopted support for wrapping iterators or manipulating what they returned. An iterator was something that you used to simply iterate over the elements in a very imperative style, and that was that.

With streams, however, things are entirely different. Streams can be explicitly parallelizable, which enables the user code and the library itself to read from them and execute them on multiple threads. Streams are designed to be transformed by Function lambdas, filtered by Predicate lambdas, and generally manipulated in the functional style that we have grown to love. Even better, they can be collected together in a variety of ways, enabling them to be plugged into any of the legacy APIs or to efficiently implement complex processing.

The life cycle of a stream is slightly more complicated than the life cycle of an iterator, because a lot more is going on. The life cycle of a stream is:

1. Creation

2. Mapping and Filtering (called the *Intermediate Steps*)

3. Collecting, Processing, or Reducing (called the *Terminal Step*)

Each of these three steps can take a wide variety of forms, and you can mix and match them like building blocks to construct practically any flow that you can envision. This is extreme flexibility and relatively easy to manage, thanks to the type systems. What is even better is that the parallelism of steps 2 and 3 are automatically handled for you by Java, so the Java runtime and libraries themselves automatically optimize your implementation.

Stream Creation

The first step, "Creation," is where you generate a stream. When generated, a stream has not yet done anything with the underlying data, just as an I/O stream has not read any bytes when you create it. The stream simply understands how to start generating data, and it provides a rich API and a significant amount of metadata for the generation of that data.

You can generate a stream from a Collection using the stream() or parallelStream() method. The stream() method generates a sequential (non-parallel) stream, which is useful when you need elements of the Collection to be processed in iteration order. If you do not have any order-of-execution requirements, however, it is always better to ask for a stream using parallelStream(). That method gives permission to the generated stream to process the elements in any order, including processing them concurrently.

It is worth noting that you *may* still get a sequential stream from parallelStream() if the Collection can't support parallelism: calling parallelStream is not demanding a stream that is parallelizable, but is giving permission for the returned stream to be parallelizable. These methods provide a bridge from the Collection API to the Stream API, so it is easy to migrate your code.[1] Similarly, if you want to generate a stream from an array, then use the Stream.of(array) method.

At the lowest level, streams can be generated using the static methods on the Stream interface. In particular, you can generate a Stream based on the Supplier functional interface using the generate method, and you can create a stream that iterates based on some initial value and an incrementing lambda using the iterate method (e.g., pass in 0 and x->x+1 as the lambda to create a stream that counts up from zero). Finally, the Stream class provides a builder class via the builder() method, so you can pass in elements to the builder and then generate the stream based on the results.

When we get into stream generation, we are entering into the lair of these strange beasts called "spliterators." Spliterators can be thought of as the larval form of streams: they enter into the cocoon through the StreamSupport.stream method and emerge as a fully formed Stream instance. They are complex enough in their own right to warrant a lengthier discussion, though, so we will get into spliterators at length when we talk about lambda and stream implementation details in Chapter 9. For the most part, users can and should stick to the Stream interface itself: rely on library support to obscure away the spliterator implementation details.

The streams you see here and in the Java SDK are not the only possibilities. Webonise Lab's FunJava library provides other ways to generate streams: In specific, that library provides a stream based on a database ResultSet, based on file contents, based on directory structures, and based on InputStream and Reader instances. We will get into the details about those stream generators in the chapters on processing files and processing database calls using streams, and you can use those implementations as models for your own stream implementations. For the sake of focus, however, in this chapter we will stick to those simpler streams provided by Java itself.

Mapping and Filtering Streams

Once you have a stream created, what can you do with it? Operations on streams are broken down into two different kinds: *intermediate* and *terminal* operations. The intermediate steps are steps that can be chained together, whereas the terminal steps terminate the stream. The processing of the stream is not kicked off until the stream reaches a terminal step, so the intermediate steps can be chained together and manipulated before the stream initiates any kind of heavyweight activity. There are two basic kinds of intermediate steps: map steps and filter steps.

---

[1]For information on how to bridge back to the Collection API from the Stream API, see the collecting/reducing step description below and the Collectors class.

The word "map" here is used in its functional sense: you take an input and you produce an output. In this case, the mapping operation will take each element of the stream, apply a function to that stream ("map the value"), and produce an output. This allows you to take a stream of one type and generate a stream of a new type: for instance, you could take a stream of ids and generate a stream of objects instantiated from a database call. Returning to our Library example, we could generate a stream of the library's books, and we could easily map that onto a stream of genres. This is what that would look like:

```
Stream<Book.Genre> genres =
  library.getBooks().parallelStream().map(Book::getGenre);
```

The map function presumes that you will be producing one output element for each input element. If you may produce zero output elements or many output elements for each input element, you instead will want to use the flatMap function. The flatMap function works the same way as the map function, except instead of producing a single element, it produces a Stream of elements. For instance, assume that you had a stream of file names, and you wanted to concatenate together all those file's contents. First, you could map the strings into Path instances, and then use the Files.lines method, which takes in a Path instance and produces a stream of its contents. You now have a map from a stream into a stream of streams: this is where flatMap will flatten that down for you. The code to do this is given in Listing 3-11. This code is made slightly more complicated by the checked exception that is thrown by the Files.lines method, but we will address how to make this code nicer in chapter 7.

Listing 3-11. Creating a stream of all the lines from files given a list of file names via Stream.flatMap

```
Function<Path, Stream<String>> readLines = path -> {
  try {
    return Files.lines(path);
  } catch (IOException ioe) {
    throw new RuntimeException("Error reading " + path, ioe);
  }
};
Stream<String> lines = Stream.of("foo.txt", "bar.txt", "baz.txt")
                            .map(Paths::get)
                            .flatMap(readLines);
```

The other common intermediary step is a filtering step. Filtering ensures that everything in the stream satisfies some test, which allows you to sift out elements that you don't want. To filter, you pass a Predicate into the Stream.filter method. Each element in the stream is put through the test. If the test returns true, the stream generates the element; if the test returns false, the stream silently discards the element. For our Library class, we could get a stream of only technical books by passing Genre.TECHNICAL::equals as our filtering Predicate. That would look like this:

```
Stream<Book> techBooks =
  library.getBooks().parallelStream().filter(Book.Genre.TECHNICAL::equals);
```

Note that the element type of the stream is not changed in filtering: we are not performing any kind of transformation on the elements themselves, but simply deciding whether to retain or reject each stream element. This is useful because you can add filters in the middle of processing to perform tests when you have the appropriate types. For instance, we can extend the Listing 3-11 example to only read the content from existing files by passing a filter; only paths for which Files.exists returns true will be retained. We implement this in Listing 3-12. There, we create the Path instances first, then pass those transient instances into Files.exists, and then pass the satisfying Path instances into our readLines lambda to generate our String instances. Our inputs are String instances and our outputs are String instances, but we are performing processing and logic on the Path instances that exist only within the stream itself.

Listing 3-12. Creating a stream of all the lines from existing files given a list of file names via Stream.filter

```
Function<Path, Stream<String>> readLines = path -> {
  try {
    return Files.lines(path);
  } catch (IOException ioe) {
    throw new RuntimeException("Error reading " + path, ioe);
  }
};
Stream<String> lines = Stream.of("foo.txt", "bar.txt", "baz.txt")
                          .map(Paths::get)
                          .filter(Files::exists)
                          .flatMap(readLines);
```

Collecting, Processing, or Reducing Streams

The mapping and filtering operations that we just discussed are the intermediary operations; you can continue to chain them together to your heart's content. Sooner or later, though, you will want to stop massaging your stream and actually do something with it. This is where the terminal operations come in. You only get one terminal operation per stream, and the stream is actually executed when the terminal operation is applied. There are three basic ways to terminate a stream: by collecting its elements, by generating side effects based on its elements, or by performing a calculation on its elements. These three ways are referred to as *collection*, *processing*, and *reducing*, respectively.

To collect streams, you need to specify what kind of collection you want as a result, and how you want to collect the elements. The Java SDK ships with many options in the Collectors class. This class produces various kinds of Collector instances. A Collector instance is responsible for consuming elements of a stream, updating some internal state based on those elements, and generating a result at the end. The built-in collectors are truly impressive: you can get the average, count the number of elements, get the min or max based on some Comparator, group elements based on some key (returning a Map of List instances), concatenate the string representation of all the results into a single String (optionally with some delimiter), and more. In Listing 3-13, we could go from our Library instance's books to a Map sorting those books by genre. Note that we use the groupingByConcurrent method in order to maintain the permission to execute in parallel. This is one of those moments where comparing the Stream API code to more traditional Java code truly exposes the power of functional programming.

Listing 3-13. Grouping Books by Genre Using Streams

```
Map<Book.Genre, List<Book>> booksByGenre =
    library.getBooks().parallelStream()
        .collect(Collectors.groupingByConcurrent(Book::getGenre));
```

Sometimes you do not want to collect together the results, but you just want to generate some side effect. The classic example would be printing out the results of a stream execution. To do this, you use the Stream.forEach method, just as you would do on a Collection. The one major difference is that the Stream.forEach method makes no guarantees about the order of execution: a parallel stream may well generate results in any order it chooses. If you really want to ensure ordering, you need to use the

Stream.forEachOrdered method. This method provides the same functionality as forEach, but with the added contract that the elements are processed in the order the stream generates them (called "encounter order"). In general, if you are reaching for Stream.forEach (and especially if you are reaching for Stream.forEachOrdered), you should take a long breath and reconsider if there is a better way for you to be handling the situation, such as a custom Collector. Programming by side effects is almost never the right answer, and is always a long-term hindrance for maintenance.

The last common terminal operation is called *reducing*, and it is an initially strange maneuver coming from functional programming.[2] The idea is that you pass in some initial value, and a function takes an element and returns an element with the same type as the initial value. The result of that function is passed along to the next element. The results of these executions are daisy-chained until the entire stream is consumed, and then the final result is returned. This chained execution is extremely powerful, and once you get the knack of it, it becomes easy to implement very complicated operations with very simple code. If you wanted to roll your own string concatenation, for instance, you could implement your reduction this way:

```
String booksString =
        library.getBooks().parallelStream()
          .map(Book::toString)
          .map(str -> str + "\n")
          .reduce("", String::concat);
```

Conceptually, what this will do is generate a stream of books, convert each book to its string representation, append a carriage return to each of those string representations, and then reduce that resulting stream. The reduction step will start with an empty string and concatenate the results. The first concatenation will concatenate the empty string with the first book; the next concatenation will take the result from the first and concatenate the second book; the next concatenation will take the result from the second and concatenate the third book; and it will go on like this until there are no more books, finally returning the result.

This warrants a word to the wise. The reduce operation is an extremely powerful operation, and it will almost certainly become a Golden Hammer[3] for you at some point; as you become more proficient with it, you will start reaching for reduce to terminate all your strings. This is not a bad impulse, because it shows that you are thinking in a functional way. If, however, you start wanting to pass in more state to your reduce operation than simply the previous result, then what you really want is a custom Collector instance or a wrapped Collector instance (c.f. Collectors.collectingAndThen). Keep this in mind, and you will keep your code readable and functional while also producing more reusable code.

Primitive Streams

Before we leave this introduction to streams, it is important to know that there are specific streams for the int, long, and double primitive types. You generate these streams by using Stream class methods: mapToInt/flatMapToInt, mapToLong/flatMapToLong, mapToDouble/flatMapToDouble. As you might expect, they provide some performance overhead compared to passing around object wrappers, although it's generally not enough to be significant for application code. More importantly, they provide APIs that fit the shape of many existing methods. For instance, IntStream has a method called mapToObj that takes a function that maps an int to an Object. The shape of that function perfectly fits the method List.get(int), so you can call intStream.map(List::get).

---

[2]While talking to functional programmers, they may also refer to the reduce operation as *inject* or *fold*.
[3]The term "Golden Hammer" comes from the popular quip: "If all you have is a hammer, everything looks like a nail." If you only have a hammer, and you are really excited about having it, then what you have is a Golden Hammer.

Lambda's Domain in Review

Java 8 provides a new abstraction: you can now abstract away the concept of processing a domain. You begin with a stream, and whether that value is coming from a map, a collection, or somewhere else, the resulting processing code is exactly the same. You can now get away from the logic of iterating over your source, and focus on what you want to do with the elements that it provides. As we have seen in this chapter, streams are this abstraction. In addition, there are some convenient shorthand methods. These shorthand methods are especially useful for converting legacy code to a more functional style. In the next chapter, we will look at how to handle data sources that are outside of our applications: interacting with the outside world makes these functional structures more complicated. This complication will actually show the power of functional programming to deal with awkward code and let you focus on the attention.

CHAPTER 4

■ ■ ■

I/O with Lambdas

So far, our exploration of lambdas and streams has existed in the well-controlled world of code. Sometimes, however, your code has to talk to the outside world. This chapter is where we enter into lambdas in the real world: instead of showing what is possible with lambdas in the abstract, we are getting into what programming with lambdas looks like in the grittiness of real code. This is a world where you end up having to work around a lot of unfortunate legacy code in Java, and where the nice theory and simple examples of lambdas give way to some of the gritty complexity. The important part for you is to understand how to work with that complexity in order to create a nicer development experience and more productive, stable code.

For our first case, we will be interacting with files. Through this chapter, we will implement a number of useful file utilities. We will implement code that will handle all the boilerplate for constructing and cleaning up a temporary file, allowing the user of the code to focus on working with the temporary file. And we will implement a method that will read through all the lines of the file, and another that will read through all the lines of certain files in the directory.

We chose files as a starting point because the file system is an obnoxiously unstable bit of reality. Many inexperienced developers will write file system code with many undocumented assumptions about the world outside the codebase and beyond the type system. These assumptions hold true throughout development, but then explode on production. The developer, confused, then utters the infamous words: "It works on my machine."

To deal with this problem, Java introduced the idea of checked exceptions. A checked exception is a way of stating that the method depends on some reality that is beyond the state of the program itself. Unchecked exceptions are there for when the programmer screwed up and passed something they shouldn't have or called a method at the wrong time. Checked exceptions, on the other hand, are for when something went wrong beyond the control of the application itself. The IOException type hierarchy describes various different ways that trying to perform I/O can fail for an application. The checked exception is the way of requiring the programmer to deal with the instability of the outside world.

Languages with less expressive type systems ignore this instability, and unwise developers circumvent the handling for these potential errors. This creates an illusion of clean code, but that illusion will be brutally shattered when a virus scanner locks a file that your code is trying to write, or some other oddity of the outside world deviates from the pristine presumptions of your code. Forcing you to deal with certain exceptions was a wise design, although many developers seem quick to dismiss it. I would dismiss it, too, except that I keep encountering programs that explode unhelpfully on I/O errors because people, languages, and tools circumvented the safety check.

Checked exceptions exist for a reason: sometimes you really do need to be responsive to an error condition. Unfortunately, they are not amenable to functional code at all. A mathematical function has an input and an output and no side effects: functional code wants to be as close to a mathematical function as possible. In Java 8 terms, this means that lambdas should not throw exceptions, and you cannot pass methods throwing a checked exception as an implementation for a functional interface (Function, Consumer, or Supplier). Upon encountering this, many programmers will simply turn the checked exception into an unchecked exception and move on. This is circumventing the safety of your system. Instead, we'd like to retain the safety while still behaving nicely in our functional world.

In the functional world, you only have two options for handling a situation: you will deal with it either upon input or upon output. If you are dealing with exceptional circumstances in a functional world, this means that you are either going to be passing exception handlers as an argument, or you will be passing information about exception occurrences as part of the return value. Working with exceptions this way may seem strange, but that is simply the experience of learning a new paradigm. This way of working with exceptions may also seem complicated, but the reality is that it is handling the complication intrinsic in I/O. The difference between engineers and artists is that engineers are punished for ignoring the real world.

Throughout the rest of this chapter, we will begin with a simple task: working with a temporary file. We will see where the exceptions arise, and work with both input and output styles of handling them. Then we will build our more advanced file systems from there. So let's get started.

Temporary Files and the Hole in the Middle

In the first chapter, we saw how inversion of control was an object-oriented way of performing a functional callback. There's a common pattern in the functional world where a function performs some setup at the beginning, some cleanup at the end, and then calls back into the user code to figure out what to do in the middle. My friend, mentor, and co-blogger, Brian Hurt, refers to this as the "hole in the middle" pattern. When dealing with temporary files, that's exactly what we want: we want to create the temporary file at the start, and we want to ensure the temporary file is cleaned up at the end, and allow the users to do what they would like with the file in the middle. The basic pattern will look like this:

```
<RETURN_T> RETURN_T withTempFile(Function<FunFile, RETURN_T> function) {
    File file = null;
    try {
      file = File.createTempFile("funfile", "tmp");
      return function.apply(file);
    } finally {
      if (file != null) file.delete();
    }
}
// This is not valid Java code: read on!
```

The setup of the temporary file is our `File.createTempFile(String,String)` call. The cleanup is the `file.delete()` call. The `function.apply` call is the hole in the middle, which the caller will fill in for us. But, of course, this is not valid Java code: there is the unhandled `IOException` that needs to be addressed. As we discussed previously, we have two options: handling the exception on input via a callback, and handing the exception on output via the return value. Let's take a look at both of these approaches in turn.

Exception Handling via Input: Passing in an Exception Handler

If you take a look at the basic pattern above, you can actually think of it as having two holes in the middle: one that is the standard behavior, and one that is the exceptional behavior. Therefore, you could take two callbacks: one implementing the standard behavior, and one implementing the exceptional behavior. A naïve implementation would look like this:

```
<RETURN_T> RETURN_T withTempFile(
  Function<FunFile, RETURN_T> function,
  Consumer<IOException> exceptionHandler
) {
```

```
    File file = null;
    try {
      file = File.createTempFile("funfile", "tmp");
      return function.apply(file);
    } catch(IOException ioe) {
      exceptionHandler.consume(ioe);
    } finally {
      if(file == null) file.delete();
    }
  }
}
// This is not valid Java code: read on!
```

There are three problems with this code. One problem is that it uses null for the file, when null is not a valid value. Another is a problem with the logic of this code. The last problem is an API problem. The compiler would catch the second problem. The first problem should be caught by your newfound sensibility, where reading null in code is like hearing nails on a chalkboard. The third problem is by far the subtlest, and will only be caught once you have experience manipulating methods as lambdas.

The first problem is the fact that we are using null. Starting in Java 8, you should only use null if you want to get a NullPointerException. In all other cases when you would use null, you should use the Optional class instead. The Optional class is the implementation of the "option" or "maybe" pattern common in functional programming, and it is how functional languages avoid even having a concept of null or any equivalent to the NullPointerException. The Optional class is a container that holds up to one single element, and provides convenient ways to act on the contained element if it exists. If we rewrite the code using Optional, we eliminate the possibility of a NullPointerException and get more readable code. It looks like this:

```
<RETURN_T> RETURN_T withTempFile(
  Function<FunFile, RETURN_T> function,
  Consumer<IOException> exceptionHandler
) {
    Optional<File> file = Optional.empty();
    try {
      file = Optional.of(File.createTempFile("funfile", "tmp"));
      return file.map(function).get();
    } catch(IOException ioe) {
      exceptionHandler.consume(ioe);
    } finally {
      file.ifPresent(File::delete);
    }
  }
}
// This is still not valid Java code: read on!
```

This code still won't compile, however, which brings us to our second problem. The second problem in our code is that we do not have a return value in the case of the exception handler. If you get into the catch block, and you execute the consumer, then what is there return value of the method? An old-school Java sensibility would be to return null in this case, but null is how you get to the hated NullPointerException. We can do better. Instead of taking a Consumer, we can take a Function, and so the user specifies the return value in either case. The resulting code looks like this:

```
<RETURN_T> RETURN_T withTempFile(
  Function<FunFile, RETURN_T> function,
  Function<IOException, RETURN_T> exceptionHandler
) {
    File file = null;
    try {
      file = File.createTempFile("funfile", "tmp");
      return function.apply(file);
    } catch(IOException ioe) {
      return exceptionHandler.apply(ioe);
    } finally {
      if (file != null) file.delete();
    }
  }
// This is not the Java code you are looking for: read on!
```

At this point, the users can specify the return value in either case, which means they can do what they would like with the method. If they realize how evil null is, they can return null. If they want to return Optional.empty() or some other default value, they can do that. It is maximal flexibility.

There is just one remaining problem with the code above: the order of the arguments is wrong. In traditional Java code, the order of arguments was largely an implementation detail. When you are writing a function in a functional style, the order of arguments is very significant. Consider the functional contract for this method: it is a bifunction that takes two functions as arguments. The first argument is the standard implementation callback, and the second argument is the error handling callback. Consider how this works as a lambda, however. If you want to do partial function application, you do it on the first argument, which is the specification of how to process the file. That implementation is likely to be very specific to the caller's context. On the other hand, the error handling is more likely to be common throughout an application. Therefore, it is more useful to have the error handling as the first argument, so that the error handling can be partially applied, leaving the temp file processing free to be implemented. The resulting method is in Listing 4-1.

Forcing the caller to handle the exception is more intuitive to the classical Java programmer. However, there are two major issues with this approach. The first is that the calling code is rather ugly, since you have two functional callbacks on top of each other. It just reads funny to a programmer used to the imperative style in idiomatic Java. The second and more significant issue is that the functional interface is a bifunction, which does not fit in many cases. You can't call Stream.map on a bifunction: you need a function for that. To address both of these issues, we can handle the exception in the return value, which is what we will do in the next section.

Listing 4-1. Temp File Creation with a Callback for Exceptions

```
<RETURN_T> RETURN_T withTempFile(
  Function<IOException, RETURN_T> exceptionHandler,
  Function<FunFile, RETURN_T> function
) {
    Objects.requireNonNull(exceptionHandler,
      "exception handler for I/O exceptions");
    Objects.requireNonNull(function, "function to apply to temp file");
    Optional<File> file = Optional.empty();
    try {
```

```
        file = Optional.of(File.createTempFile("funfile", "tmp"));
        return file.map(function).get();
    } catch (IOException e) {
        return exceptionHandler.apply(e);
    } finally {
        file.ifPresent(File::delete);
    }
}
```

Exception Handling via Output: Capturing Execution Results

It's not how people normally think of it, but you can consider the checked exception to be a part of the API of the method. Think of it in terms of postconditions: when the method execution completes, either the method will have returned a value or it will have thrown an exception. Being good object-oriented programmers, you can encapsulate those alternatives into an object. The result is a more functional (and function-friendly) style of programming.

The first thing that we will need is a class to capture these results. We could use the Optional class, but it does not have a way to communicate what the exception was. So let's build out something like the Optional class, but optionally containing our exception. We can call it our Result class. But before we use it, let's understand what we're using. Listing 4-2 contains the entire class definition, but don't let it scare you: we will walk through it piece by piece, and it is actually quite simple. In the process, we will also get to see the power of the Optional class's API.

Listing 4-2. The Result Class

```
import java.util.*;
import java.util.function.*;

/**
 * A class which represents a result of some processing, which is either
 * an exception or an object of the given type.
 */
public class Result<RESULT_T> {

  private final Optional<RESULT_T> result;
  private final Optional<Exception> exception;

  /**
   * Constructs an instance to wrap the given result.
   *
   * @param result The result; may not be {@code null}
   */
  public Result(RESULT_T result) {
    Objects.requireNonNull(result, "result to wrap");
    this.result = Optional.of(result);
    this.exception = Optional.empty();
  }

  /**
   * Constructs an instance to wrap the given exception.
   *
```

```java
 * @param e The exception; may not be {@code null}.
 */
public Result(Exception e) {
  Objects.requireNonNull(e, "exception to wrap");
  this.result = Optional.empty();
  this.exception = Optional.of(e);
}


/**
 * Provides the result as an optional.
 *
 * @return The result in an option, if there is any; otherwise, the
 * empty optional. Never {@code null}.
 */
public Optional<RESULT_T> getResult() {
  return result;
}

/**
 * Provide the exception represented by this result, or the empty optional
 * if there is no such exception.
 *
 * @return The exception represented by this result.
 */
public Optional<Exception> getException() {
  return exception;
}

/**
 * Returns whether this instance was constructed with a result.
 *
 * @return Whether we have a result.
 */
public boolean hasResult() {
  return result.isPresent();
}

/**
 * Gets the result, if present; otherwise, throws a
 * {@link java.util.NoSuchElementException} with the exception
 * in the suppressed field.
 *
 * @return The result, if present.
 * @throws java.util.NoSuchElementException If there is no result.
 */
public RESULT_T getOrDie() {
  return result.orElseThrow(() -> {
      NoSuchElementException ex = new NoSuchElementException(
        "No element in result"
      );
      ex.addSuppressed(getException().orElseThrow(() ->
        new RuntimeException("INTERNAL ERROR"))
```

```
        );
        return ex;
      }
    );
}

/**
 * Executes the given function against this result, if we have a result.
 *
 * @param function The function to apply; never {@code null}
 * @return The result of the function in an {@link java.util.Optional} if
 *         we have a result, or the empty optional if there was no result.
 */
public <RETURN_T> Optional<RETURN_T> ifPresent(
    Function<? super RESULT_T, RETURN_T> function
) {
    Objects.requireNonNull(function, "the function to apply");
    return result.map(function);
}


/**
 * Executes the given consumer against this result, if we have a result.
 * Otherwise, does nothing.
 *
 * @param consumer The consumer to apply; never {@code null}
 */
public void ifPresent(Consumer<? super RESULT_T> consumer) {
    Objects.requireNonNull(consumer, "the consumer to apply");
    result.ifPresent(consumer);
}


/**
 * Executes the given function against this exception, if we have one.
 *
 * @param function The function to apply; never {@code null}
 * @return The result of the function in an {@link java.util.Optional} if
 * we have an exception, or the empty optional if there was no exception.
 */
public <RETURN_T> Optional<RETURN_T> ifNotPresent(
    Function<? super Exception, RETURN_T> function
) {
    Objects.requireNonNull(function, "the function to apply");
    return exception.map(function);
}


/**
 * Executes the given consumer against this exception, if we have
 * an exception. Otherwise, does nothing.
 *
 * @param consumer The consumer to apply; never {@code null}
 */
```

```java
  public void ifNotPresent(Consumer<? super Exception> consumer) {
    Objects.requireNonNull(consumer, "the consumer to apply");
    exception.ifPresent(consumer);
  }
  /**
   * Executes the given function against the result, if we have a result.
   *
   * @param function The function to apply; never {@code null}.
   * @return The result of processing the function, which may be
   *         this exception, the exception during processing, or the
   * object returned by the function; never {@code null}.
   */
  public <RESULT2_T> Result<RESULT2_T> map(
    Function<RESULT_T, RESULT2_T> function
  ) {
    Objects.requireNonNull(function, "mapping function");
    try {
      return new Result<>(function.apply(getOrDie()));
    } catch (Exception e) {
      return new Result<>(e);
    }
  }

  /**
   * Applies the given consumer if there is a result; otherwise, does nothing.
   *
   * @param resultHandler The handler for results; never {@code null}
   * @return {@code this} for chaining
   */
  public Result<RESULT_T> whenResult(Consumer<RESULT_T> resultHandler) {
    Objects.requireNonNull(resultHandler, "result handler");
    result.ifPresent(resultHandler);
    return this;
  }

  /**
   * Applies the given consumer if there is an exception; otherwise,
   * does nothing.
   *
   * @param exceptionHandler The handler for exceptions; never {@code null}
   * @return {@code this} for chaining
   */
  public Result<RESULT_T> whenException(Consumer<Exception> exceptionHandler) {
    Objects.requireNonNull(exceptionHandler, "exception handler");
    exception.ifPresent(exceptionHandler);
    return this;
  }

  /**
   * Applies the given consumer if there is an exception of the given type;
   * otherwise, does nothing.
   *
```

```
 * @param exceptionHandler The handler for exceptions; never {@code null}j
 * @param exceptionClasses The classes being handled by this handler;
 *                         never {@code null}
 * @return {@code this} for chaining
 */
public <EXCEPTION_T extends Exception> Result<RESULT_T> whenException(
  Consumer<? super EXCEPTION_T> exceptionHandler,
  Class<? extends EXCEPTION_T>... exceptionClasses
) {
  Objects.requireNonNull(exceptionHandler, "exception handler");
  Objects.requireNonNull(exceptionClasses, "exception classes to handle");
  exception.ifPresent(e -> {
      Stream<Class<? extends EXCEPTION_T>> classesStream =
        Stream.of(exceptionClasses);
      Optional<Class<? extends EXCEPTION_T>> match = classesStream.filter(
        c -> c.isInstance(e)
      ).findAny();
      match.ifPresent(exceptionClass -> {
          EXCEPTION_T ex = exceptionClass.cast(e);
          exceptionHandler.accept(ex);
        }
      );
    }
  );
  return this;
}
}
```

The first things to note are the constructors and the accessors: the class encapsulates two `Optional` instances: one representing the result, and one representing the exception that was thrown. A given result can either be a result or an exception that was thrown, so one of these will be the empty optional and the other one will be populated.

The `hasResult()` method shows a common theme. It simply delegates to the `result.isPresent()` method, and this class will regularly end up simply delegating to the appropriate `Optional` instance method. In this case, we check if we have a result by checking if the result is present.

The `getOrDie()` method provides a convenient way for us to get at the result if we really know that the result is present. If the caller is wrong and the result is not present, it will throw a `NoSuchElementException` with the resulting exception as a suppressed exception. This is implemented via the `orElseThrown` method, which either returns the result or throws the exception provided by a `Supplier`. Our `Supplier` implementation will put the exception into the stack trace of the `NoSuchElementException`, which should help debugging. (The "INTERNAL ERROR" exception is only ever reached if both the exception and the result were initially populated as `null`, which should simply never happen.)

The `map` function will transform the result, if it exists; otherwise, it will construct a new result and pass the exception along. This creates a way to act upon the result without losing the exception information. In most case when you reach for `getOrDie()`, you really want `map()`.

The `ifPresent` and `ifNotPresent` methods provide a convenient way to consume the result or the exception if they are present. This, along with `map()`, allows the user to specify an implementation without having to worry about the state of the result, which makes for a very readable API. Note that the big difference with `ifPresent()`/`ifNotPresent()` and `map()` is the return value: `ifPresent()`/`ifNotPresent()` loses information but converts to the more common Optional type, while `map()` retains information but stays with the present type.

The when methods provide support for a fluent API, which allows you to write functional code that looks like imperative code to the reader. They return the current object for chaining, so you can call the methods in order, providing something that looks a lot like a try/catch block with exceptions at the end.

The very last when method is for catching multiple types of exceptions, and it is a great demonstration of the power of Java 8. Thanks to type inference, the consumer's argument will be automatically set to the broadest common superclass of the methods to be caught. The traditional implementation would involve null, if blocks, and loops, but those are all replaced by the Optional and Stream class methods.

Using this Result class, we can encapsulate the result of a method call. Instead of returning a RETURN_T, we return a Result<RETURN_T>. When the method executes, it will construct a Result instance with either the return value of the user's function, or with the IOException that was thrown. An initial pass at the code might look something like this:

```
<RETURN_T> Result<RETURN_T> withTempFile(Function<File, RETURN_T> function) {
    Objects.requireNonNull(function, "function to apply to temp file");
    Optional<File> file = Optional.empty();
    try {
      file = Optional.of(File.createTempFile("funfile", "tmp"));
      return new Result<>(file.map(function).get());
    } catch (IOException e) {
      return new Result<>(e);
    } finally {
      file.ifPresent(File::delete);
    }
} // This code would work, but could do with improvement: read on!
```

This code bears a striking resemblance to the code in Listing 4-1. If you let your eyes blur a little bit and just look at the profile of the function in the whitespace, you will see that the method has the same shape. Any time that you have two methods with the same shape, you are missing an opportunity for code reuse. In this case, the code is almost identical except on the return lines: in Listing 4-1, the return lines delegate to user-given code. In our new method, we want to call the Return class constructors at that point. We can pass the Return class constructors into the Listing 4-1 code as the user-given code, thereby delegating the actual implementation of the temp file into a single place. The resulting delegation code is given in Listing 4-3, and it is extremely simple. This demonstrates again how powerful the new paradigm is in our postfunctional Java world.

Listing 4-3. Temp File Creation with Exceptions Encapsulated in the Return Value

```
/**
 * Creates a temporary file, passes it into the given function, and
 * deletes the temporary file when the function is complete.
 *
 * @param function The behavior to implement with the temporary file,
 *                 which may not return {@code null}; may not be {@code null}
 * @return The result of the given function
 */
public static <RETURN_T> Result<RETURN_T> withTempFile(
  Function<File, RETURN_T> function
) {
  Objects.requireNonNull(function, "function to apply to temp file");
  Function<File, Result<RETURN_T>> resultify = function.andThen(Result::new);
  return withTempFile(Result::new, resultify);
}
```

Consuming Our Temp File Function

In a purely functional world, there is always a return value: a program is simply a function that takes the string arguments and system environment variables as input and produces an exit code as output. However, in a postfunctional language such as Java 8, we often want to use side effects instead of return values. This is why the Consumer class is useful. Unfortunately, the API that we have provided so far only accepts functions, which means that the user always has to specify a return value. Furthermore, when you take a reference to a method with one argument but returning void, you get an instance of the Consumer interface. If we want to allow users to pass in methods with that shape, we need to accept the Consumer interface.

This isn't too tricky, but it does require a bit of finagling. Of course, we want to build off of our existing APIs instead of duplicating functionality. This means that we will need some bridge from the Consumer that our user passes into the Function that our API desires. The difference between Consumer and Function is the return value: Consumer returns void while Function returns a value. For our bridge, we will return a default value. We could return null, but null is the evil path to NullPointerException. The other default non-value is Optional.empty(), so we can use that. The resulting code looks like Listing 4-4.

Listing 4-4. Bridge from a Consumer to a Function

```
/**
 * Convert a consumer to a function that consumes the argument and returns
 * {@link java.util.Optional#empty()}.
 *
 * @return A function that consumes the argument and returns the
 *          empty option.
 */
static <T> Function<T, Optional<A>> functionise(Consumer<T> consumer) {
  return a -> {
    consumer.accept(a);
    return Optional.empty();
  };
}
```

Now that we have that method, we can create our new API. The simple case is one where we require the user to pass the IOException handler. In this case, we have an API just like our previous version in Listing 4-1, but we take two Consumer instances instead of two Function instances. The user is responsible for deciding how to handle the IOException, should it occur, as well as how to handle the normal case. The code for this is in Listing 4-5.

Listing 4-5. Method Accepting a Consumer to Process a Temporary File, and Calling a Callback on Error

```
/**
 * Creates a temporary file, passes it into the given consumer, and
 * deletes the temporary file when the function is complete.
 *
 * @param consumer The consumer to call with the temporary file, which is
 *          never {@code null}; may not be {@code null}
 * @param exceptionHandler The handler for when an {@code IOException}
 *          occurs; may not be {@code null}
 */
public static void withTempFile(
  Consumer<IOException> exceptionHandler,
  Consumer<FunFile> consumer
```

```
) {
  Objects.requireNonNull(exceptionHandler,
    "exception handler for I/O exceptions");
  Objects.requireNonNull(consumer,
    "consumer to apply to temp file");
  Function<IOException, Optional<Object>> exceptionFunction =
    functionise(exceptionHandler);
  Function<File, Optional<Object>> consumerFunction = functionise(consumer);
  withTempFile(exceptionFunction, consumerFunction);
}
```

With all this functional niceness in place, we should really finish with an API that will feel natural to the Java traditionalists. This would mean that a function that takes a consumer, and throws an exception if an IOException occurs. In this case, we will create a container for the exception. The exception handler will store the exception into the consumer. When the method returns, we can check to see if the container is set, and throw the exception if it is. We need the container because variables used in lambdas are implicitly final, which means that we cannot set a variable that is defined outside of the lambda. This implementation will actually use null, because Optional is immutable, and other options (such as using a List) are more obscuring than clear. The code is given in Listing 4-6.

Listing 4-6. Method Accepting a Consumer to Process a Temporary File, and Throwing an Exception on Error

```
/**
 * Creates a temporary file, passes it into the given consumer, and
 * deletes the temporary file when the function is complete.
 *
 * @param consumer The consumer to call with the temporary file, and
 *                 it is never {@code null}; may not be {@code null}.
 * @throws java.io.IOException If an exception occurs.
 */
public static void withTempFile(Consumer<File> consumer) throws IOException {
  AtomicReference<IOException> reference = new AtomicReference<>(null);
  Consumer<IOException> exceptionHandler = reference::set;
  withTempFile(exceptionHandler, consumer);
  if (reference.get() != null) throw reference.get();
}
```

Listing 4-6 is also an excellent example about why you shouldn't release Zalgo. (See the "Don't Release Zalgo" in chapter 2.) The withTempFile method guarantees that if it will execute its argument, then that argument will be executed before the method returns. Because of that, we know that the if(reference.get() != null) line will execute after the exceptionHandler implementation executes. If the exceptionHandler sometimes executed later, then our code would break under some uncertain (undoubtedly surprising and unfortunate) circumstances.

Reading All the Lines of Files in a Directory

Now that we have exercised our real-world lambda skills, it is time to take on something more involved. For our next goal, we will print out all the lines of the files in a directory. This will give us a chance to decompose a more complex problem, and to see how to combine streams. By the time we are done with this exercise, you should have a good sense for how streams can be manipulated, both while working with I/O and more generally.

When programming in a functional style, it really pays to first stop and think about what you really want to accomplish. First, let's consider the shape of the function that we want. We know that we want to act on a `java.io.File` instance, so we should either take that a file as input or make it as a method of something that extends the `File` class. The output side is trickier. We do not know what a user is going to do with the lines of the file. We could take a `Consumer` to process them, but it's both simpler and more flexible to return the lines. We could read all the lines into some kind of `Collection`, but that requires all the lines to be read into memory, and it prevents any processing from occurring until the lines are done being read. So it is best to return a `Stream`, which provides flexibility and support for concurrent processing. But a stream of what?

The return value may not be as obvious at it initially seems. A `Stream` of `String` instances seems like the obvious choice, but that is only kind of right. At any point in time, we could have an `IOException` thrown, and when you are dealing with things like navigating directories, you should absolutely expect them. Our pattern so far in this chapter has been to create two methods: one that accepts a `Consumer` to process the errors, and one that returns `Result` objects. Although duplication of the API is made simple through functional programming, it is certainly annoying and it clutters the class. Let's try for a different approach.

The new approach to processing the class will still use the `Result` class for elements in the `Stream`, but we will give our users a new tool. We will provide a class that is constructed with a `Consumer`, and which processes a Stream of Result instances to remove the exceptional cases. This gives the user the ability to specify how to handle exceptions after the fact, and convert the `Stream` of `Results` of `Strings` into the much more familiar `Stream` of `Strings`. So now we have two things to write: the method that will take a `File` and produce a `Stream` of `Results` of `Strings`, and a post-processor class that will turn a `Stream` of `Results` of `Strings` into a `Stream` of `Strings`. Now it is time to start thinking about implementations, starting with the post-processor.

Complex Stream Processing Using Creative Flattening

This is where we will really get into a fancy `Stream` stunt, and the real power of a `Stream` will come out. The difficulty is that we have a fairly complex operation on a stream. We want to handle and then remove elements from the stream meeting a certain criteria: in this case, we want to handle and remove `Result` instances that contain exceptions.

If you glance over the `Stream` API, it first seems like we want to perform a map operation: we want to take in types of `Result<String>` and return a `String`, and the map method is how you transform the type if the `Stream`. The map method looks like this:

```
<R> Stream<R> map(Function<? super T,? extends R> mapper)
```

The problem is that we do not have a one-to-one mapping: not every input will produce an output. We could return an `Option`, but what does that gain us? Why wouldn't we just stick with our `Result` type instead? If we get fixated with the map method, we could then create a two-part system, first performing the map and then performing the `filter` to remove elements. If we were to go down that point, we would not be leveraging the type system to tell us that the `Result` has been handled, and we would be creating a possibility for an error to creep in between when the `Result` is handled and where it is removed. A better alternative is to use `flatMap`.

The `flatMap` method is based on the concept of "flattening," which is a functional structure that takes in a container of containers, and produces a single "flat" container with all the elements of all the containers. Consider that you had a list that looked like this:

```
List<List<String>> list = Arrays.asList(
  Arrays.asList("Eddard Stark", "Catelyn Tully", "Benjen Stark"),
  Arrays.asList("Lysa Telly", "Jon Arryn", "Robin Arryn"),
  Arrays.asList("Cersei Lannister", "Robert Baratheon")
);
```

Then the flattened list contains all the elements of those inner lists, but without the inner list structure. It would look like this:

```
List<String> flatList = Arrays.asList(
 "Eddard Stark", "Catelyn Tully", "Benjen Stark",
 "Lysa Telly", "Jon Arryn", "Robin Arryn",
 "Cersei Lannister", "Robert Baratheon"
);
```

The flatMap method allows you to perform a corresponding operation on a Stream. This is the API:

```
<R> Stream<R> flatMap(Function<? super T,? extends Stream<? extends R>> mapper)
```

You can pass in a function that takes an element of the stream and returns a new Stream of any type. All those returned streams are concatenated together and processed. This is how we will concatenate the results together for the files that we read, which is what the API is really designed for. However, it can also be used when you have an optional return value from a mapping operation. To do this, we will return Stream. empty() when there is no result, and Stream.of(element) when we have a result. Here is the resulting class:

Listing 4-7. Result Mapping Function

```java
import java.util.*;
import java.util.function.*;
import java.util.stream.*;

/**
 * A class intended to be passed to
 * {@link Stream#flatMap(java.util.function.Function)} to process
 * {@link Result} instances. The class is constructed with an exception handler
 * that will be passed any exceptions, and the {@link #apply(Result)} method
 * will return a stream containing the result (if any). The stream has 0
 * elements if the {@link Result} instance had no result, and has 1 element if
 * the instance had a result.
 */
public class ResultMap<RESULT_T>
  implements Function<Result<RESULT_T>, Stream<RESULT_T>>
{

  private final Consumer<Exception> exceptionHandler;

  /**
   * Constructs an instance that will delegate to the given exception handler.
   *
   * @param exceptionHandler The handler for exceptions in the stream; never
   *                         {@code null}
   */
```

```
  public ResultMap(final Consumer<Exception> exceptionHandler) {
    Objects.requireNonNull(exceptionHandler, "exception handler");
    this.exceptionHandler = exceptionHandler;
  }

  /**
   * Applies this function to the given argument.
   * If the result container has a result, a stream containing only that result
   * is returned.
   * If the result container has an exception, the exception handler is called
   * and the empty stream is returned.
   * If the argument is {@code null}, the empty stream is returned.
   *
   * @param resultContainer The container for results; may be {@code null}.
   * @return a 0 or 1 element stream with the result, if any.
   */
  @Override
  public Stream<RESULT_T> apply(final Result<RESULT_T> resultContainer) {
    // Handle any obnoxious boundaries with short-circuiting
    if (resultContainer == null) return Stream.empty();

    // First argument is what to do with exceptions,
    // Second argument is what to do with results
    return resultContainer.map(
                              error -> {
                                exceptionHandler.accept(error);
                                return Stream.empty();
                              },
                              Stream::of
    );
  }
}
```

It's truly beautiful how simple functional programming makes this kind of processing. For an added benefit, consider how simple it would be to unit test this kind of class, exercising its API completely. (If you would like to go see, look up this class in Webonise Lab's FunJava library.) With our class available, let's create a place to use it by generating our stream.

Streaming all the Lines of all the Files in a Directory

With our support class in place, we can now turn toward the main piece of our functionality. We want to process a java.io.File and return a Stream of Result instances, each containing either an IOException or a String of the line of the file. The general breakdown of the implementation will be this:

```
File dir => Stream<Result<String>>:
        For each file in dir, execute...
                File file => Stream<Result<String>>:
                        Return all the lines in file
```

This would be a rather imperative implementation. From a functional standpoint, we actually want three methods. Can you see where? The trick is to realize that walking the directory is a useful trick, and there is no reason to couple that useful trick to the details about what to do when you get there. One helpful approach to get to this functional decomposition is to be very strict about your method doing only one thing, keeping in mind that the average Java developer's concept of "one thing" is probably far too broad: printing all the lines of all the files in a directory is not one thing; walking the files in a directory is one thing—and even that is a pretty big thing. It helps if you first do a back-of-the-napkin style of design before you write any code. If it takes more than one line to describe a function, you're doing something wrong. One functional decomposition of the problem looks like this:

Given:

```
[Lines] File file => Stream<Result<String>>
        Return all the lines in file
[Walk] File dir => Stream<File>
        For each file in dir, return the file in the stream
```

Implement:

```
File dir => Stream<Result<String>>
        Apply dir to Walk and flatMap the result to Lines
```

Those are the three functions we will implement now. Since all three of them take a File as the first argument, we will implement them on a subclass of File, which we will call FunFile. (This class is available in the also project, should you want to see it in production.)

Let's begin with the Lines method, since it will be the simplest. The java.nio.file.Files class, introduced in Java 7, has been extended with a number of useful Stream-generating static methods, including Files.lines. Unfortunately, despite the name, the Files class acts mostly on Path instances. Furthermore, the API produces a Stream of String objects and throws an IOException. This method signature makes the method ill-suited for working within streams, but its core functionality is exactly what we want: we just need to make the API match what we are looking for. The implementation of our wrapper is given in Listing 4-8. Keep in mind that this is attached to a class extending java.io.File.

Listing 4-8. FunFile.getLines()

```java
/**
 * If this file is a plain file, provides the lines of the file (read as
 * UTF-8) without the line-termination characters as a stream.
 * Otherwise, returns a single {@link Result} instance with an
 * {@link IOException}.
 *
 * @return The lines of the file; never {@code null}
 */
public Stream<Result<String>> getLines() {
  if (!isFile()) {
    return Stream.of(new Result<>(new IOException(
      "File is not a plain file: " + toString()
    )));
  }
  try {
    return Files.lines(toPath()).map(Result::new);
  } catch (IOException ioe) {
    return Stream.of(new Result<>(ioe));
  }
}
```

Before we leave the getLines() method, it is worth taking a sidebar to discuss the error condition handling in this method. If the underlying file is not a "plain file" (e.g., it is a directory), we return an IOException in the stream. The API requires that the file is a plain file, and so it not being a plain file is a violation of the API. The general rule is that checked exceptions are used for errors caused by changes in the execution environment, and unchecked exceptions are used for API violations. If a really good programmer wouldn't see the exception, it is an unchecked exception; if the exception occurs because of something beyond the control of the program, it's a checked exception. In this case, it's arguably appropriate to use an unchecked exception, because it is a violation of the API. However, it is also possible that the file is not a plain file because it no longer exists. It might also return false because Java couldn't determine the file type from the file system for some reason, which can happen with NFS. As a result, we are going with the standard checked exception error approach, even if it is an API violation.

Now that we have the getLines() method, we need the Walk method to walk the tree. This reveals a slight ambiguity in our API definition: when we say "all the files in the directory," do we mean "all the files that are immediate children of the directory," or do we mean "all the files that are children of the directory, regardless of intervening directory depth"? In other words, is this a recursive listing or a simple listing? We can code it easily enough to support both approaches by taking an extra parameter: if true, we will recourse into subdirectories; if false, we won't.

The implementation of the Walk method is very straightforward, and given in Listing 4-9. We use Files. list(Path) to implement the walk, and then map the results into a FunFile using the new FunFile(Path) constructor. The bulk of the method (in terms of lines of code) is spent implementing the recursion: in addition to handling directories and files distinctly, we also want to ensure that we don't end up in an endless loop, so we have to check the canonical path.

Listing 4-9. The FunFile.listFiles(boolean) Method

```java
/**
 * Returns a stream of the plain files in the directory, recursing into
 * subdirectories if the {@code recurse} argument is {@code true}.
 *
 * @param recurse Whether to recurse into subdirectories
 * @return The plain files in the directory; never {@code null}
 */
public Stream<Result<FunFile>> listFiles(boolean recurse) {
  if (!isDirectory()) {
    return Stream.of(new Result<>(new IOException(
      "File is not a directory: " + toString()
    )));
  }
  try {
    final String thisPath = this.getCanonicalPath();
    return Files.list(toPath()).map(FunFile::new).flatMap(file -> {
        if (recurse && file.isDirectory()) {
          final String filePath;
          try {
            filePath = file.getCanonicalPath();
          } catch (IOException ioe) {
            return Stream.of(new Result<>(ioe));
          }
          if (!thisPath.equals(filePath)) {
            return file.listFiles(true);
          } else {
            return Stream.empty();
```

```
        }
    } else if (file.isFile()) {
        return Stream.of(new Result<>(file));
    } else {
        return Stream.empty();
    }
    }
    );
} catch (IOException ioe) {
    return Stream.of(new Result<>(ioe));
}
}
```

Now we just have to glue the two together. Again, we will take a `boolean` to determine whether or not we will recurse into subdirectories. The stream of files that we will be consuming is a `Stream` of `Result` instances, so we have to decide what to do with errors and what to do with results. Errors will just get passed along, wrapped as a `Stream` and then flattened back into the stream. The `FunFile` instances in the stream, however, will have their `getLines()` method called, which will return a stream and then that stream will be flattened into the stream. The result will be a flat stream of lines (and errors) generated by reading the lines out of all of the files. That is Listing 4-10. All the work of this chapter built up to that one, simple method.

Listing 4-10. The FunFile. getLinesInDirectory(boolean) Method

```
/**
 * Provides all the lines of all the files in a directory. If this file
 * is not a directory, return a stream with a single element, which is a
 * single {@link Result} instance with an {@link IOException}. Otherwise,
 * return the concatenated stream of trying to read all the lines of all
 * the files in the directory using {@link #getLines()}, recursing into
 * subdirectories if the {@code recurse} argument is {@code true}.
 *
 * @param recurse Whether to recurse into subdirectories
 * @return The lines of all the files; never {@code null}
 */
public Stream<Result<String>> getLinesInDirectory(boolean recurse) {
    if (!isDirectory()) {
        return Stream.of(new Result<>(new IOException(
            "File is not a directory: " + toString()
        )));
    }
    Function<Exception, Stream<Result<String>>> onError =
        ex -> Stream.of(new Result<>(ex));
    Function<FunFile, Stream<Result<String>>> onResult =
        FunFile::getLines;
    return listFiles(recurse).flatMap(
        result -> result.map(onError, onResult)
    );
}
```

Summary

In this chapter, we saw lambdas in the real world. We saw how they interacted with checked exceptions, and how to work with those exceptional cases by accepting callbacks and returning encapsulated results. More importantly, we saw how to think through and develop a solution for a non-trivial problem by processing streams using our lambda tools.

In the next chapter, we will address another difficult space where lambdas and streams can make life a lot easier: database access. We will extend the approach that we laid out here, but we will get to see more about working with and transforming data elements themselves.

CHAPTER 5

■ ■ ■

Data Access with Lambdas

In the last chapter, we saw how lambdas enable us to work with files and streams. In this chapter, we will look at interacting with the database. Way back in chapter 1, we saw how lambdas can help Spring's JDBCTemplate by making it easy to implement its callback interfaces. In chapter 3, we were introduced to streams, and in chapter 4, we saw how streams can make it easier to work with file data. In this chapter, we will see the specifics of working with Java's data access structures (the `java.sql` package). This will give us an opportunity to meet another new data structure in Java 8's standard library: the spliterator.

If we are going to work with data access, we need to be working with some non-trivial database. In this chapter, we will be working with an H2 in-memory database containing an index of all the words in all the works of Shakespeare. These words are organized by line number. This means that we have a `text` table, a `line` table, a `word` table, and a `line_word` table joining `line` and `word`. The UML diagram for the tables looks like this:

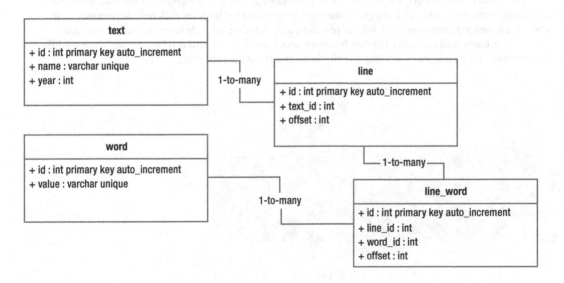

This database was loaded from the texts provided by Project Gutenberg at `http://www.gutenberg.org/ebooks/100`. In total, there are 38 texts (the sonnets are grouped as a single text). There are about 113,000 lines, about 36,000 distinct words, and almost a million words used. While this is still a relatively tiny database by corporate standards, it is big enough to slow down processing and warrant some special handling. We will walk through loading the database in Appendix A, where we will contrast imperative, object-oriented, and postfunctional approaches. For the sake of this chapter, we will start with a populated database and move through there.

With this database loaded and ready to go, let's figure out how (and why) to bring streams into the mix. Let's start with a simple request: we would like to print out all the word usages, one per line, with all the associated metadata. This might be done, for instance, if you are generating input for a Hadoop map-reduce run. The SQL we are going to run (and some sample results) are as follows:

```
SELECT t.name, l."offset", w."value", lw."offset"
FROM "text" t, word w
INNER JOIN line l ON (t.id = l.text_id)
INNER JOIN line_word lw ON (lw.line_id = l.id AND lw.word_id = w.id)
```

Text Title	Line Offset	Word	Word Offset
A LOVER'S COMPLAINT	328	Betray	5
THE WINTER'S TALE	3326	interpose	5
THE TWO GENTLEMEN OF VERONA	2041	expedition	7
ALLS WELL THAT ENDS WELL	23	Second	12
THE TRAGEDY OF ANTONY AND CLEOPATRA	3840	solemnity	7

How do we work with this query now that we can leverage lambdas? We can decompose the problem into the steps in the flow given below. By using streams, each of those four steps can be developed individually. The stream instance and its element type will bridge those independently developed steps. Because of that, we can develop the steps in whichever order and put them together at the end. If we had multiple developers, we could even assign the different steps to be built out by different developers, with each step being tied to the previous. So it's not just the execution that is made more asynchronous and concurrent by streams and lambdas: it's development, too. We will prove this out by starting in the middle, working our way to the end, and then filling in the front and tying it all together.

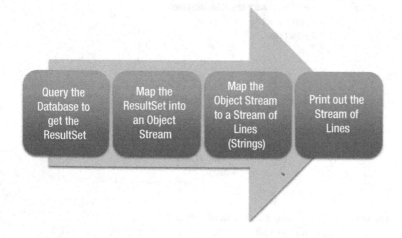

Representing the Intermediary Query Results

Java's standard SQL library represents the result set of the query as a `java.sql.ResultSet`. A result set provides a streaming set of results, so we will represent it functionally using the `java.util.function.Stream`. But what is the type of the elements of that stream? Traditionally, the answer would be a Java bean, with each field in the query result becoming a property of the Java bean: you would have getters and setters for all four of the fields in the SQL query. In a world with lambdas, however, we will instead use an immutable Java object, as given in Listing 5-1.

Listing 5-1. The Java Object Representing the Results

```java
/**
 * Functional-friendly class for storing results of querying the word
 * usage database.
 */
public class WordUsage {

  private final String textName;
  private final int lineOffset;
  private final String word;
  private final int wordOffset;

  public WordUsage(
    final String textName, final int lineOffset,
    final String word, final int wordOffset
  ) {
    this.textName = textName;
    this.lineOffset = lineOffset;
    this.word = word;
    this.wordOffset = wordOffset;
  }

  public String getTextName() {
    return textName;
  }

  public WordUsage withTextName(String textName) {
    return new WordUsage(textName, lineOffset, word, wordOffset);
  }

  public int getLineOffset() {
    return lineOffset;
  }

  public WordUsage withLineOffset(int lineOffset) {
    return new WordUsage(textName, lineOffset, word, wordOffset);
  }

  public String getWord() {
    return word;
  }
```

```java
public WordUsage withWord(String word) {
    return new WordUsage(textName, lineOffset, word, wordOffset);
}

public int getWordOffset() {
    return wordOffset;
}

public WordUsage withWordOffset(int wordOffset) {
    return new WordUsage(textName, lineOffset, word, wordOffset);
}

}
```

The immutability of the Java bean in Listing 5-1 is significant, because streams can quickly (and often transparently) move into processing on multiple threads. The Java memory model does not guarantee that an object constructed in Thread A but accessed in Thread B will necessarily have its fields intact. If you construct an object in one thread and access it in another, any given field access may return null, even if you assign it in the constructor. The reason is because different threads maintain their own distinct memory space, and the Java virtual machine will take a significant performance hit if it has to walk the entire tree and copy the objects whenever a thread modifies a field. The really obnoxious part about this is that this rule is poorly understood, and the error may not crop up until the system is under load, at which point the system is a rather unhelpful NullPointerException that appears where it should be impossible. That's a nightmare for a poor developer to debug, especially if the concurrency is obscured.

To solve this problem, the Java virtual machine gives you three options. First, you can use a synchronized block on every object that you access. This is unwieldy and error-prone. Your other two options are to annotate the field with volatile or final, either of which will solve the memory management problem. The volatile keyword tells Java that the runtime needs to check its thread-local cache against the source of truth every time you access the field. This is a bit of a performance hit, but it works as long as the object's fields are themselves thread-safe. The final keyword tells Java that the field cannot change value, and so whatever value you find at one point will be the value in the future. Since the field cannot change value, there's no need for the run time to be copying the field around the caches or checking the cache against the source of truth. In addition to solving the memory management problem without the performance hit of volatile, it also makes the object much easier to reason about, because each instance of the class has a fixed, permanent value. If the field values of an object don't change, then there is nothing that another thread can do to break your thread's reasoning about the object, so you can pretend as though you are in a single thread of execution even in a multi-threaded environment.

Whereas old style Java objects are referred to as POJOs ("Plain Old Java Objects"), objects in this new immutable style are sometimes called PIJOs ("Plain Immutable Java Objects"), pronounced "PEE-johs." Personally, I prefer the term FuJIs ("Functional Java Instances").

Note that FuJIs fit better with streams than POJOs do. Whereas as POJO's setter has a type that takes an argument and returns void, FuJI's "setters" return the type that was being modified. This means that you can use the setter as a mapping in the stream. For instance, if you wanted to set the text name to a single value for all the entries of the stream, the FuJI code is notably shorter and more readable than the POJO code, as demonstrated in Listing 5-2.

Listing 5-2. Assigning a Value to Each Element of a Stream of POJOs vs. a Stream of FuJIs

```java
import java.util.stream.*;

public class Listing2 {

  public static void main(String[] args) {
    // Set Constant Value on a Stream of POJOs
    Stream<PojoWordUsage> pojos = Stream.of(/* INSERT POJOS HERE */);
    pojos.map(pojo -> {
        pojo.setTextName("New Text Name");
        return pojo;
      }
    );

    // Set Constant Value on a Stream of FuJIs
    Stream<WordUsage> fujis = Stream.of(/* INSERT FUJIS HERE */);
    fujis.map(fuji -> fuji.withTextName("New Text Name"));
  }
}
```

If you have a template object and want to work with data assigned by the stream, then the FuJI is significantly more efficient: that code is given in Listing 5-3. In that case, we have a single POJO whose value we keep assigning, which will probably work fine as long as we guarantee that the stream is single threaded and executing in the same thread as the allocation of the object. The FuJI, on the other hand, will produce new instances of the object on every pass of the stream, which will work no matter how concurrent the stream may be. The FuJI code also happens to be shorter and more readable, too.

Listing 5-3. Mapping a Stream of Input Data to a Template POJO vs. a Template FuJI

```java
import java.util.stream.*;

public class Listing3 {

  public static void main(String[] args) {
    WordUsage template = new WordUsage("some text", 0, "word", 1);
    PojoWordUsage pojoTemplate = new PojoWordUsage("some text", 0, "word", 1);
    Stream<Integer> lineOffsets = Stream.of(/* INSERT LINE OFFSETS HERE*/);

    // Using POJO Template (not threadsafe)
    Stream<PojoWordUsage> assignedPojos = lineOffsets.map(offset -> {
        pojoTemplate.setLineOffset(offset);
        return pojoTemplate;
      }
    );

    // Using FuJI Template (threadsafe)
    Stream<WordUsage> assignedFujis =
      lineOffsets.map(template::withLineOffset);
  }

}
```

Printing Out the Results

To implement the functionality to print out the lines, all we need to know is that we are working with a Stream of WordUsage instances. If we know that we are working with a stream, and we know the definition of the WordUsage class, then we can implement the next step. We do not need any more details. This kind of distinction was part of the promise of object-oriented software, and it has really come to pass in this postfunctional world. The reason it can happen is because the stream provides an abstraction for the flow of control of the application. Before, Java provided abstractions over data. With streams, you can now pass in the flow of control itself to a part of the application, and that part of the application decides what to do with it.

In this case, we will be receiving the processed WordUsage instances, and we will be responsible for first converting the WordUsage instances into a tab-separated value (TSV) output format, and then passing the resulting stream somewhere to print the output. Printing out the stream of output string instances is easy enough, so we will leave that to the end. First, let's figure out how to convert the WordUsage instances. There are two simple approaches we could take, and we'll consider both of them.

If we have the ability to manipulate to the WordUsage class, then we can add that method right onto the class. The resulting method can then be passed into the stream as a mapping function. The method that we would add to the WordUsage class would look like this:

```
public String toTSV() {
  return String.format("%s\t%d\t%s\t%d",
    textName, lineOffset, word, wordOffset);
}
```

Given a stream of WordUsage instances, we would then just pass in WordUsage::toTSV as a mapping function. This will instruct the stream to apply the instance method to each element of the stream. If the stream of WordUsage instances was named source, then the mapping call would look like this:

```
source.map(WordUsage::toTSV)
```

That is certainly the easiest way to do it, and it keeps the implementation details of how to convert a WordUsage into a TSV within the WordUsage class itself. This will help prevent "code rot," where code becomes less functional over time. One of the major causes of code rot is when a calling code site makes assumptions about the object being called. Those assumptions may hold in the present moment, but if the class changes, it may not be obvious you need to change the code. To see how this plays out, let's consider our alternative approach: using a lambda to map a WordUsage to a TSV.

In this case, the code that became our toTSV() method would instead be defined inline. This approach is commonly the default for non-functional programmers coming into a postfunctional language, and also for Java developers who have recently discovered and become enamored with lambdas. If the source stream of WordUsage instances was called source, then the inline lambdas would look like this:

```
source.map(wordUsage ->
  String.format("%s\t%d\t%s\t%d",
      wordUsage.getTextName(), wordUsage.getLineOffset(),
      wordUsage.getWord(), wordUsage.getWordOffset()
  )
);
```

This would work just fine for the moment. It is less readable than the method version, because you do not get to use the semantic toTSV method name. If you want to figure out that the output value is TSV, the developer has to be able to read the format string and then recognize that is TSV. So the method approach has that advantage. But there is an even bigger (yet more subtle) problem with this approach.

Imagine that we changed WordUsage to have a "segment number." For the sonnets, this would be the sonnet number. For the plays, this would be the act number, with preface material having segment number 0. Someone implementing this would go into WordUsage, and he would update that class to use the segment number throughout its code, and then all its tests would pass and the class would generally look great. Our lambda code would compile and execute just fine, and all our tests would pass. But the resulting data would be corrupt: for any given text, it would look like there were two different words at line offset 1, word offset 1. Until someone analyzed and validated the data, there would be no way to detect that corruption. Once upon a time, the code worked very well. Due to a change in the code over time, the code ceased to work properly. That is code rot.

What we are seeing is the advantage of the object-oriented principle of encapsulation. The fact is that the getters on our WordUsage instance are a violation of encapsulation in spirit, if not technically: they directly expose implementation details about the class. It is possible for us to change those implementation details sometime in the future, but doing so in any significant way—such as adding a new field and redefining what an existing field means—invites code rot.

The lesson here is that lambdas are powerful things. Even more powerful than lambdas themselves, however, is the ability for Java 8 to leverage object-oriented best practices (such as encapsulation) in combination with functional behaviors (such as mapping stream elements). This is why postfunctional languages are so incredibly powerful when used properly: it really does mix the best of both paradigms.

Now that we have converted our stream of WordUsage instances into a stream of tab-separated value (TSV) strings, we need to print them out. Doing this is simple: we will get our hands on a `PrintWriter` or `PrintStream` instance, and then have the stream execute in its `println` method for each element. In our case, we will use `System.out` for our `PrintStream` instance, and `output` as the output stream of String elements. In that case, the resulting code looks like this:

```
output.forEach(System.out::println);
```

This demonstrates the use of a given instance's method as a lambda: we are literally taking the particular instance of `System.out`, and the invocation of `println` on that particular instance, and converting that into a lambda. That's a lot of lifting for a couple of colons, and that's the power of Java 8. With all of this established, we can return to the start: downloading from the database.

Mapping the ResultSet to a Stream

The task of mapping the `ResultSet` instance to a `Stream` instance is not as trivial as we may perhaps like. If we take a look at the Stream class, it is an interface. If it were a small, well-defined interface such as the Iterator class, we could just implement a direct bridge. Unfortunately, it's a huge interface with some very tricky (and ambiguous) definitions, so it is not something we are going to want to implement directly. We will take a look at four ways of implementing our bridge from ResultSet to Stream:

1. Using `Stream.Builder` to construct a stream up front.

2. Using `Stream.of` and `Stream.flatMap` to construct the stream on demand.

3. Implementing the `Stream` built on `Spliterators.AbstractSpliterator`.

4. Mapping the `ResultSet` into an `Iterator` and then into a `Spliterator` and then into a `Stream`.

Each of these four approaches has advantages and disadvantages, which we will see when we consider their implementations. The result of all four approaches will be a Stream of WordUsage instances, and that stream can get plugged immediately into all the work that we have done in the other sections of this chapter.

In each of these cases, we will have the specific mapping from the current ResultSet row to the WordUsage instance. This part of the implementation is the same throughout, so we will add it directly onto our WordUsage class as a static method and reference it from there. This will allow the code samples to stay more obviously focused on the infrastructure. This method is given in Listing 5-4. With the method in place, we can start into our four implementations.

Listing 5-4. The WordUsage-from-ResultSet Mapping Method

```
/**
 * Returns a new instance of this class based on the current row of a
 * result set. The results within the result set are expected to be
 * as follows:
 * <p>
 * <b>1.</b> The string title of the text<br />
 * <b>2.</b> The line offset within the text<br />
 * <b>3.</b> The word itself<br />
 * <b>4.</b> The word offset within the line<br />
 *
 * @param rs The result set whose current row should be read;
 *           never {@code null}.
 * @return A {@link WordUsage} constructed from the query results.
 */
public static WordUsage fromResultSet(ResultSet rs) throws SQLException {
  Objects.requireNonNull(rs, "result set to read from");
  return new WordUsage(
      rs.getString(1),  // title
      rs.getInt(2),     // line offset
      rs.getString(3),  // word
      rs.getInt(4)      // word offset
  );
}
```

Method One: Building a Stream Using the Stream Builder

The simplest way to dynamically build a Stream is using `Stream.Builder`. The Stream.Builder class follows the standard "builder" design pattern. This design pattern is an object with two phases: an *accumulation* phase and a *build* phase. The object starts in the *accumulation* phase. During this phase, it takes in elements. At some point, a trigger method is called that converts the builder into the build phase. In the build phase, the builder is a factory, and produces instances of the desired class.

In our case, we will provide WordUsage instances into the Stream.Builder. We will do this by iterating through the result set in the familiar way, constructing the instances, and passing them in. All of this happens in the calling code's thread of execution, and a fully populated stream is returned to the caller. If there is any exception in populating this stream, it is propagated directly to the caller. The code for the Stream.Builder approach is in Listing 5-5.

Listing 5-5. Using a Stream Builder to Convert a ResultSet to a Stream

```
public static Stream<WordUsage> createStream(ResultSet rs)
  throws SQLException
{
  Stream.Builder<WordUsage> builder = Stream.builder();
  while (rs.next()) {
    WordUsage usage = WordUsage.fromResultSet(rs);
    builder.add(usage);
  }
  return builder.build();
}
```

The primary advantage of this approach is that it is very familiar to Java developers. This is your standard way of building up a collection. Its next major advantage is that the stream built by the stream builder is extremely flexible, allowing parallel execution and other behind-the-scenes optimizations. Finally, this approach also makes reasoning about the ResultSet and the stream very easy: you know that there will not be a data access or data conversion error once this method returns, and the result set (and its resources) can be closed with the method returns.

The primary disadvantage of this approach is that it is a resource hog. It hogs the thread of execution, preventing anything else from being done by that thread until all the results are read. It also hogs memory, because the entire stream has to be buffered into memory before any of it can be processed. Both of these disadvantages are minor if the data set is small, and they get more serious as the data set becomes larger. With even a moderately large data set (such as ours), this is not a good fit. With a smaller data set, however, the simplicity of the approach might well outweigh its inefficiencies.

Method Two: Building a Stream Using Stream.of and Stream.flatMap

When we are looking to move from a ResultSet to a Stream, our problem is that we have trouble getting into the Stream API. This approach gets into the Stream API by constructing a single-element stream holding just the ResultSet. We will then use the `Stream.flatMap` method that we saw last chapter to explode the ResultSet into the resulting objects.

In this approach, the stream consisting of a single element will be constructed through `Stream.of(resultSet)`. The `Stream.of` method takes any number of arguments, and will construct a highly efficient stream containing those elements in argument order. Unlike the `Stream.Builder` approach, where objects can be determined and passed in at run time after the builder is initiated, the elements of `Stream.of` all need to be provided immediately at the point when the method is invoked.

To convert the stream from a single ResultSet into the mapped elements, we will use `Stream.flatMap`. As we saw in the last chapter, this allows each element of the source stream to be mapped into zero or more elements of the result stream. In our case, the single ResultSet element of the source stream is mapped into one WordUsage element for each row of the ResultSet.

The catch we have here is that we will need to leave the ResultSet open until all the rows are processed. In order to close the ResultSet at the appropriate time, we can use `Stream.onClose(Runnable)`. This method allows you to hook a callback to be executed when the stream is closed. It is not often used, but it does enable you to delegate responsibility for resource management to stream itself. This is very useful for keeping your code clean and not threading resources through calls in your codebase.

The one catch with using `Stream.onClose(Runnable)` is that you need to use the returned `Stream`. Some Java developers will register the handler with onClose and presume that the stream instance itself has been modified. This may, in fact, be the case. However, the Stream API allows the stream implementation to return an entirely new instance with the handler attached, and so you want to be sure that you use that returned instance.

So we can now pull all this together. We will use Stream.of to create the single-element stream with a ResultSet. That stream will have the ResultSet registered with it, so that the stream will close the ResultSet. We will have a flatMap call that will be passed the iteration and stream building code: that code will be just like we had in the previous section. This code is given in Listing 5-6.

Listing 5-6. Using Stream.of and Stream.flatMap to Convert a ResultSet to a Stream

```java
public static Stream<WordUsage> createStream(ResultSet resultSet)
  throws SQLException
{
  Stream<ResultSet> rsStream = Stream.of(resultSet).onClose(() -> {
      try {
        resultSet.close();
      } catch (SQLException ignore) {}
    }
  );
  return rsStream.flatMap(rs -> {
      Stream.Builder<WordUsage> builder = Stream.builder();
      try {
        while (rs.next()) {
          WordUsage usage = WordUsage.fromResultSet(rs);
          builder.add(usage);
        }
      } catch (SQLException sqle) {
        // TODO Handle exceptions
      }
      return builder.build();
    }
  );
}
```

There are a number of advantages to this approach. The ResultSet is not processed until the stream is actually exercised, which defers the expensive read from the ResultSet until and unless it is actually needed. Exceptions that arise while reading the data are moved from the caller's flow into the flow of the stream, which is a more appropriate place for them to be. The resulting stream will be the highly optimized stream coming out of the Stream.Builder still, which is a major payoff. Finally, all the setup work for the stream handling is allowed to take place before the execution of the result set and the processing, which will streamline the execution.

The disadvantage of this approach is that it is still a hog, even if it is a deferred hog. All the results have to be cached into memory before any of them can be processed. Also, the ResultSet must be fully read before any result can be processed. This means that we cannot leverage the time waiting for the database processing and network latency to process results that have already come in. We would like to start our processing as quickly as possible, and that is where the next couple of alternatives come into play.

Mapping the ResultSet with Result-Based Error Handling

Another issue with this approach in Listing 5-6 is error handling: we are going to have a SQLException instance being thrown, but what are we supposed to do with it? In Listing 5-6, we left a TODO and silently swallowed it. We could wrap it in a RuntimeException and throw the unchecked exception, but then we are ignoring an exception that we almost certainly want to be handling, and probably making a mess of our types in the process. We can use the funjava.Result type from the FunJava library to solve this problem.

In the last chapter, we started working with Funjava Result_type in order to capture the error handling and make it an explicit part of the stream flow. We can take advantage of that result again. Instead of our createStream method taking just a ResultSet, we will also require it to provide us an error handler. Instead of registering the close with the Stream's onClose handler, we will perform the close immediately in the processing flow. The caller will provide the implementation of error handling, and we will apply it using the ResultErrorHandler class, just as we saw in the last chapter. The result is a much more robust implementation of that method, and it is given in Listing 5-7.

Listing 5-7. Using the Result Type for a More Robust Stream.of and Stream.flatMap Conversion

```
public static Stream<WordUsage> createStream(
  ResultSet resultSet, Consumer<Exception> errorHandler
)
    throws SQLException {
  return Stream.of(resultSet).flatMap(rs -> {
      Stream.Builder<Result<WordUsage>> builder = Stream.builder();
      try {
        while (rs.next()) {
          try {
            WordUsage usage = WordUsage.fromResultSet(rs);
            builder.add(Result.of(usage));
          } catch(SQLException sqle) {
            builder.add(Result.of(sqle));
          }
        }
      } catch (SQLException sqle) {
        builder.add(Result.of(sqle));
      } finally {
        try {
          rs.close();
        } catch (SQLException sqle) {
          builder.add(Result.of(sqle));
        }
      }
      return builder.build();
    }
  ).flatMap(new ResultErrorHandler<>(errorHandler));
}
```

Method Three: Building a Stream Using an AbstractSpliterator

In both of the previous cases, we built out the stream of results in memory, and then returned the entire stream. This meant that we had to wait for all of the I/O to resolve before doing any processing, and we had to store all the results in memory at the same time. If you have enough data to warrant an external database, then those are probably not acceptable qualities in a solution. This solution, as well as the next, both offer an alternative approach. These solutions will integrate the iteration of the result set into the stream processing itself, meaning that the results can be processed piecemeal.

This solution will follow the more traditional Java approach: if you want to implement an interface, find the abstract class which implements the interface, and build your implementation by extending that abstract class. However, there is no AbstractStream to inherit from. Instead, we have to go a bit deeper. This is where we meet the Spliterator.

Java 8 introduces a new type called Spliterator. A spliterator is like an iterator, in that its job is to produce a sequence of elements. Just like an iterator, the sequence of elements could be finite or infinite, but it's usually finite. The big difference between an iterator and a spliterator is that the spliterator has the ability to "split." The concept of splitting a spliterator is that you break one spliterator into two, with some portion of the elements returned by the original spliterator and some portion of the elements returned by a new spliterator.

Assume that you had a spliterator of English letters, "A" to "Z." You could draw "A," "B," and "C" from your spliterator, and then split it. At this point, the spliterator might start to provide only the remaining consonants ("d," "f," "g," "h," "j"…) and return a new spliterator for the remaining vowels ("e," "i," "u"…). These two spliterators would then be entirely independent, and could be executed in any order without any interdependency. The rule is just that no element should be lost in the split, and no element should be duplicated by the split spliterators.

In Java 8, spliterators provide the elements that will become the stream elements. All the various stream operations are really operations on spliterators and the elements that come out of them. You generate a stream from a spliterator by passing in the spliterator instance into the StreamSupport.stream(Spliterator, boolean) method. The second argument specifies whether the resulting stream is "parallel" or "sequential": a parallel stream is allowed to operate on elements in any order and operate on multiple elements at the same time; a sequential stream will always execute within the caller's thread, and will conclude processing an earlier element before processing the next. If a previous element might alter the interpretation of a later element, then you have to create a sequential stream. If the elements are capable of being processed distinctly, then you should create a parallel stream. By default, streams in Java are sequential, because that is the safe answer. If it is at all possible, however, you should use parallel streams by calling stream.parallel() and using the returned stream. A concrete example of these different modes is given in Listing 5-8.

Listing 5-8. Results of Running a Stream in Parallel vs. in Sequence

```java
import java.util.stream.*;

public class Listing8 {

  public static void main(String[] args) throws Exception {
    IntStream stream;

    // Sequential stream—commonly default mode
    stream = IntStream.range(1, Integer.MAX_VALUE);
    stream.sequential().mapToObj(i -> {
        System.out.println("Mapping " + i + " to string");
        return Integer.toString(i);
      }
    ).forEach(System.out::println);

    /* Example output sampling
        Mapping 34438924 to string
        34438924
        Mapping 34438925 to string
        34438925
        Mapping 34438926 to string
        34438926
        Mapping 34438927 to string
        34438927
        Mapping 34438928 to string
        34438928
```

```
        Mapping 34438929 to string
        34438929
        Mapping 34438930 to string
        34438930
*/

// Parallel stream—commonly requires explicit call to .parallel()
stream = IntStream.range(1, Integer.MAX_VALUE);
stream.parallel().mapToObj(i -> {
    System.out.println("Mapping " + i + " to string");
    return Integer.toString(i);
    }
).forEach(System.out::println);

/* Example output sampling
    Mapping 298035702 to string
    298035702
    Mapping 298035703 to string
    298035703
    Mapping 298035704 to string
    298035704
    Mapping 298035705 to string  ← Thread change
    Mapping 405565 to string
    405565
    Mapping 405566 to string
    405566
    Mapping 405567 to string
    405567
*/
    }
}
```

There are a number of ways to implement spliterators in Java 8. Most of the functionality for creating spliterators is contained within the Spliterators (note the "s") class. Another common way to create a spliterator is to start with a stream and call stream.spliterator(). The final common way to create a spliterator is to build it from an iterator, which we will explore in the next section. In this section, we implement a spliterator using the AbtractSpliterator base class provided within the Spliterators class. We will then use that result to construct the stream.

The core method to implement for the AbstractSplitorator base class is tryAdvance. This method takes a Consumer, which represents the downstream behavior. The code is responsible passing any newly generated element into the consumer. The method returns true if a new element was generated, and returns false if it is exhausted.

We do not want to tie this code directly into our particular implementation. We don't want this for two reasons: first, we'd like to simplify our classes and maintain clear distinctions in our code; second, by staying focused, we will create a valuable bit of reusable code. In that case, our class can rely on the user to specify the transformation. Since almost every interesting method on the ResultSet type throws a SQLException, we can't take a simple functional interface: instead, we will provide an abstract method that throws a SQLException, and then handle the exception in our tryAdvance method. Assuming our class has the ResultSet stored in a field named resultSet, then the resulting methods are given in Listing 5-9.

Listing 5-9. The tryAdvance Method for the ResultSetSpliterator

```
/**
 * Given a {@link ResultSet} instance on a current row, return a
 * {@code RESULT_T} instance for that row.
 * This code should not call {@link java.sql.ResultSet#next()} or
 * otherwise mutate the result set: it should be treated as read-only.
 *
 * @param resultSet The result set to load.
 * @return The result instance.
 * @throws SQLException If an error occurs.
 */
protected abstract RESULT_T processRow(ResultSet resultSet)
  throws SQLException;

/**
 * If a remaining element exists, performs the given action on it,
 * returning {@code true}; else returns {@code false}.  If this
 * Spliterator is {@link #ORDERED} the action is performed on the
 * next element in encounter order.  Exceptions thrown by the
 * action are relayed to the caller.
 *
 * @param action The action
 * @return {@code false} if no remaining elements existed
 * upon entry to this method, else {@code true}.
 * @throws NullPointerException if the specified action is null
 */
@Override
public boolean tryAdvance(final Consumer<? super RESULT_T> action) {
  Objects.requireNonNull(action, "action to be performed");
  try {
    if (resultSet.isClosed() || !resultSet.next()) {
      return false;
    }
    RESULT_T result = processRow(resultSet);
    if (result == null) {
      throw new NullPointerException("Returned null from processRow");
    } else {
      action.accept(result);
      return true;
    }
  } catch (SQLException sqle) {
    throw new RuntimeException("SQL Exception while processing result set",
      sqle);
  }
}
```

The constructor for this class will have to extend the AbstractSpliterator constructor. That constructor takes two arguments: the estimated size of the spliterator and the characteristics of the spliterator. The estimated size of the spliterator is just that: it is a vague estimation of the number of elements returned. If the size of the spliterator is not known at all, then the magic value Long.MAX_VALUE is used. The second argument is the characteristics of the spliterator, and this is how you suggest to the runtime how your spliterator can be used.

There are a number of characteristics, and they are treated as a bitfield. The two most important are IMMUTABLE and CONCURRENT, and those specify the relationship of the spliterator to the source. If the spliterator's view of the source cannot be changed, then the spliterator should specify IMMUTABLE. This will be the case with our ResultSet spliterator, since the results of a SQL query cannot be changed. Alternatively, if the spliterator's view of the source can be concurrently modified, then the spliterator should specify CONCURRENT. This could be the case in a spliterator that acted on a thread-safe collection or a memory-mapped file.

There are a few other characteristics that a spliterator can have. Unlike IMMUTABLE and CONCURRENT, which are mutually exclusive, these are more distinct: none of the following characteristics excludes the others. The most significant is ORDERED. This characteristic guarantees that elements will be processed in "encounter order," which is the iteration order for the spliterator. If you pass ORDERED to a spliterator, you will have an API that is akin to a sequential stream — there's still some wiggle room for parallelism in the implementation, but not much. If you are ORDERED, you can also be SORTED. If your spliterator is SORTED, then either your spliterator has a comparator attached, or the elements are sorted according to their natural ordering. This allows some optimizations for sorting, and also allows the results of the spliterator to be processed in parallel and then sorted back into order. The DISTINCT flag signals that each element of the spliterator is distinct from every other element. This signals that no additional work is needed to filter out redundant values, such as in Stream.distinct(). The NONNULL characteristic asserts that no result from the spliterator will ever be null, which allows some safety checks to be bypassed. Finally, the SIZED and SUBSIZED characteristics both assert that the estimated size for the spliterator is accurate. SUBSIZED additionally guarantees that spliterators that are split off this spliterator will themselves be SIZED and SUBSIZED: in other words, SUBSIZED means that not only is the total number of elements known, but if there is a breakout of elements into distinct spliterators, then the partial sizes are also known.

In our case, every row will create an instance, so we can use the NONNULL characteristic. Since it is best to avoid null in general, we can make this directly in our class. In our particular case, we also know that every resulting WordUsage instance is distinct from the others, so we can use the DISTINCT characteristic. However, this is not necessarily the case for every SQL query. We do not know the total number of instances we will create, so we cannot be SIZED. We also don't have any ordering in our current query and don't really have any need for an ordering, so we won't be ORDERED. Finally, the results of the SQL query cannot be modified during our iteration, so we can return the IMMUTABLE option. With that decided, we can build out the constructor, giving us the class in Listing 5-10.

Listing 5-10. The ResultSetSpliterator with Constructor

```
import java.sql.ResultSet;
import java.sql.SQLException;
import java.util.*;
import java.util.function.*;

/**
 * A {@link java.util.Spliterator} that traverses a
 * {@link java.sql.ResultSet}. When the result set is exhausted,
 * it will be automatically closed. Implementing classes must implement
 * {@link #processRow(java.sql.ResultSet)} to
 * specify how to convert a row into a result object.
 */
public abstract class ResultSetSpliterator<RESULT_T>
  extends Spliterators.AbstractSpliterator<RESULT_T>
{
```

```java
private static final int CHARACTERISTICS =
    Spliterator.IMMUTABLE | Spliterator.DISTINCT | Spliterator.NONNULL;
private final ResultSet resultSet;

/**
 * Constructor.
 *
 * @param resultSet The result set to process; may not be {@code null}.
 * @param additionalCharacteristics Relevant characteristics beyond
 *                      {@link java.util.Spliterator#IMMUTABLE}
 *                      and {@link java.util.Spliterator#NONNULL},
 * or {@code 0} if none
 */
public ResultSetSpliterator(
    final ResultSet resultSet,
    final int additionalCharacteristics
) {
    super(Long.MAX_VALUE, CHARACTERISTICS | additionalCharacteristics);
    Objects.requireNonNull(resultSet, "result set");
    this.resultSet = resultSet;
}

// See Listing 5-9 for more code that goes here
}
```

There is just one problem left to solve: closing the ResultSet. If the user passes the ResultSet into this object, and then closes the ResultSet, this spliterator may not have been called. We saw this issue before in streams, and we used the onClose callback to handle it. Unlike streams, spliterators do not have a concept of being closed, so we will have to build it ourselves. What we would like is for the ResultSet to be closed when we finish working our way through it. The ResultSet might also be holding up a Statement or a Connection, too, and so we would like to give the user the option to close those, as well. To support this, our constructor will take a variable number of AutoCloseable instances, and we will close them whenever we exhaust the result set. This involves adding a doClose() method and a call to that method when the ResultSet is exhausted. The result of updating our class is in Listing 5-11.

Listing 5-11. Completed ResultSetSpliterator Class

```java
import java.sql.ResultSet;
import java.sql.SQLException;
import java.util.*;
import java.util.function.*;

/**
 * A {@link java.util.Spliterator} that traverses a {@link java.sql.ResultSet}.
 * When the result set is exhausted, it will be automatically closed.
 * Implementing classes must extend {@link #processRow(java.sql.ResultSet)} to
 * specify how to convert a row into a result object.
 */
public abstract class ResultSetSpliterator<RESULT_T>
    extends Spliterators.AbstractSpliterator<RESULT_T>
{
```

```
private static final int CHARACTERISTICS =
  Spliterator.IMMUTABLE | Spliterator.NONNULL;
private final ResultSet resultSet;
private final AutoCloseable[] toClose;

/**
 * Constructor.
 *
 * @param resultSet The result set to process; may not be {@code null}.
 * @param additionalCharacteristics relevant characteristics beyond
 *                                  {@link java.util.Spliterator#IMMUTABLE}
 *                                  and {@link java.util.Spliterator#NONNULL},
 *                                  or {@code 0} if none
 * @param toClose Optional additional autocloseables (such as
 *                {@link java.sql.Connection}) to close when the result
 *                set is exhausted; may be {@code null}
 *                (equivalent to empty).
 */
public ResultSetSpliterator(
    final ResultSet resultSet, final int additionalCharacteristics,
    final AutoCloseable… toClose
) {
  super(Long.MAX_VALUE, CHARACTERISTICS | additionalCharacteristics);
  Objects.requireNonNull(resultSet, "result set");
  this.resultSet = resultSet;
  if (toClose == null) {
    this.toClose = new AutoCloseable[0];
  } else {
    this.toClose = toClose;
  }
}


/**
 * Given a {@link ResultSet} instance on a current row, return a
 * {@code RESULT_T} instance for that row.
 * This code should not call {@link java.sql.ResultSet#next()} or
 * otherwise mutate the result set: it should
 * be treated as read-only.
 *
 * @param resultSet The result set to load.
 * @return The result instance.
 * @throws SQLException If an error occurs.
 */
protected abstract RESULT_T processRow(ResultSet resultSet)
  throws SQLException;

/**
 * If a remaining element exists, performs the given action on it,
 * returning {@code true}; else returns {@code false}.  If this
 * Spliterator is {@link #ORDERED} the action is performed on the
 * next element in encounter order. Exceptions thrown by the
```

```
 * action are relayed to the caller.
 *
 * @param action The action
 * @return {@code false} if no remaining elements existed
 * upon entry to this method, else {@code true}.
 * @throws NullPointerException if the specified action is null
 */
@Override
public boolean tryAdvance(final Consumer<? super RESULT_T> action) {
  Objects.requireNonNull(action, "action to be performed");
  try {
    if (resultSet.isClosed() || !resultSet.next()) {
      doClose();
      return false;
    }
    RESULT_T result = processRow(resultSet);
    if (result == null) {
      throw new NullPointerException("Returned null from processRow");
    } else {
      action.accept(result);
      return true;
    }
  } catch (SQLException sqle) {
    throw new RuntimeException(
      "SQL Exception while processing result set", sqle);
  }
}

private void doClose() {
  try {
    if (resultSet != null && !resultSet.isClosed()) resultSet.close();
  } catch (SQLException ignore) {}
  for (int i = 0; i < toClose.length; i++) {
    try {
      AutoCloseable closeMe = toClose[i];
      toClose[i] = null;
      if (closeMe != null && closeMe != resultSet) closeMe.close();
    } catch (Exception ignore) {}
  }
}
}
```

With our utility class finally built, we can build our stream for the WordUsage query. We will simply declare an instance of the ResultSetSpliterator that delegates its ResultSet handling to our WordUsage. fromResultSet utility method. Since we will return a distinct WordUsage each time, we can pass the DISTINCT characteristic. We also pass it the connection from the ResultSet, so that it will close the connection as soon as the spliterator is exhausted. With that spliterator constructed, we will then pass in the spliterator to generate a parallel stream. That resulting code is in Listing 5-12.

Listing 5-12. Generating a New Stream Using ResultSetSpliterator

```java
public static Stream<WordUsage> createStream(
  Connection conn, ResultSet resultSet
) throws SQLException {
  Spliterator<WordUsage> usages =
    new ResultSetSpliterator<WordUsage>(
      resultSet, Spliterator.DISTINCT, conn
    ) {
      @Override
      protected WordUsage processRow(final ResultSet resultSet)
        throws SQLException
      {
        return WordUsage.fromResultSet(resultSet);
      }
    };
  Stream<WordUsage> stream = StreamSupport.stream(usages, true);
  return stream;
}
```

Method Four: Building a Stream from an Iterator

Although building out a spliterator was very educational, it was also a lot of work. If you do not need that level of control, you can build a spliterator from an iterator, and then build a stream from there. There are two bridge methods that get from an Iterator to a Spliterator: Spliterators.spliterator (Iterator, long, int) and Spliterators.spliteratorUnknownSize (Iterator, int). The former is used when you know the size of the elements that will be iterated over; the latter is for when you do not know the size. The former is notably more efficient than the latter, so if you can figure out the size ahead of time, definitely use it. In both cases, you pass the characteristics of the spliterator as the final argument.

Building an iterator for a ResultSet is notably simpler than building a spliterator. Our iterator implementation is therefore a simplification of our spliterator implementation in Listing 5-11. The only catch is that the single tryAdvance method of the Spliterator is two distinct methods in the Iterator class: hasNext() and then next(). Because of this, we will need to be able to store some state about whether or not there is a next element. This is a ternary variable: it can either be true, false, or unknown. This is one of the few legitimate uses of null: by using the Boolean type, we can get those three states. The implementation of our iterator is given in Listing 5-13.

Listing 5-13. ResultSetIterator Implementation

```java
import java.sql.ResultSet;
import java.sql.SQLException;
import java.util.*;

/**
 * An {@link java.util.Iterator} that traverses a {@link java.sql.ResultSet}.
 * When the result set is exhausted,
 * it will be automatically closed. Implementing classes should extend
 * {@link #processRow(java.sql.ResultSet)} to
 * specify how to convert a row into a result object.
```

```
 */
public abstract class ResultSetIterator<RESULT_T>
  implements Iterator<RESULT_T>
{

  private final ResultSet resultSet;
  private final AutoCloseable[] toClose;
  private volatile Boolean hasNext = null;

  /**
   * Constructor.
   *
   * @param resultSet The result set to process; may not be {@code null}.
   * @param toClose   Optional additional autocloseables (such as
   *                  {@link java.sql.Connection}) to close
   *                  when the result set is exhausted; may be {@code null}
   *                  (equivalent to empty).
   */
  public ResultSetIterator(final ResultSet resultSet, final AutoCloseable... toClose) {
    Objects.requireNonNull(resultSet, "result set");
    this.resultSet = resultSet;
    if (toClose == null) {
      this.toClose = new AutoCloseable[0];
    } else {
      this.toClose = toClose;
    }
  }

  /**
   * Given a {@link java.sql.ResultSet} instance on a current row,
   * return a {@code RESULT_T} instance for that row.
   * This code should not call {@link java.sql.ResultSet#next()} or
   * otherwise mutate the result set: it should
   * be treated as read-only.
   *
   * @param resultSet The result set to load.
   * @return The result instance.
   * @throws java.sql.SQLException If an error occurs.
   */
  protected abstract RESULT_T processRow(ResultSet resultSet)
    throws SQLException;

  private void doClose() {
    try {
      if (!resultSet.isClosed()) resultSet.close();
    } catch (SQLException ignore) {}
    for (int i = 0; i < toClose.length; i++) {
      try {
        AutoCloseable closeMe = toClose[i];
        toClose[i] = null;
        if (closeMe != null && closeMe != resultSet) closeMe.close();
```

```java
      } catch (Exception ignore) {}
    }
  }

  /**
   * Returns {@code true} if the iteration has more elements.
   * (In other words, returns {@code true} if {@link #next} would
   * return an element rather than throwing an exception.)
   *
   * @return {@code true} if the iteration has more elements
   */
  @Override
  public boolean hasNext() {
    try {
      if (hasNext == null) {
        hasNext = !resultSet.isClosed() && resultSet.next();
      }
    } catch (SQLException sqle) {
      throw new RuntimeException(
          "Could not determine if we have a next element", sqle
      );
    }
    if (!hasNext) doClose();
    return hasNext;
  }

  /**
   * Returns the next element in the iteration.
   *
   * @return the next element in the iteration
   * @throws java.util.NoSuchElementException if the iteration has no
   *                                          more elements
   */
  @Override
  public RESULT_T next() {
    if (!hasNext()) {
      throw new NoSuchElementException("No elements remaining");
    }
    try {
      return processRow(resultSet);
    } catch (SQLException sqle) {
      throw new RuntimeException("Error while processing elements", sqle);
    } finally {
      hasNext = null;
    }
  }
}
```

With this iterator, it is now the user's responsibility to know what characteristics to pass in when creating the spliterator. We saw from the last section that we can pass in DISTINCT, IMMUTABLE, and NONNULL. Once we create that spliterator, we will pass it into the `StreamSupport.stream` just like last time. This code is in Listing 5-14.

Listing 5-14. Creating a Stream from a ResultSetIterator

```
public static Stream<WordUsage> createStream(
  Connection conn, ResultSet resultSet
) throws SQLException {
  Iterator<WordUsage> usages =
    new ResultSetIterator<WordUsage>(resultSet, conn) {
      @Override
      protected WordUsage processRow(final ResultSet resultSet)
        throws SQLException
      {
        return WordUsage.fromResultSet(resultSet);
      }
  };
  Spliterator<WordUsage> spliterator =
    Spliterators.spliteratorUnknownSize(usages,
      Spliterator.NONNULL | Spliterator.DISTINCT | Spliterator.IMMUTABLE
    );
  Stream<WordUsage> stream = StreamSupport.stream(spliterator, true);
  return stream;
}
```

In this case, this final solution is just as fast as the solution before. From an API standpoint, we have moved the responsibility for understanding and deciding the characteristics to the user, and we have forced him to make the call to `Spliterators.spliteratorUnknownSize`. Those are both less than optimal, but they are hardly onerous. Given the situation, this is the solution that I would go with in my code. But it won't work in all situations.

Specifically, you will want to implement your own spliterator if you can be very efficient with the splits. If you can split your work load in an intelligent and efficient way, then providing your own implementation for `Spliterator.trySplit` is a huge win. A `ResultSet` — and any other kind of single-stream processing, like any `java.io.Stream` — does not really give you much to work with. But if you do encounter a situation where you can be smart about `trySplit`, then certainly implement your own `Spliterator`.

Pulling It All Together

We are finally ready to pull it all together: the stream and all its various parts. We will use the `ResultSetSpliterator` implementation, since we have it and it has the nicest user API. We will then map that into tab-separated values using the `WordUsage.toTSV()` method. Finally, we will print the tab-separated values as a String out to our standard out. The code for this is given in Listing 5-15.

Listing 5-15. Query with Mapping and Printing Out

```java
import java.sql.Connection;
import java.sql.ResultSet;
import java.sql.SQLException;
import java.util.*;
import java.util.stream.*;

public class Listing15 {

  public static void main(String[] args) throws Exception {
    Database.createDatabase();
    Connection conn = Database.getConnection();
    Stream<WordUsage> stream = createStream(conn, Database.queryResults(conn));
    stream.map(WordUsage::toTSV).forEach(System.out::println);
  }

  public static Stream<WordUsage> createStream(
    Connection conn, ResultSet resultSet
  ) throws SQLException {
    Spliterator<WordUsage> usages =
      new ResultSetSpliterator<WordUsage>(
        resultSet, Spliterator.DISTINCT, conn
      )
    {
      @Override
      protected WordUsage processRow(final ResultSet resultSet)
        throws SQLException
      {
        return WordUsage.fromResultSet(resultSet);
      }
    };
    Stream<WordUsage> stream = StreamSupport.stream(usages, true);
    return stream;
  }
}
```

That is a lot of power for a very little bit of code. It is also extremely extensible, and it is very clear where the process steps fit into the workflow, and what is workflow and what is the implementation of steps. This is an excellent example of the powerfully expressive postfunctional coding style of Java 8, even when having to interact with ugly and difficult legacy code.

CHAPTER 6

■ ■ ■

Lambda Concurrency

The Java programming language is, at its core, a series of instructions. These instructions are executed in sequence. By default, you only ever have one of these series going at a time. However, if you have multiple processing cores on your machine, or if you have any kind of I/O, then this single series of instructions suddenly becomes very inefficient. If your program has a lot to do, but its single stream has to wait for the "read" I/O instruction to complete before doing anything else, then your program is wasting time. If you have four processing cores, but only one stream of instructions, then you are at best only using a quarter of your potential power. The solution to this is to have multiple streams of instructions executing at the same time within your program, which is called concurrency.

If you have read anything about lambdas in Java 8, you've probably heard the words "lambda" and "concurrency" used in the same breath. Concurrency seems to be one of the driving interests in adopting lambdas, but exactly why lambdas help with concurrency is often left as an exercise to the reader. In this chapter, we will see how and why lambdas play so nicely with concurrency. We are going to take a look at the primary Java concurrency technologies, starting with the venerable Thread class and ultimately building up to a highly concurrent system using streams. These streams are not the I/O streams: these are streams of processing. What we will see is that lambdas make it easy to pass around instructions that can be executed across multiple streams: while Java technically always had this capability, lambdas make the code readable, and streams make implementing it easy.

It is easy for conversations about concurrency to wander off into the abstract, and even easier for examples of concurrency to be trivially simple. To avoid this, we will use a consistent example throughout this chapter, and simply solve this problem in different ways. (This practice of repeatedly solving a familiar problem in different ways is called a code kata, a term coined by Dave Thomas.) In our case, the "problem to solve" will be printing primes of increasing size: we will use Java's BigInteger class to generate primes starting with 1 bit long and going up to 50,000 bits long. In order to make room for our concurrency, we will say that the generated values do not need to be printed in order. The reference implementation is given in Listing 6-1: in that listing, we generate the primes in a serial fashion.

Listing 6-1. Reference Implementation of Prime Generation

```java
// PrimeFactory.java
import java.math.BigInteger;
import java.util.*;
import java.util.concurrent.*;

public class PrimeFactory {

  /**
   * Returns a number that has bit length {@code bitLength} and is
   * probably prime. The odds of the value being prime are the same as
   * {@link BigInteger#probablePrime(int, java.util.Random)}.
```

```java
 *
 * @param bitLength The bit length of the resulting prime; must be
 * @return A random {@link java.math.BigInteger} of bit length
 *         {@code bitLength} which is probably prime.
 * @see java.math.BigInteger#probablePrime(int, java.util.Random)
 */
public static BigInteger ofLength(int bitLength) {
  return ofLength(bitLength, ThreadLocalRandom.current());
}

/**
 * Returns a number that has bit length {@code bitLength} and is
 * probably prime. The odds of the value being prime are the same as
 * {@link BigInteger#probablePrime(int, java.util.Random)}.
 *
 * @param bitLength The bit length of the resulting prime; must be
 * @param rand      The random bit generator to use.
 * @return A random {@link java.math.BigInteger} of bit length
 *         {@code bitLength} which is probably prime.
 * @see java.math.BigInteger#probablePrime(int, java.util.Random)
 */
public static BigInteger ofLength(int bitLength, Random rand) {
    if (bitLength <= 0) {
      throw new IllegalArgumentException(
        "Bit length must be positive; was " + bitLength);
    }
    return new BigInteger(bitLength, ThreadLocalRandom.current());
  }

}

// DemoRunner.java
import java.util.*;

/*
* Responsible for running the demonstrations we have in this chapter.
 */
public class DemoRunner {

  /**
   * The number of runs we will do per demo to get our timings. Must be odd.
   */
  public static final int RUN_COUNT = 3;

  /**
   * The maximum bitlength of primes to generate.
   */
  public static final int MAX_BITLENGTH = 50000;

  /**
   * The interface for this chapter demos need to implement.
   */
```

```java
  public interface Demo {

    /**
     * Implementation of generating primes up to a certain bitlength. The demo
     * should generate each prime and then print it to standard out.
     */
    void generatePrimesToBitLength(int bitLength);
  }

  /**
   * Runs the demo {@link #RUN_COUNT} times and then prints the median time.
   *
   * @param demo The demo to run; never {@code null}
   */
  public static void run(Demo demo) {
    Objects.requireNonNull(demo, "demo");
    long[] timings = new long[RUN_COUNT];
    for (int i = 0; i < timings.length; i++) {
      System.out.println("START ROUND " + (i+1));
      long startTime = System.currentTimeMillis();
      demo.generatePrimesToBitLength(MAX_BITLENGTH);
      long endTime = System.currentTimeMillis();
      timings[i] = endTime - startTime;
    }
    Arrays.sort(timings);
    long medianTime = timings[timings.length / 2];
    System.out.println("All timings: " + Arrays.toString(timings));
    System.out.println("Median time: " + medianTime + "ms");
  }

}

// Listing1.java
import java.math.BigInteger;
import java.util.*;

public class Listing1 {

  public static void printPrimes(int maxBitLength) {
    Random rand = new Random();
    for (int i = 0; i < maxBitLength; i++) {
      BigInteger prime = PrimeFactory.ofLength(i + 1, rand);
      System.out.println(prime.toString());
    }
  }

  public static void main(String[] args) {
    DemoRunner.run(Listing1::printPrimes);
  }
}
```

The timing given by our DemoRunner is not scientific, but it will do for basic comparisons. On my computer, Listing1.printPrimes takes roughly 50 seconds to complete. (On your computer, it could take much longer; if you are running the code at home and it takes too long, reduce MAX_BITLENGTH to get a more reasonable result.) My computer, however, is barely breaking a sweat: only four of my eight cores are busied at all, and they hang out at about 50% utilization each. Let's see if we can use concurrency to make better use of our hardware.

We will start by using classic Java threads; those are what most developers are probably familiar with. Lambdas help somewhat here. However, thread management was tricky, and people wanted to use thread pools, so Java introduced the concept of Executors to simplify things. Lambdas help even more with executors. Most important, however, we get the concept of streams of execution in Java 8, which truly leverage the power of lambdas to make concurrency easy. We will see precisely how by the end of the chapter.

Lambdas and Classic Java Threading

The first Java concurrency structure was the Thread class, and it still underlies all the other concurrency structures in the Java language. Lambdas work well with the Thread class, because the Thread class is built around the Runnable interface. As we saw in chapter 2, a lambda is implicitly converted into an interface implementation through type inference, so you can write this code:

```
Runnable r = () -> System.out.println("Hello, World!");
```

The Thread class has a constructor that takes a Runnable. In the world with Java 8 lambdas, this means that the Thread class has a constructor that takes a lambda: that lambda is converted into a Runnable by the compiler. This means that lambdas make writing Thread code much simpler: instead of having an anonymous inner class or some distant interface implementation, you can simply pass your lambda right in.

A naïve approach to using the Thread class to solve our kata is to spawn a thread for each value to be calculated. Unfortunately, threads are not cheap, and you will quickly exhaust the resources of your virtual machine that way. Instead, we will spawn a certain number of threads, and split the work to be done evenly among them. Those threads will do the CPU-intensive work, so we will have one of those per processor core. We will have another thread that will be responsible for printing the values to standard out, since that is the I/O intensive work, and having multiple threads attempting to write to standard out is a bottleneck. Both these threads will be defined by passing the lambda right in.

Now, one catch with threads is that they swallow errors by default. If you provide some work for a thread to do, and that work explodes with a RuntimeException, then the thread just silently dies. In order to get some kind of error messaging, you have to set a Thread.UncaughtExceptionHandler instance. This can be set either on the thread or globally, but the same type inference stunt will help make this code readable: Thread.UncaughtExceptionHandler is an interface, so we can implement it inline. This code:

```
Thread.setDefaultUncaughtExceptionHandler(
  new Thread.UncaughtExceptionHandler() {
    @Override
    public void uncaughtException(final Thread t, final Throwable e) {
      System.err.println("Exception in " + t + ": " + e);
    }
  }
);
```

Just became this:

```
Thread.setDefaultUncaughtExceptionHandler((t, e) -> {
    System.err.println("Exception in " + t + ": " + e);
    }
);
```

The code for this entire implementation is given in Listing 6-2.

Listing 6-2. Using Lambdas to Define Thread Instances

```
import java.math.BigInteger;
import java.util.*;
import java.util.concurrent.*;
import java.util.concurrent.atomic.*;

public class Listing2 {

  private static void joinThread(Thread t) {
    try {
      t.join();
    } catch (InterruptedException e) {
      e.printStackTrace();
    }
  }

  public static void printPrimes(int maxBitLength) {
    Thread.setDefaultUncaughtExceptionHandler((t, e) -> {
        System.err.println("Exception in " + t + ": " + e);
      }
    );

    int processorCount = Runtime.getRuntime().availableProcessors();

    BlockingQueue<String> primes = new LinkedBlockingQueue<String>();

    Thread[] threads = new Thread[processorCount];
    for (int t = 0; t < threads.length; t++) {
      int modulus = t;
      threads[modulus] = new Thread(() -> {
        for (int i = 0; i < maxBitLength; i++) {
          int bitLength = i + 1;
          if (bitLength % processorCount == modulus) {
            BigInteger prime = PrimeFactory.ofLength(bitLength);
            primes.add(prime.toString());
          }
        }
      }
      );
      threads[modulus].start();
    }
```

```java
    AtomicBoolean doneSignal = new AtomicBoolean(false);
    Thread printer = new Thread(() -> {
      List<String> myPrimes = new ArrayList<>(threads.length);
      for (Thread.yield(); !doneSignal.get(); Thread.yield()) {
        primes.drainTo(myPrimes);
        if (myPrimes.isEmpty()) {
          // Take an extra breather
          Thread.yield();
        } else {
          System.out.println(String.join("\n", myPrimes));
          myPrimes.clear();
        }
      }
    }
    );
    printer.start();

    for (int t = 0; t < threads.length; t++) {
      joinThread(threads[t]);
    }
    doneSignal.set(true);
    joinThread(printer);
  }

  public static void main(String[] args) {
    DemoRunner.run(Listing2::printPrimes);
  }
}
```

The main class just delegates to printPrimes. That method defines our exception handler and creates a queue for the prime strings. We then launch a thread for each processor. Each of those threads will generate an even portion of the primes, and put them into a blocking queue. Then we launch another thread whose sole job it is to read off that queue and print out the values. We need some way to tell that printer thread that we are done, so we have to declare a signal that the printer is required to monitor on each loop. This whole thing feels rather like a Rube Goldberg machine.

On my computer, this code runs in about 14.5 seconds, and we are happily saturating all the processors. However, this code is pretty ugly: we are doing something extremely simple, and there is a bunch of ceremony and noise obscuring that simple effort. All of that ceremony and noise is necessary because of the fact that we are working with the Thread class directly. Working with threads this way is incredibly awkward, which is why Java introduced executors. In the next section, we will see that lambdas help clean those up, too.

Lambdas and Executors

The ExecutorService and its related classes are convenient wrappers around the Thread class. They provide the proven and standard patterns of thread execution: there are executors for responsively sized thread pools, executors for fixed sized thread pools, executors that will generate threads on demand and then cache them, and executors that wrap a single thread. If you find yourself wanting to do something with threads fancier than the executors can support, then you are either working on a PhD thesis or doing something wrong.

In all these cases, the usage is the same: you pass an instance of the Callable interface into the executor, and it returns a Future instance that is a handle on the result. That Future instance also provides access to any error that occurred during the processing. This usage has three major advantages over the Runnable approach done by threads: first, you can return a value from your concurrent processing; second, your errors are not silently swallowed (assuming you get the result from the Future); and third, a thread can only run one Runnable instance, but an executor's thread can run handle multiple Callable instances. Just like with the Thread's inline Runnable implementation, though, we can provide our Callable implementation inline using lambdas. This makes the code much simpler to read.

We can see these advantages in play when we rewrite our kata using the executors. Instead of coming up with a clever way to divvy up the work evenly, we will simply add all the work to be done into our primary processing executor. Just like before, that executor will have as many threads as we have processors, and it will be responsible for the CPU-intensive work. We will hand the I/O intensive work off to another executor, which will be a single thread. Since the hand-off is cleaner, we can set the I/O intensive thread to be maximum priority, ensuring that it executes as much as possible: we see again there that lambdas make the code much more readable, since we can specify the ThreadFactory implementation inline. The code for this kata is given in Listing 6-3.

Listing 6-3. Using Lambdas to Define ExecutorService Work Instances

```java
import java.math.BigInteger;
import java.util.*;
import java.util.concurrent.*;

public class Listing3 {

  public static void printPrimes(int maxBitLength) {
    ExecutorService executor =
      Executors.newFixedThreadPool(Runtime.getRuntime().availableProcessors());
    ExecutorService printExecutor = Executors.newSingleThreadExecutor(r -> {
        Thread t = new Thread(r);
        t.setPriority(Thread.MAX_PRIORITY);
        return t;
      }
    );

    // The resulting work
    List<Future<?>> futures = new ArrayList<>(maxBitLength);

    for (int i = 0; i < maxBitLength; i++) {
      int bitLength = i + 1;
      Future<String> stringFuture = executor.submit(() -> {
          BigInteger prime = PrimeFactory.ofLength(bitLength);
          return prime.toString();
        }
      );
```

```
        futures.add(printExecutor.submit(() -> {
                String primeString = stringFuture.get();
                System.out.println(primeString);
                return null;
            }
        )
    );
    }

    // Signal that there will be no more tasks added
    executor.shutdown();
    printExecutor.shutdown();

    // Wait for everything to complete and check for errors
    futures.parallelStream().forEach(future -> {
        try {
            future.get();
        } catch (InterruptedException | ExecutionException e) {
            e.printStackTrace();
        }
      }
    );
    }

    public static void main(String[] args) {
        DemoRunner.run(Listing3::printPrimes);
    }
}
```

This code is much nicer compared to Listing 6-2. There is no need for us to declare flags or hand-off queues; instead, we just pass one Future into the work for another, and we work with the resulting futures. We still get our saturated processor cores, and we still get our dedicated thread to I/O. You may be concerned about the overhead incurred by the executor classes as opposed to our "hand-tuned" implementation, but the result is actually half a second faster on my computer, coming in at 14.0 seconds.

If you were paying close attention, you probably caught the invocation of futures.parallelStream(). We saw in the last chapter how streams can be set to process in parallel, with the result being some additional transparent concurrency. Here, the parallelism allows us to check the futures for errors very quickly, and all it cost was a method call. That is very powerful, but we are not quite ready to get into that concurrency approach: we will get there in a later section of this chapter. There is still more to be done here with Java's preexisting concurrency tools!

Lambdas and the ThreadPoolExecutor

This gives you the basic idea about how lambdas make life with executors so much nicer. There is one particular place, however, where the ability to define interface implementations inline is incredibly helpful, and that's with the ThreadPoolExecutor.

The ThreadPoolExecutor is an extremely customizable implementation of the ExecutorService class. Many programmers (including your author) really like to twiddle knobs, and this class gives you plenty of knobs to keep you busy. Some of those knobs are numerical values, but there are many callbacks available for this class. Each of those callbacks is an interface, which means that there are suddenly many places where lambdas make your life much easier. It is, however, possible to have too much of a good thing. It is a great example of the limits of lambdas to provide clarity.

The problem is that the ThreadPoolExecutor has this constructor:

```
public ThreadPoolExecutor( int corePoolSize,
                           int maximumPoolSize,
                           long keepAliveTime,
                           TimeUnit unit,
                           BlockingQueue<Runnable> workQueue,
                           ThreadFactory threadFactory,
                           RejectedExecutionHandler handler )
```

The temptation in Java 8 is to want to provide the threadFactory and handler inline. Unfortunately that leads to code that looks like this:

```
ThreadPoolExecutor tpe = new ThreadPoolExecutor(
    processorCount,
    processorCount * 2 + 1,
    1L, TimeUnit.SECONDS,
    new ArrayBlockingQueue<>(processorCount * 4 + 1),
    r -> {
      Thread t = new Thread(r);
      t.setPriority(Thread.MAX_PRIORITY);
      return t;
    },
    (rejected, executor) -> {
      BlockingQueue<Runnable> fullQueue = executor.getQueue();

      // Wait for the timeout
      try {
        boolean submitted = fullQueue.offer(
          rejected,
          1L, TimeUnit.SECONDS
        );
        if (submitted) return;
      } catch (InterruptedException e) {
        // Fall through
      }

      // If we get here, the queue is well and truly full
      // First, execute our work
      rejected.run();

      // Next, execute another piece of work to be nice
      // (This slows down the producer thread & might break a deadlock.)
      Runnable otherWork = fullQueue.poll();
      if (otherWork != null) otherWork.run();
    }
);
```

That code is extremely hard to follow, especially if you did not just look up the constructor. The problems here are threefold: first, there are too many arguments in the constructor, so it is hard to keep straight what is supposed to do what; second, the multiple lambdas in the row create some deep nesting, and make it hard to see where one lambda stops and another begins; third, the lambda implementations themselves are very long, which makes it hard to see where the constructor ends and the following code begins. These problems may seem obvious to the reader, but to the API designer and the writer, it's a very natural path to this code. You will probably inadvertently write this code sometime soon.

The best practice is to only have one lambda per method call. Since any single-element interface is prone to being made into a lambda, you should limit your methods to only have one of those. However, we are dealing with a violation of this best practice, and since it is in the Java SDK, it is not likely to be fixed any time soon. When working with legacy code, the solution to this problem is to use semantic variables: create and assign them first, and then pass them into the constructor.

```java
int processorCount =
  Math.max(1, Runtime.getRuntime().availableProcessors());
int corePoolSize = processorCount;
int maxPoolSize = processorCount * 2 + 1;
long threadTimeoutMag = 1L;
TimeUnit threadTimeoutUnit = TimeUnit.SECONDS;
BlockingQueue<Runnable> queue =
  new ArrayBlockingQueue<>(processorCount * 4 + 1);
ThreadFactory threadFactory = r -> {
  Thread t = new Thread(r);
  t.setPriority(Thread.MAX_PRIORITY);
  return t;
};
RejectedExecutionHandler rejectHandler = (rejected, executor) -> {
  BlockingQueue<Runnable> fullQueue = executor.getQueue();

  // Wait for the timeout
  try {
    boolean submitted = fullQueue.offer(rejected, 1L, TimeUnit.SECONDS);
    if (submitted) return;
  } catch (InterruptedException e) {
    // Fall through
  }

  // If we get here, the queue is well and truly full
  // First, execute our work
  rejected.run();

  // Next, execute another piece of work to be nice
  // (This also slows down the producer thread and might break a deadlock.)
  Runnable otherWork = fullQueue.poll();
  if (otherWork != null) otherWork.run();
};
```

```
ThreadPoolExecutor tpe = new ThreadPoolExecutor(
    corePoolSize,
    maxPoolSize,
    threadTimeoutMag, threadTimeoutUnit,
    queue,
    threadFactory,
    rejectHandler
);
```

This creates a bunch of variables cluttering your scope. The solution for that, of course, is to move things into their own method. Given the sheer number of lines of code, this is probably a good idea. The lambda-to-interface conversions can also be done in their own methods. The resulting code is in Listing 6-4. Note that this code provides convenient extension points for subclasses: it's just another example of how cleaning up hard-to-read code also results in better-structured code. This demonstrates the simplest way to tell a good practice from a bad one: a bad practice has collateral damage; a good practice has collateral benefits.

Listing 6-4. ThreadPoolExecutor Creation and Using Lambdas Responsibly

```
protected ThreadFactory createThreadFactory() {
  return r -> {
    Thread t = new Thread(r);
    t.setPriority(Thread.MAX_PRIORITY);
    return t;
  };
}

protected RejectedExecutionHandler createdRejectedExecutionHandler() {
  return (rejected, executor) -> {
    BlockingQueue<Runnable> fullQueue = executor.getQueue();

    // Wait for the timeout
    try {
      boolean submitted = fullQueue.offer(rejected, 1L, TimeUnit.SECONDS);
      if (submitted) return;
    } catch (InterruptedException e) {
      // Fall through
    }

    // If we get here, the queue is well and truly full
    // First, execute our work
    rejected.run();

    // Next, execute another piece of work to be nice
    // (This also slows down the producer thread and might break a deadlock.)
    Runnable otherWork = fullQueue.poll();
    if (otherWork != null) otherWork.run();
  };
}
```

```java
public ThreadPoolExecutor createThreadPoolExecutor() {
  int processorCount = Math.max(1,
    Runtime.getRuntime().availableProcessors());
  int corePoolSize = processorCount;
  int maxPoolSize = processorCount * 2 + 1;
  long threadTimeoutMag = 1L;
  TimeUnit threadTimeoutUnit = TimeUnit.SECONDS;
  BlockingQueue<Runnable> queue =
    new ArrayBlockingQueue<>(processorCount * 4 + 1);
  ThreadFactory threadFactory = createThreadFactory();
  Objects.requireNonNull(threadFactory,
    "thread factory for thread pool executor");
  RejectedExecutionHandler rejectHandler = createdRejectedExecutionHandler();
  Objects.requireNonNull(rejectHandler,
    "rejected execution handler for thread pool executor");

  return new ThreadPoolExecutor(
      corePoolSize,
      maxPoolSize,
      threadTimeoutMag, threadTimeoutUnit,
      queue,
      threadFactory,
      rejectHandler
  );
}
```

Lambdas and Fork/Join

When we last left our bitlength prime generator, we had gotten a significant performance improvement by leveraging Java's executors. However, this took a lot of set-up and noise. Wouldn't it be nicer if you could just specify the work that you wanted to do, and not have to worry about the concurrency details? The good news is that you can, using Java's Fork/Join pools. In Java 7, that functionality existed in the SDK. In Java 8, lambdas make that functionality user friendly.

The basic concept of the Fork/Join pool is that you work on tasks that can fork additional work, and then can join that work back into the main thread. You can create and manage the underlying thread pool if you really care by using the ForkJoinPool class. However, you can also ignore the pool management entirely: you can simply provide the work to perform concurrently, fire off that work, and join that work back into your thread at some later point. It is really that simple: Java handles the rest.

Of course, there are a lot of caveats to the kind of work that you should pass into the Fork/Join framework: long-blocking work, for instance, requires some careful handling. You can read about these details in the JavaDoc for the ForkJoinTask and ForkJoinPool classes. However, for the kind of work that we are dealing with, it is absolutely perfect.

What is even better is that the Fork/Join framework works extremely nicely with streams: you can fork the work at one stage of the stream and join it in another. To implement our solution, we will define a parallel stream of numbers, ranging from 1 to our maximum bitlength. We will then map our parallel stream into a parallel stream of forked ForkJoinTask instances, each of which is generating a prime. Then we will join those tasks back (handling the errors), and then print the result to standard out. This code is given in Listing 6-5.

Listing 6-5. Using Lambdas to Define Fork/Join Tasks

```java
import java.util.concurrent.*;
import java.util.stream.*;

public class Listing5 {

  public static void printPrimes(int maxBitLength) {
    Stream.iterate(1, i -> i+1).limit(maxBitLength).parallel()
      .map(i ->
             ForkJoinTask.adapt(() -> PrimeFactory.ofLength(i)).fork()
      )
      .map(ForkJoinTask::join)
      .forEach(System.out::println);
  }

  public static void main(String[] args) {
    DemoRunner.run(Listing5::printPrimes);
  }
}
```

This code executes in about 14 seconds on my machine. That means this code is just as performant as the hand-rolled executor code before, and it is strikingly shorter. If all you are doing is CPU-intensive work, or if it is primarily CPU-intensive work with some very brief blocking work (such as reading from a private file on a local disk), then this is a perfect solution for you.

Stream Parallelism

In the last chapter, we discovered that there were sequential and parallel streams, and sequential streams were the default. And in the last section, we used a parallel stream for maximum concurrency. But what exactly is going on when we switch from sequential to parallel streams? To see the difference, we can run the code in Listing 6-6.

Listing 6-6. Code to Demonstrate the Difference Between Sequential and Parallel Streams

```java
// NumberStreamFactory.java
import java.util.stream.*;

public class NumberStreamFactory {

  /**
   * Returns a parallel stream which returns the {@code int} values from 1 to {@code value}.
   *
   * @param value The value to count up to; must be positive.
   * @return A stream that returns 1, 2, ..., {@code value}.
   */
```

```java
  public static Stream<Integer> countTo(int value) {
    if (value <= 0) {
      throw new IllegalArgumentException("Need a positive value to count up to, but we were
      given " + value);
    }
    return Stream.iterate(1, i -> i + 1).limit(value).parallel();
  }

}

// Listing6.java
public class Listing6 {

  public static void main(String[] args) {
    System.out.println("\n\n\nPARALLEL");
    NumberStreamFactory.countTo(200).parallel().map(i -> {
        System.out.println("map: " + i +
          " Thread: " + Thread.currentThread().getName());
        return i;
      }
    ).forEach(i ->
          System.out.println("forEach: " + i +
            " Thread: " + Thread.currentThread().getName())
    );

    System.out.println("\n\n\nSEQUENTIAL");
    NumberStreamFactory.countTo(200).sequential().map(i -> {
        System.out.println("map: " + i +
          " Thread: " + Thread.currentThread().getName());
        return i;
      }
    ).forEach(i ->
          System.out.println("forEach: " + i +
            " Thread: " + Thread.currentThread().getName())
    );

  }
}


/* SAMPLE RESULT

PARALLEL
map: 13 Thread: ForkJoinPool.commonPool-worker-4
map: 132 Thread: main
map: 163 Thread: ForkJoinPool.commonPool-worker-1
map: 32 Thread: ForkJoinPool.commonPool-worker-3
forEach: 32 Thread: ForkJoinPool.commonPool-worker-3
map: 182 Thread: ForkJoinPool.commonPool-worker-2
forEach: 182 Thread: ForkJoinPool.commonPool-worker-2
map: 33 Thread: ForkJoinPool.commonPool-worker-3
...
```

```
SEQUENTIAL
map: 1 Thread: main
forEach: 1 Thread: main
map: 2 Thread: main
forEach: 2 Thread: main
map: 3 Thread: main
forEach: 3 Thread: main
map: 4 Thread: main
forEach: 4 Thread: main
map: 5 Thread: main
forEach: 5 Thread: main
map: 6 Thread: main
forEach: 6 Thread: main
map: 7 Thread: main
forEach: 7 Thread: main
...

*/
```

As we can see, sequential streams are simple: they execute in the caller's thread. As much as possible, they perform the entire stream of operations for an element before moving onto the next. There are, however, some operations (such as `stream.sorted()`) that require processing the entire stream: the stream can't know if the current element is the smallest until it has consumed the entire stream. Therefore, this call acts as a barrier: the particular element of the stream cannot move beyond it before the subsequent elements are processed.

The parallel streams are more interesting. If you have sufficient elements, they will delegate some of their work into the common `ForkJoinPool` instance. This is the same thread pool in which our Fork/Join tasks executed, which shows how nicely those frameworks play together. Some of the work may still done locally (such as number 132), but in any case, the same thread will execute as far along the stream as possible (as demonstrated by numbers 32 and 182).

However, you should have absolutely no presumption that elements of the stream are processed in order, or that they are processed promptly after they are generated – we generated 182 items out of the stream before we processed our sixth item, number 33. If we had a stream where each element was a gigabyte in size, we would be in trouble! The stream generation itself can get very far ahead of the processing, and those elements remain cached in memory until they are processed. Therefore, it is always best if parallel streams generate very small elements (such as indexes or lines of text), and you build those small elements into larger elements as part of your stream processing.

Another thing to watch out for is the fact that your Fork/Join tasks will share the common Fork/Join pool with the stream operations themselves. Therefore, you should never have your stream operation wait for your Fork/Join task to resolve unless you are using `ForkJoinTask.join()` or `ForkJoinTask.invoke()` – those two methods will cause the current thread to process the task itself if it is not yet started. Any other dependency on a Fork/Join task resolving, whether directly or indirectly, is potentially setting yourself up for a deadlock.

However, if you can generate a stream of small elements, if your stream operations do not block for very long, and you can be slightly careful about your Fork/Join tasks, then the stream parallelism is an easy way to get significant concurrency gains out of your Java applications. You simply specify what you want to have happen and let the runtime do the concurrency management and the optimization for you. All of this can be done with readable code because lambdas make it possible to pass around behavior as simply as data.

Conclusion

I hope that you can now see the power of lambdas and streams to make concurrent code relatively easy. The code becomes very readable, and you separate out the execution details from the work to be done. This is truly one of the most impressive parts of post-functional code.

Note that there is still a time and a place for the other approaches. A single thread is useful as a one-time fire-and-forget hook, or long-running background daemon tasks. Executors are useful when you have a variety of work to be done and need more control over the thread pooling. The fork/join framework works extremely well for recursive problems. But for the very common case of tying together a stream of operations, lambdas and the stream frameworks are a powerful and welcome addition to the Java SDK.

■ ■ ■

## CHAPTER 7

Lambdas and Legacy Code

At this point in this book, you have seen all the wonderful things that lambdas can do for your codebase. But what about the huge pile of legacy code that is out there? There is a lot of code to be merged into this new reality, and a lot of Java developers are commited to projects that have to drag forward those balls of mud. How can lambdas make their life easier?

Furthermore, the new Java 8 APIs are very impressive, but there are many APIs in the Java SDK that have not yet been updated for the brave new lambda world. How do you take advantage of lambdas with APIs that are not at all intended to support it?

The good news is that the Java language's developers have been long concerned about this issue. Java is by its nature a conservative language, so the language developers could not break any of the existing Java code with radical language changes. The language developers could, however, add in new features and provide new powers and new APIs. Most important, they provided key functionality to bridge legacy code into our new world. That functionality, combined with a few key practices, means there is only a minor bit of code necessary to gain all the power of lambdas, even from code that has no idea about them.

Resources and Exceptions

The most awkward legacy pattern in Java is the "try-with-resource" pattern. This is where a stateful object – usually either an I/O object or a pool – needs to be put from an initial condition into an operational condition before you can use it, and then that stateful object also needs to be cleaned up when your user operation is completed on it. This pattern is widely adopted and conceptually works quite nicely with object-oriented programming. However, the implementation of this pattern has never worked well in Java, and the language has struggled with ways to improve it since the start.

Initially, this pattern required you to declare a variable outside of a scope, then enter into a try/catch block. It was 14 additional lines of code required for each resource, which looked something like this:

```
InputStream in = null;
try {
  in = acquireInputStream();
  // Do something with "in"
} finally {
  if (in != null) {
    try {
      in.close();
    } catch (IOException closeException) {
      // What now?
    }
    in = null;
  }
}
```

This creates the question of what to do with the closeException that may be thrown. If an exception is thrown while working with the resource, and then another exception is thrown while closing the resource, then what? If you throw closeException, the original exception (which is probably actually useful) is lost. The usual solution was to simply ignore the closeException, often hidden inside a method called something like closeQuietly(InputStream in). This method could also then ignore null values. This made the code significantly shorter and somewhat more readable:

```
InputStream in = null;
try {
  in = acquireInputStream();
  // Do something
} finally {
  closeQuiety(in);
  in = null;
}
```

There are some subtle problems with this code, however. At first glance, they may seem trivial, but they won't be trivial when they crop up in your production code. The most significant of these subtle problems is that this code ignores any exception that occurs on close, which is exactly when buffered streams, compression streams, and cryptographic streams will throw their exceptions. This code will silently discard those exceptions, leaving the calling code (and the debugging developer) to think everything is just fine. This code pattern also still leaks the resource's variable into the surrounding scope. If you forgot to assign the resource to null, you would then leak the object itself, preventing its timely garbage collection. The resource handling can also get lost or confused easily if there are catch clauses attached to the try, as well, and multiple resources would require nesting these structures within each other. The whole thing just has a kind of ugliness to it still.

In an attempt to resolve this ugliness, Java 7 introduced the "try-with-resources" syntax structure. This allows you to declare your resources at the start of the try block, and it would automatically close the resources. You can assign anything that implements java.lang.AutoCloseable as a resource. That resource will be closed automatically when the try block completes. If an exception is thrown on close, then the exception will be propagated up to the caller. If there was already an exception thrown and an additional exception is thrown on close, than that additional exception is attached to the first as a suppressed exception: the stack trace will reveal the original exception as the primary cause, and the close exception as an additional suppressed exception. As an added benefit, you have clearly delimited boundaries for your variables, and the compiler guarnatees that they will be closed when you exit the block. Overall, this gives the kind of exception handling that people are looking for, and the code looks like this:

```
public void closeQuietlyTryWithResource() {
  try(InputStream in = acquireInputStream()) {
    // Do something
  } catch(IOException exception) {
    // Handle exception, which may include close exceptions
  }
}
```

Unfortunately, this plays poorly with the syntax of lambdas. The try-with-resources block is not a single statement, so if you want your try-with-resources as a body of a lambda, you immediately have to wrap that call in a pair of brackets, such as this:

```
Consumer<Object> consumer = it -> {
  try (InputStream in = acquireInputStream()) {
    // Do something
  } catch (IOException exception) {
    // Handle exception, which may include close exceptions
  }
};
```

Note also that we have to put the lambda within the try-with-resources block itself, or we have to execute the lambda before we exit the try-with-resources block. If you assign the lambda within the try-with-resources block, exit the try-with-resources block, and then try to call the lambda, the input stream will be closed. The order of operations will be as follows:

1. Enter try-with-resources block.

2. Assign the lambda.

3. Exit try-with-resources block, closing the input stream.

4. Call the lambda.

A demonstration of this error is in Listing 7-1. When you walk through it in this way, the error seems obvious. However, this is an easy mistake to make, and it can be quite tricky to detect in practice. It can be especially tricky to detect if you are calling into code that releases Zalgo. If you remember from chapter 2, a developer "releases Zalgo" any time calling code sometimes executes immediately and sometimes executes in a deferred manner. If your code releases Zalgo, then you might pass your resource into that code expecting it to be executed immediately. However, when it executes in that deferred manner, you will have a race condition: the try-with-resource block will call at some point in the future, and the calling code will read the input stream at some other point in the future. Which one comes first is at the capricious whim of the thread scheduler. The result will be intermittent closed input streams: you will get exceptions when the reading code occasionally loses the race.

Listing 7-1. Calling a Lambda after Its Resources Are Closed

```
import java.io.IOException;
import java.io.InputStream;
import java.io.UncheckedIOException;
import java.util.function.*;

public class Listing1 {

  public static void main(String[] args) {
    Consumer<Object> consumer = null;
    try (InputStream in = acquireInputStream()) {
      consumer = it -> {
        try {
          System.out.println("Trying to read!");
          in.read();
        } catch (IOException ioe) {
```

```
          throw new UncheckedIOException("read error", ioe);
        }
      };
    } catch (IOException ioe) {
      throw new UncheckedIOException("input stream error", ioe);
    }
    consumer.accept(new Object());
  }

  public static InputStream acquireInputStream() {
    return new InputStream() {
      @Override
      public int read() throws IOException {
        return 1;
      }

      @Override
      public void close() throws IOException {
        System.out.println("Closing!");
        super.close();
      }
    };
  }

}

/* RESULT
Closing!
Trying to read!
*/
```

All in all, the try-with-resources approach is not too bad, although it is already getting a bit noisy. You have to be careful about which blocks are nested in which way, but that is very manageable. The bigger problem is that if you have a return value from your function, then the return from the catch block has to match the return from the try block. The natural reaction for many Java developers will be to return null at this point, but that is just opening up the possibility of encountering a NullPointerException, since it expects the consumer to handle the situation while making it easy for them to ignore the situation. There are three better options depending on your circumstance: unchecked exceptions, an exception-handling caller, or a Result object.

Handling Resources by Throwing an Unchecked Exception

A very popular and very common solution is to handle checked exceptions by converting them to unchecked exceptions and rethrowing them. This passes the responsibility for addressing the situation back to the caller, and the exception will probably traverse quite a ways back up through the execution stack before it encounters an exception handler. Hopefully, wherever that is will be well-suited for handling the exceptional circumstance in an intelligent way.

Java 8 introduced some support for this programming convention: the java.io.UncheckedIOException class, which explicitly exists to wrap checked IOException instances in an unchecked wrapper. Since IOExceptions are at the root of the most common exception classes, this class provides a means to convert most common exceptions into the unchecked form. The best way to do this is to use the UncheckedIOExcept ion(String,IOException) constructor, which allows you to also attach a message for human consumption to the point of conversion; in general, the more information you can provide in the case of an exception, the better off you will be. For an example of this usage, see Listing 7-2.

Listing 7-2. An UncheckedIOException Wrapping an IOException

```
import java.io.ByteArrayInputStream;
import java.io.IOException;
import java.io.InputStream;
import java.io.UncheckedIOException;
import java.util.function.*;

public class Listing2 {

  public static InputStream createInputStream() throws IOException {
    return new ByteArrayInputStream("foobar".getBytes());
  }

  public static void call(Consumer<Object> c) {
    c.accept(new Object());
  }

  public static void main(String[] args) {
    call(it -> {
        try (InputStream in = createInputStream()) {
          throw new IOException("And with a kiss, I die!");
        } catch (IOException e) {
          throw new UncheckedIOException(
            "Error working with input stream", e);
        }
      }
    );
  }
}

/* RESULT
Exception in thread "main" java.io.UncheckedIOException: Error working with input stream
        at Listing1.lambda$main$0(Listing1.java:22)
        at Listing1$$Lambda$1/558638686.accept(Unknown Source)
        at Listing1.call(Listing1.java:14)
        at Listing1.main(Listing1.java:18)
Caused by: java.io.IOException: And with a kiss, I die!
        at Listing1.lambda$main$0(Listing1.java:20)
        ... 4 more
*/
```

If you look at the stack trace in Listing 7-2, you can begin to see some of the stack trace noise generated by Java's lambda implementation. We will get into why that is there and how to read it in the next chapter. What we can tell already, however, is that we get the exact source lines from the lambda itself (the lambda$main$0 lines), along with the location where the lambda was called (the Listing1.call line). This should make sense, since calling the lambda is simply executing the function interface method for it (the Listing1$$Lambda$1/558638686.accept line). The original exception is also given to us in the "Caused by" line, just like we are used to. All in all, this is very familiar and comfortable.

However, things become much more interesting when you start using parallel streams. In this case, the exception will be thrown from the context of the ForkJoinWorkThread instances. This is going to create significantly more noise in the stack trace, and it obscures our ability to backtrack the call stack. To see where the difficulty lies, let's build out an example. In this example, we will explode when we execute the 100th line. Let's take a look at the result in Listing 7-3.

Listing 7-3. Unhandled Exception Terminating a Stream

```java
import java.io.ByteArrayInputStream;
import java.io.IOException;
import java.io.InputStream;
import java.io.UncheckedIOException;
import java.util.*;
import java.util.concurrent.atomic.*;
import java.util.function.*;
import java.util.stream.*;

public class Listing3 {

  public static InputStream generateInputStream() {
    return new ByteArrayInputStream("foobar".getBytes());
  }

  public static Stream<Integer> generateParallelStream() {
    final int elements = 1000;
    List<Integer> toReturn = new ArrayList<>(elements);
    for (int i = 0; i < elements; i++) {
      toReturn.add(i);
    }
    return toReturn.parallelStream();
  }

  public static Function<Integer, Integer> generateMap() {
    AtomicInteger counter = new AtomicInteger(0);
    return i -> {
      int count = counter.incrementAndGet();
      try (InputStream in = Listing3.generateInputStream()) {
        if (i == 100) {
          throw new IOException(
            "And with a kiss, I die! (After " + count + " executions)");
        }
        return i;
```

```
    } catch (IOException ioe) {
      throw new UncheckedIOException(
        "Error working with input stream", ioe
      );
    }
  };
}

public static void main(String[] args) {
  generateParallelStream().map(generateMap()).forEach(System.out::println);
}
}

/* RESULT (with a few hundred lines of numbers cut off the front)
...
794
245
190
402
15
57
957
58
16
403
191
Exception in thread "main" java.io.UncheckedIOException: Error working with input stream
        at Listing3.lambda$generateMap$1(Listing3.java:35)
        at Listing3$$Lambda$1/1149319664.apply(Unknown Source)
        at java.util.stream.ReferencePipeline$3$1.accept(
            ReferencePipeline.java:193)
        at java.util.ArrayList$ArrayListSpliterator.forEachRemaining(
            ArrayList.java:1359)
        at java.util.stream.AbstractPipeline.copyInto(AbstractPipeline.java:512)
        at java.util.stream.AbstractPipeline.wrapAndCopyInto(
            AbstractPipeline.java:502)
        at java.util.stream.ReduceOps$ReduceTask.doLeaf(ReduceOps.java:747)
        at java.util.stream.ReduceOps$ReduceTask.doLeaf(ReduceOps.java:721)
        at java.util.stream.AbstractTask.compute(AbstractTask.java:316)
        at java.util.concurrent.CountedCompleter.exec(CountedCompleter.java:731)
        at java.util.concurrent.ForkJoinTask.doExec(ForkJoinTask.java:289)
        at java.util.concurrent.ForkJoinPool$WorkQueue.runTask(
            ForkJoinPool.java:916)
        at java.util.concurrent.ForkJoinPool.scan(ForkJoinPool.java:1689)
        at java.util.concurrent.ForkJoinPool.runWorker(ForkJoinPool.java:1644)
        at java.util.concurrent.ForkJoinWorkerThread.run(ForkJoinWorkerThread.java:157)
Caused by: java.io.IOException: And with a kiss, I die! (After 489 executions)
        at Listing3.lambda$generateMap$1(Listing3.java:31)
        ... 14 more
*/
```

117

The stack trace in Listing 7-3 is not nearly as nice as the version in Listing 7-2. We still have the lambda references in our stack trace, but they are references to where the lambda is declared; there is no reference at all to the main method, which is where our lambda is wired into the stream. The code goes straight from rather generic stream infrastructure to the place in the source where the lambda was declared. This can make it tricky to figure out where the code is actually called; imagine if the lambda was defined in some other class and reused in multiple streams – from experience, that exception would be very tricky to debug based on the stack trace.

The other thing to note is that we have gotten well into our processing before this failed: we exploded on the 304th execution. That means we had 303 executions that completed successfully. Some of those were printed out. Some of those, however, may not have been; it depends on how far down the pipeline they got when the explosion occurred. Worse, we did not even try any of the numbers after we saw the explosion: a single explosion will terminate the entire stream. So we have some of our elements in a completed state, some in an intermediate state, and some that were never even initiated. The explosion just left things in an ugly place.

The final issue with this approach is that we have reintroduced exception swallowing, although we a very sneaky about it. The good news is that we will always get an exception. However, if multiple threads have exceptions, then we will only see the first. It is possible that multiple threads threw exceptions simultaneously: for instance, if they were all doing database queries when the database went down. Yet, in that case, you will only see the first exception, even though there were multiple problems.

Sometimes, these limitations are okay. Sometimes, your work really is all-or-nothing, or it is safe to rerun multiple times, even if things were in indeterminate states. In these cases, the mapping of exceptions to unchecked exceptions works just fine. However, if you want to try to salvage work from intermittent errors, then you are going to need something more clever.

Handling Resources with an Exception-Handling Caller

Since Java 8 is a post-functional language, we can apply an object-oriented solution to our problem. The object that we want will encapsulate the try-with-resources logic and the error handling, so that the user can provide just the desired implementation. The object can then be queried after the map has run to deal with any exceptions that arise.

The idea here is that we will have some code up front and some code at the end, and an opening for user-defined code in the middle. My friend, mentor, and co-blogger, Brian Hurt, refers to this as the "hole in the middle pattern." Spring calls this "inversion of control," and it was one of the key strengths of the early Spring APIs, most especially Spring JDBC. In our case, the code up front is the creation of the resource (the "try" part of the try-with-resources block) and the exception handling (the "catch" part of the try-with-resources block). The opening for user-defined code in the middle is the code that takes the resource and the stream value and returns the mapped value for the stream.

For the implementation, we will create this class along with two single-method interfaces: one that defines how to make a resource, and one that defines how to process the resource. We will intend for the user to implement these interfaces using lambdas. These interface methods will allow the user to throw checked exceptions, so the user is totally free to do what they would like. The class itself will encapsulate the creation of the resource and the handling of return values and exceptions.

There is a catch to this very neat theory: we have to return something in the case of an exception. A legacy Java developer is again going to reach for null out of habit, but this is a bad habit. Java 8 provides the Optional class, which represents a value that may or may not be set. This is a better option, because the Optional class cannot lead you to accidentally raise a NullPointerException; the API provides many better alternatives for getting the value, including representing the common get-and-if-null-explode code pattern.

The result of our stream will therefore be an Optional container of the type that the map itself would normally return. We can filter out empty Optional types using the filter method for streams, which makes it very easy to clean up the streams from any exceptional elements. The empty elements do provide some value, too: they enable us to discover that an error occurred in our stream, so we could provide somewhat more intelligent behaviors.

This class, its interfaces, and a demonstration of its call are all given in Listing 7-4. The class implementation itself is rather ugly. This is because there are a lot of type variables and strange syntax floating around, and it is made worse by the fact that interfaces cannot be members of classes: they are always static. However, the resulting API and usage is actually quite nice.

Listing 7-4. Handling Resources with an Object Using Optional

```
import java.io.ByteArrayInputStream;
import java.io.IOException;
import java.io.InputStream;
import java.util.*;
import java.util.concurrent.*;
import java.util.concurrent.atomic.*;
import java.util.function.*;
import java.util.stream.*;

public class Listing4 {

  public static class ResourceExceptionHandler
    <RESOURCE_T extends AutoCloseable>
  {

    public static interface FunctionWithResource
      <RESOURCE_T extends AutoCloseable, IN_T, OUT_T>
    {
      OUT_T apply(RESOURCE_T resource, IN_T value) throws Exception;
    }

    public static interface ResourceMaker
      <RESOURCE_T extends AutoCloseable>
    {
      RESOURCE_T create() throws Exception;
    }

    private final ResourceMaker<RESOURCE_T> init;
    private final ConcurrentMap<Object, Exception> exceptions =
      new ConcurrentSkipListMap<>();

    public ResourceExceptionHandler(final ResourceMaker<RESOURCE_T> init) {
      Objects.requireNonNull(init,
        "ResourceMaker (initialization code for resource)");
      this.init = init;
    }

    public Map<Object, Exception> getExceptions() {
      return exceptions;
    }
```

```java
    public Function<Integer, Optional<Integer>> map(
        FunctionWithResource<RESOURCE_T, Integer, Integer> f
    ) {
      return i -> {
        try (RESOURCE_T resource = init.create()) {
          return Optional.of(f.apply(resource, i));
        } catch (Exception e) {
          exceptions.put(i, e);
          return Optional.empty();
        }
      };
    }

  }

  public static InputStream generateInputStream() {
    return new ByteArrayInputStream("foobar".getBytes());
  }

  public static Stream<Integer> generateParallelStream() {
    final int elements = 1000;
    List<Integer> toReturn = new ArrayList<>(elements);
    for (int i = 0; i < elements; i++) {
      toReturn.add(i);
    }
    return toReturn.parallelStream();
  }

  public static ResourceExceptionHandler.FunctionWithResource
    <InputStream, Integer, Integer> generateMap()
  {
    AtomicInteger counter = new AtomicInteger(0);
    return (in, i) -> {
      int count = counter.incrementAndGet();
      if (i == 100) {
        throw new IOException(
          "And with a kiss, I die! (After " + count + " executions)");
      }
      return i;
    };
  }

  public static void main(String[] args) {
    // Create the handler for exceptions
    ResourceExceptionHandler handler =
      new ResourceExceptionHandler(Listing4::generateInputStream);
```

```
    // Perform the stream processing
    Function<Integer, Optional<Integer>> mapFunction =
      handler.map(generateMap());
    generateParallelStream()
        .map(mapFunction)
        .filter(Optional::isPresent).map(Optional::get)
        .forEach(System.out::println);

    // Work with the exceptions
    Map<Object, Exception> exceptions = handler.getExceptions();
    exceptions.forEach((key, val) -> {
        System.out.println(key + ": " + val);
        val.printStackTrace(System.err);
      }
    );
  }
}
```

This approach, however, requires that we have the extra handling in place to extract the values from within their Optional container. There is another alternative based on flatMap, which we first saw back in chapter 3: we could have our values return a stream, and the stream can be empty or it can be populated with a single element. This allows us to sidestep the Optional type and its extraction, although it hides any symptom of the error from the stream itself. Still, the API is overall a bit nicer, even if you have to call the flatMap method to perform what is effectively a simple map operation. This code is given in Listing 7-5.

Listing 7-5. Handling Resources with an Object Using flatMap

```
import java.io.ByteArrayInputStream;
import java.io.IOException;
import java.io.InputStream;
import java.util.*;
import java.util.concurrent.*;
import java.util.concurrent.atomic.*;
import java.util.function.*;
import java.util.stream.*;

public class Listing5 {

  public static class ResourceExceptionHandler
    <RESOURCE_T extends AutoCloseable>
  {

    public static interface FunctionWithResource
      <RESOURCE_T extends AutoCloseable, IN_T, OUT_T>
    {
      OUT_T apply(RESOURCE_T resource, IN_T value) throws Exception;
    }

    public static interface ResourceMaker<RESOURCE_T extends AutoCloseable> {
      RESOURCE_T create() throws Exception;
    }
```

```java
  private final ResourceMaker<RESOURCE_T> init;
  private final ConcurrentMap<Object, Exception> exceptions
    = new ConcurrentSkipListMap<>();

  public ResourceExceptionHandler(final ResourceMaker<RESOURCE_T> init) {
    Objects.requireNonNull(init,
      "ResourceMaker (initialization code for resource)");
    this.init = init;
  }

  public Map<Object, Exception> getExceptions() {
    return exceptions;
  }

  public Function<Integer, Stream<Integer>> map(
      FunctionWithResource<RESOURCE_T, Integer, Integer> f
  ) {
    return i -> {
      try (RESOURCE_T resource = init.create()) {
        return Stream.of(f.apply(resource, i));
      } catch (Exception e) {
        exceptions.put(i, e);
        return Stream.empty();
      }
    };
  }

}

public static InputStream generateInputStream() {
  return new ByteArrayInputStream("foobar".getBytes());
}

public static Stream<Integer> generateParallelStream() {
  final int elements = 1000;
  List<Integer> toReturn = new ArrayList(elements);
  for (int i = 0; i < elements; i++) {
    toReturn.add(i);
  }
  return toReturn.parallelStream();
}

public static ResourceExceptionHandler.FunctionWithResource
  <InputStream, Integer, Integer> generateMap()
{
  AtomicInteger counter = new AtomicInteger(0);
  return (in, i) -> {
    int count = counter.incrementAndGet();
```

```
    if (i == 100) {
      throw new IOException(
        "And with a kiss, I die! (After " + count + " executions)");
    }
    return i;
  };
}

public static void main(String[] args) {
  // Create the handler for exceptions
  ResourceExceptionHandler handler =
    new ResourceExceptionHandler(Listing5::generateInputStream);

  // Perform the stream processing
  Function<Integer, Stream<Integer>> flatMapFunction =
    handler.map(generateMap());
  generateParallelStream()
      .flatMap(flatMapFunction)
      .forEach(System.out::println);

  // Work with the exceptions
  Map<Object, Exception> exceptions = handler.getExceptions();
  exceptions.forEach((key, val) -> {
      System.out.println(key + ": " + val);
      val.printStackTrace(System.err);
    }
  );
  }
}
```

In both of these cases, we have a nice separation of concerns: our stream works the happy path, and then we deal with the exceptions later on. The code itself is rather ugly and touchy, which is why it is best to write it once and be done with it. The APIs provided above, along with others, are available in the FunJava project under the name funjava.io.FunResource.

While this approach provides the clear distinction between the "happy path" of the stream and exception handling later on, sometimes that distinction cannot be kept clear. Sometimes you want to be able to handle exceptions as part of the processing. In that case, you want to keep the information about the exception within the same stream. This is the point when we use a Result object.

Handling Resources Using a Result Object

Consider a stream where you want to process files. The files, however, may or may not exist, and if they do not exist, that has a specific meaning, as well. For instance, the files may be optional user-specified files, and if the file is not uploaded, then you want to use a default. In this case, you will want to keep the information about an IO error within the stream itself, so that you can process that error within the stream. This makes the handler approach we saw in the last section ill-suited, because you do not want to be querying another object to find out what happened earlier in the same stream. The unchecked exception situation would break consistently and get you nowhere. Instead, what you are looking for is a Result object.

We saw the Result object before. It is a cousin of the Optional type, in that it holds a value that may or may not exist. However, the Result object will hold either the return value or an exception. These are the only two options out of any non-void Java computation. The Result type, like the Optional type, can provide a convenient API for accessing its contents.

We used the Result object before, but let's look at how such a type could be reimplemented now. What we want is to store either a return value or an exception, which means that we can have two fields. We expect only one of them to be null at any point in time; the other should be non-null. If you pass in a return value, we call that a "successful" Result instance. If you pass in an exception, we call that a "failure" Result instance. Since the type of the result and exception fields will depend on the caller's contexts, we will make them type variables. In order to make for a nicer usage for the user, we can use static methods instead of exposing constructors: the static methods trick the Java type system into doing more type inference work for you, instead of having to repeat type information all over your code. We will also provide five accessors into our state: two boolean accessors that just check if the result is successful or a failure; two direct accessors that return the state of their field; and a combined accessor that returns the successful value if it is successful and explodes with the failure value if it is a failure. Using this type, we can then implement our basic inline stream error handling. The Result implementation and the error handling are demonstrated in Listing 7-6.

Listing 7-6. Handling Resources with a Result Type

```java
import java.io.ByteArrayInputStream;
import java.io.IOException;
import java.io.InputStream;
import java.util.*;
import java.util.concurrent.atomic.*;
import java.util.function.*;
import java.util.stream.*;

public class Listing6 {

  public static class Result<SUCCESS_T, FAILURE_T extends Exception> {

    private final SUCCESS_T success;

    private final FAILURE_T failure;

    private Result(final SUCCESS_T success, final FAILURE_T failure) {
      if (success == null && failure == null) {
        throw new IllegalArgumentException(
          "Success and failure cannot both be null");
      }
      if (success != null && failure != null) {
        throw new IllegalArgumentException(
          "Success and failure cannot both be non-null");
      }
      this.success = success;
      this.failure = failure;
    }
```

```java
public static <SUCCESS_T, FAILURE_T extends Exception>
  Result<SUCCESS_T, FAILURE_T> ofFailure(FAILURE_T failure)
{
  Objects.requireNonNull(failure, "failure to assign is null");
  return new Result(null, failure);
}

public static <SUCCESS_T, FAILURE_T extends Exception>
  Result<SUCCESS_T, FAILURE_T> ofSuccess(SUCCESS_T success)
{
  Objects.requireNonNull(success, "success to assign is null");
  return new Result<>(success, null);
}

public boolean isSuccess() { return success != null; }

public boolean isFailure() { return failure != null; }

/**
 * Provides the result on successful, or throws the failure exception
 * on failure.
 *
 * @return The success value on successful.
 * @throws FAILURE_T If this result is not successful.
 */
public SUCCESS_T get() throws FAILURE_T {
  if (success != null) return success;
  throw failure;
}

/**
 * Returns the success value, or {@code null} if this result is a failure.
 *
 * @return The success value or {@code null}.
 */
public SUCCESS_T getSuccess() {
  return success;
}

/**
 * Returns the failure, or {@code null} if this result is successful.
 *
 * @return The failure value or {@code null}.
 */
public FAILURE_T getFailure() {
  return failure;
}
```

```java
    @Override
    public String toString() {
      if (isSuccess()) {
        return "SUCCESS[" + success + "]";
      } else {
        return "FAILURE[" + failure + "]";
      }
    }
  }

  public static InputStream generateInputStream() {
    return new ByteArrayInputStream("foobar".getBytes());
  }

  public static Stream<Integer> generateParallelStream() {
    final int elements = 1000;
    List<Integer> toReturn = new ArrayList(elements);
    for (int i = 0; i < elements; i++) {
      toReturn.add(i);
    }
    return toReturn.parallelStream();
  }

  public static Function<Integer, Result<Integer, IOException>> generateMap() {
    AtomicInteger counter = new AtomicInteger(0);
    return i -> {
      int count = counter.incrementAndGet();
      try (InputStream in = Listing3.generateInputStream()) {
        if (i == 100) {
          return Result.ofFailure(
              new IOException(
                "And with a kiss, I die! (After " + count + " executions)")
          );
        }
        return Result.ofSuccess(i);
      } catch (IOException ioe) {
        return Result.ofFailure(ioe);
      }
    };
  }

  public static void main(String[] args) {
    // Perform the stream processing
    generateParallelStream()
        .map(generateMap())
        .forEach(result -> {
            if (result.isFailure()) {
              result.getFailure().printStackTrace(System.err);
              System.err.flush();
```

```
        } else {
          System.out.println(result.getSuccess());
          System.out.flush();
        }
      }
    );
  }

}
```

This approach is safer and cleaner in that it requires the user to be more intentional about error handling, while also giving them the information necessary to perform that error handling. It also allows you to handle errors while the stream is being processed, instead of having to wait until afterwards. The downside of this approach is that it is not as easy to wrap existing resource-based code: you have to wrap your results in the Result object in the first place, as opposed to wrapping the whole method that you are trying to implement in some helper object.

When you are working with resources in Java, you are working with syntactic sugar of a different flavor: it is not especially kind to post-functional code, but it was a very nice benefit for the imperative code that came before it. Your particular approach to bridging the paradigm depends on the needs of your particular system, but the sooner you can encapsulate the ugliness and move entirely into the post-functional world, the happier your code will be.

Bridging Collections and Streams

Before Java introduced streams, its primary bulk mode of operation was through the Collection API. There were efforts to create bulk collection operations (called "comprehensions"), and even some efforts to turn the Iterator class into something strongly resembling the contemporary stream. However, the API is really not intended for post-functional kinds of work, and there were consistently rough edges that worked poorly with the stream approach: this is why Java introduced an entirely new set of APIs.

The good news is that it is easy to go from an instance of the collection type to a stream: simply call the collection.stream() or collection.parallelStream() method for a sequential or parallel stream, respectively. For an instance of the Map type, you will first need to specify whether you want the map's key set, entry set, or values collection, and then you can get the stream of your choice from there. Both the Map type and the Collection type also have a forEach method that takes a consumer: it is effectively a shorthand for collection.stream().forEach(Consumer), and this method should probably supplant your for loops in any case when you do not need to know the index.

Going from a stream back to a collection, however, is somewhat trickier. There is no .toList() method on the Stream type, as nice as that would be. One option is to use one of the methods of converting the stream into an array, and then using Arrays.asList(Array) to get your desired list. The result will be a fixed-sized (but not immutable) list of all the stream elements. A basic demonstration of that approach is given in Listing 7-7, and if that is the approach that you want to take, be sure to read the next section on arrays.

Listing 7-7. Bridging Streams to Collections via toArray()

```java
import java.util.*;
import java.util.stream.*;

public class Listing7 {

  public static Stream<Integer> generateParallelStream() {
    final int elements = 1000;
    List<Integer> toReturn = new ArrayList<>(elements);
    for (int i = 0; i < elements; i++) {
      toReturn.add(i);
    }
    return toReturn.parallelStream();
  }

  public static void main(String[] args) {
    // Perform the stream processing
    List<Object> list = Arrays.asList(generateParallelStream().toArray());
  }

}
```

If you have some existing list that you want to add an element into, then you can simply use the List.add method as your consumer. That method technically returns boolean, and so it is not precisely the accurate shape for the Consumer, but Java will allow you to bend the rules here. If you have a list that exists before your stream operations, then simply pass that list's list::add method into the stream's forEach, and you are fine. A similar approach will work for adding stream elements to an existing set. The only caveat is that if you are using a parallel stream, you want to make sure that you are using a thread-safe collection, since its add method will be called from multiple threads. This approach is demonstrated in Listing 7-8.

Listing 7-8. Bridging Streams to Collections Using Add

```java
import java.util.*;
import java.util.concurrent.*;
import java.util.stream.*;

public class Listing8 {

  public static Stream<Integer> generateParallelStream() {
    final int elements = 1000;
    List<Integer> toReturn = new ArrayList<>(elements);
    for (int i = 0; i < elements; i++) {
      toReturn.add(i);
    }
    return toReturn.parallelStream();
  }
```

```
public static void main(String[] args) {
  // Perform the stream processing
  List<Integer> list = new CopyOnWriteArrayList<>();
  generateParallelStream().forEach(list::add);
}

}
```

Note that if the collection you want to add elements to is not thread-safe, and your stream is a parallel stream, then you can use a `Collection.synchronizedList(List)` (or related method) to synchronize it. This can be done inline, which would create a line like this:

```
generateParallelStream().forEach(Collections.synchronizedList(list)::add);
```

If you want your stream to produce an immutable list or set, then the simplest approach is to use Google's Guava library. Among other immutable types, the Guava library provides an ImmutableList and ImmutableSet (among other immutable types), and it provides builder types for each of these immutable types. The add method for these builder types works just as well as the add method of the list that we saw before. These builders are also all thread-safe, so they are safe to use with parallel streams. An example of this usage is given in Listing 7-9. This approach works particularly well if you simply build up your collection within one method and then return it to the user as your final step.

Listing 7-9. Bridging Streams to Collections Using a Builder

```
import com.google.common.collect.ImmutableList;

import java.util.*;
import java.util.stream.*;

public class Listing9 {

  public static Stream<Integer> generateParallelStream() {
    final int elements = 1000;
    List<Integer> toReturn = new ArrayList<>(elements);
    for (int i = 0; i < elements; i++) {
      toReturn.add(i);
    }
    return toReturn.parallelStream();
  }

  public static void main(String[] args) {
    // Perform the stream processing
    ImmutableList.Builder<Integer> builder = ImmutableList.builder();
    generateParallelStream().forEach(builder::add);
    ImmutableList list = builder.build();
  }

}
```

Finally, if you want to get particularly fancy and highly efficient about things, you can use the Collector part of the Stream API. The Collector part of the Stream API provides a kind of specialized reduce logic, where the result is a composite of the existing elements. Many examples of Collector implementations can be found in the `java.util.stream.Collectors` class. Among these are `Collectors.toList()`, `Collectors.toSet()`, and `Collectors.toCollection(Supplier)`. Each of those methods returns a Collector instance, and that is passed to `stream.collect(Collector)`. Both `Collectors.toList()` and `Collectors.toSet()` do exactly what they sound like: they return a List or Set. However, there is no guarantee given about the extent of the mutability of the resulting collection, nor its serializability, nor its thread safety. If you want to be more specific about what you are getting back, you call `Collectors.toCollection(Supplier)`. The Supplier is responsible for supplying collections of the type you want, and it is presumed that each time the supplier is called, it will supply a new instance. Because of that, the simplest thing to pass as a supplier is the constructor itself, such as `CopyOnWriteArrayList::new`. This results in code that looks like Listing 7-10, which is both terse and highly performant.

Listing 7-10. Bridging Streams to Collections Using a Collector

```java
import java.util.*;
import java.util.concurrent.*;
import java.util.stream.*;

public class Listing10 {

  public static Stream<Integer> generateParallelStream() {
    final int elements = 1000;
    List<Integer> toReturn = new ArrayList<>(elements);
    for (int i = 0; i < elements; i++) {
      toReturn.add(i);
    }
    return toReturn.parallelStream();
  }

  public static void main(String[] args) {
    // Perform the stream processing
    List<Integer> list = generateParallelStream()
      .collect(Collectors.toCollection(CopyOnWriteArrayList::new));
  }

}
```

Bridging Arrays and Streams

Going back and forth between arrays and streams is really quite wonderfully simple. To get a stream from an array, use `Stream.of(array)`. To get an array from a stream, you have two choices: either accept an array of `Object` instances and call `Stream.toArray()`; or pass that method a way to construct an array of a given size, and it will return the constructed array. The simplest way to define the supplier is to pass in the array constructor, such as `Integer[]::new`. Both going into and out of arrays is demonstrated in Listing 7-11.

Listing 7-11. Bridging Arrays and Streams

```java
import java.util.stream.*;

public class Listing11 {

  public static Integer[] generateArray() {
    final Integer[] elements = new Integer[1000];
    for (int i = 0; i < elements.length; i++) {
      elements[i] = i;
    }
    return elements;
  }

  public static void main(String[] args) {
    Integer[] array = generateArray();
    Stream<Integer> stream = Stream.of(array);
    array = stream.toArray(Integer[]::new);
  }

}
```

Making Interfaces More Lambda Friendly

Many of the interfaces in the Java SDK only have one non-default method on them. This is true of Runnable, Callable, AutoCloseable, and many of the other most common interfaces. These interfaces can be implemented directly using a lambda by simply using the lambda where the interface is expected. We have seen this trick regularly in our code, most recently in Listing 7-5, where we returned a lambda as our implementation of ResourceExceptionHandler.FunctionWithResource in generateMap(). So those single-method interfaces work quite nicely with lambdas already. Most of the remaining interfaces are very large, such as Collection, and clearly out of reach of a single lambda as its entire implementation.

However, there are a small number of interfaces in the SDK – and quite a few in user code – which have only a few non-default methods, and you might really want to be able to define its implementation inline through lambdas. This is a very useful trick, but you can't define more than one method at a time using a lambda, and we need to define multiple methods at the same time. How do we do it?

This is where some serious creativity comes in. The trick is to define a new single method that can be used to drive the implementation of all the other methods. The user then specifies that new method, and our code will delegate to that new method's implementation. This new method and the delegating implementations go into a new interface that extends our target interface.

For instance, let's say that we wanted to create an Iterator that you could define with a lambda. There are two non-default methods on Iterator: hasNext() and next(). Both have to do with the next element, but the former tests for existence without advancing while the latter advances. Therefore, our single method will need to operate in both an advancing and non-advancing mode. Since hasNext also may look beyond the end of the iterator, where there are no elements, our single method will need to return its result optionally. The result is this method:

```java
Optional<E> maybeNext(boolean advance);
```

With that method in hand, we can define the other two methods in the iterator using default methods. For next(), we call maybeNext and pass in true to advance. We get back an Optional result, and we use the Optional API to either return its contained value or throw a NoSuchElement exception. For hasNext(), we call maybeNext and pass in false to avoid advancing. Then we simply let the caller know if the result is present. All of this goes into our new interface, which extends Iterator. Now users can assign the lambda into this type in order to get an Iterator out. This code, and a demonstration of how it works, is in Listing 7-12.

Listing 7-12. Making Iterator More Lambda Friendly

```java
import java.util.*;
import java.util.concurrent.atomic.*;

public class Listing12 {

  public interface LambdaIterator<E> extends Iterator<E> {

    Optional<E> maybeNext(boolean advance);

    default E next() {
      return maybeNext(true).orElseThrow(NoSuchElementException::new);
    }

    default boolean hasNext() {
      return maybeNext(false).isPresent();
    }
  }

  public static Iterator<String> generateIterator() {
    String[] values = new String[]{"Hello", " ", "World"};
    AtomicInteger nextI = new AtomicInteger(0);
    LambdaIterator<String> it = advance -> {
      if (nextI.get() >= values.length) return Optional.empty();
      String result = values[nextI.get()];
      if (advance) nextI.incrementAndGet();
      return Optional.of(result);
    };
    return it;
  }

  public static void main(String[] args) {
    Iterator<String> it = generateIterator();
  }

}
```

The big trick with this approach is that you have to come up with the clever single method that can handle all the needs of any given method. Your super-method does have access to the other methods in the interface, but if you use those other methods, then you need to be extremely careful not to produce a recursive loop. Coming up with a good, single method is the kind of problem that should excite you as a developer.

Implementing Abstract Classes via Lambdas

Lambdas and interfaces go hand in hand in Java 8. They are really two different syntaxes for the same underlying functionality. However, abstract classes can also get some help from the addition of lambdas. The syntax is not as nice, but it is more clear than the classic inline class definition.

Like with interfaces, the goal is going to be to reduce the implementation of all the undefined methods into a single statement. In this case, however, we will be attempting to build a constructor that takes a lambda instead of simply a lambda. The user will have to call our constructor (which is less nice), but this gives us significantly more to work with: in addition to the implementation lambda, we can also accept other configuration values.

To see how this works specifically, let's look at `AbstractCollection`. Let's say that we wanted to be able to implement an `AbstractCollection` through a lambda. The two abstract methods on `AbstractCollection` are the following:

```
public abstract Iterator<E> iterator()
public abstract int size()
```

We will want to implement both of those by passing a lambda and possibly some other arguments into a constructor. We can certainly accept the size as an argument in the constructor, which leaves the `iterator()` method for our lambda implementation. We will therefore require the user to provide us something like a `Supplier<Iterator<E>>` as our lambda argument. Of course, we will provide an interface type for that supplier, so that users understand exactly what we need. We will call this kind of a `Collection`, `LambdaCollection`.

To demonstrate using our `LambdaCollection`, let's consider that we wanted to be able to treat the lines of a file as a Collection, and we were willing to do it in an inefficient (yet effective) way. In that case, we could define a way to go from the lines of the files to an iterator over the lines of the files, and this would be our lambda. We would also have to do one trip through the file at the outset to get the size. We demonstrate the code for `LambdaCollection` and this case in Listing 7-13.

Listing 7-13. Using a Lambda to Implement an Abstract Type

```java
import java.io.File;
import java.io.IOException;
import java.io.UncheckedIOException;
import java.nio.file.Files;
import java.nio.file.Path;
import java.util.*;

public class Listing14 {

  public static class LambdaCollection<E> extends AbstractCollection<E> {

    private final int size;
    private final Listing14.LambdaCollection.IteratorFactory<E> factory;

    /**
     * Defines the means of acquiring an {@link java.util.Iterator}.
     */
    public interface IteratorFactory<E> {
```

```java
  /**
   * Creates a new instance of an {@link java.util.Iterator}.
   * The iterator should be a fresh iterator each time this
   * method is called, but it should always iterate over the
   * same source.
   *
   * @return A new {@code Iterator}; never {@code null}.
   */
  Iterator<E> create();

}

  public LambdaCollection(int size, IteratorFactory<E> factory) {
    this.size = size;
    this.factory = factory;
  }

  /**
   * Returns an iterator over the elements contained in this collection.
   *
   * @return an iterator over the elements contained in this collection
   */
  @Override
  public Iterator<E> iterator() {
    return factory.create();
  }

  @Override
  public int size() {
    return size;
  }
}

public static Path generateFile() throws IOException {
  File file = File.createTempFile("example", "tmp");
  file.deleteOnExit();
  Path path = file.toPath();
  Files.write(path, "this\nis\nour\nfile".getBytes("UTF-8"));
  return path;
}

public static void main(String[] args) throws Exception {
  Path file = generateFile();
  Collection<String> collection = new LambdaCollection<>(
      (int) Files.lines(file).count(),
      () -> {
```

```
    try {
      return Files.lines(file).iterator();
    } catch (IOException ioe) {
      throw new UncheckedIOException(
        "Error reading lines from " + file, ioe);
    }
  }
 );
 }

}
```

The key thing to recognize from Listing 7-13 is that we delegate our abstract method implementation to a lambda. That lambda is passed into the constructor. That is the basic pattern for using lambdas to implement abstract methods. You may be tempted to accept multiple lambdas into a constructor, and thereby to implement more and more abstract elements. Don't do this for two reasons: first, because it encourages people to create ad hoc classes when they should have reusable classes; second, because it is hard to read, and Java already has an inline class definition format that works well for this case. That is one particular case where lambdas make things less readable, not more.

The Transparent Optional Trick

There is one last very useful trick for working with legacy code. This trick is a way to deal with null values. When Java encounters a null value, it throws the obnoxiously omnipresent NullPointerException. The message for the NullPointerException looks like this:

```
Exception in thread "main" java.lang.NullPointerException
```

As a Java developer with practically any experience understands, that is a totally unhelpful message. For one thing, it's not even clear what is null, so it could be anything on that line that caused the problem. There is also no state of the application that is communicated in that error message. This message is of extremely limited utility, and it is part of the reason why null should be driven entirely from your codebase as quickly as possible. Now that we have Optional, there is absolutely no need for null.

Of course, legacy code did not have Optional, and the legacy developers may not have been so enlightened as we now are. However, we can be rid of the null values and provide more useful error messaging at the same time in a transparent way. The trick is to use an optional value internally, while providing a (mostly) consistent API externally. The requirement for the consistent API is that we throw a NullPointerException if the value is null, which we can do using the Optional.orElseThrow(Supplier<Exception>) method. Additionally, we provide a way to get the value as an Optional, so people who really do want to check whether or not the value exists can do so that way. The intent would be that the code would eventually migrate over to the accessors acting directly on the Optional type instead, so we can deprecate the old setter. As a syntactic convenience, it is nice to leave a setter that directly sets the value via Optional.ofNullable(Object): if you provide that overload of the setter, then the caller doesn't have to do their own wrapping of the raw value. An example of this implementation is given in Listing 7-14.

Listing 7-14. Example of a Bean Migrating Toward Optionals

```java
import java.util.*;

public class SomeBean {
    private int id = 0;
    private Optional<String> name = Optional.empty();

    public SomeBean() {
    }

    public SomeBean(final int id, final String name) {
      this.id = id;
      this.name = Optional.ofNullable(name);
    }

    public int getId() {
      return id;
    }

    public void setId(final int id) {
      this.id = id;
    }

    @Deprecated
    public String getName() {
      return name.orElseThrow(
        () -> new NullPointerException(
                  "No name provided for: " + this.toString()
              )
      );
    }

    public Optional<String> getNameOptional() {
      return name;
    }

    public void setName(final String name) {
      this.name = Optional.ofNullable(name);
    }

    public void setName(final Optional<String> name) {
      this.name = (name == null ? Optional.empty() : name);
    }

    @Override
    public String toString() {
      return "SomeBean{" +
          "id=" + id +
          ", name=" + name.orElse(null) +
          '}';
    }

}
```

Developing Backwards

Before we close out this conversation, it is also worth noting that it is often important to develop backwards. If you are working on an open source library or are otherwise unsure about the skill of the developer reading your code, then you need to take special care. Not every Java developer has read this book yet, and so this new post-functional programming paradigm can seem very strange to them. For instance, this line of code recently came up in a project that I was working on:

```
(impl == null ? defaultImpl : impl).apply(arg);
```

If you know that impl and defaultImpl are both Function values, then it is very easy to understand what is going on there. On the other hand, it looks somewhat bizarre. It looks even stranger in the middle of a series of stream transformations. Even simple forEach calls can throw people for a loop sometimes.

Given that, care needs to be taken to be as clear as possible. If you are going to work with developers who may not be familiar with post-functional programming, be nice to them. Implement interfaces for the arguments where you expect a lambda, so that they can pass in interface implementations and have an obvious place to look for documentation. Limit the number of lambdas that you take in a method, because having too many lambdas results in a maze of callbacks. Generally, be very clear that the code you are writing really is clearer and easier for them to read. Not only will this reduce the number of questions (and buggy changes!) that you are going to get, but it creates an opportunity for those developers to learn and move along.

CHAPTER 8

■ ■ ■

Lambdas in Java Bytecode

This chapter is for those who want to go deeper and understand how lambdas really work. This is your red pill vs. blue pill moment: do you want to live in a world where Java has lambdas and they work great and everything is slick and awesome, or do you want to see what is really going on beneath the surface and discover the magic of the compiler pulls? If you are happy with the lambdas as you know and love them, then skip this chapter and enjoy. If you need to know what your code really means, then hold on tight: it's time to go down the rabbit hole.

The reality is that lambdas are an illusion. Java lambdas are entirely a construct of the compiler. The compiler converts your Java code with its lambdas into more primitive operations within a lower-level language. Understanding that conversion can help you understand exactly what is going on, which can be useful in situations such as debugging and optimization.

However, before we step into this new world, there are some necessary caveats. This chapter is written based on Oracle's Java compiler, and specifically version 1.8.0_05. It is entirely possible (although extremely unlikely) that Oracle will completely overhaul their lambda implementation in a future release, and certainly likely that there will be refinements as we go along. Alternative Java compilers might well have very different implementations, as well. So if you are following along with your own Java compiler at home, and you notice some subtle difference, then that is what happened. Those kinds of changes are what you have to expect to see when you look under the hood.

We also need to be up front that this chapter is not a comprehensive introduction to Java compilers and the resulting underlying bytecode language. That language has its own semantics, and those semantics are tricky and technical. We will just start to get into some of those semantics through the course of this chapter. We are staying focused on lambdas and what they do, so anything extraneous to lambdas is irrelevant to this excursion.

If you are still with me after all that warning, then you probably know that Java code itself does not compile directly to bytes that are executed by the operating system. Instead, the Java compiler (henceforth, "javac") compiles to another intermediate form, which is executed by the Java Virtual Machine (henceforth, "JVM"). This intermediate form is called the Java bytecode. Bytecode, however, has no concept of lambdas. It also has no concept of try-with-resources blocks, enhanced for-loops, or many of the other structures within Java. Instead, the compiler converts those Java structures into an underlying form in bytecode.

In this chapter, we will see how the compiler converts lambda commands in the Java language into structures within the Java bytecode language. We will begin by getting comfortable with reading bytecode, and then we will move on to seeing how particular kinds of lambda structures are converted into bytecode. But before we get to the lambdas, we need to get the basics.

Hello, Bytecode

Normal human beings do not read bytecode. However, Java ships with a tool called "javap" that takes in a class file and renders its bytecode in a more human-accessible version of the code. There are other tools for performing this same trick, and if you are interested in getting to know bytecode better, then you should certainly take a look at the asm toolset. However, javap ships with Oracle's SDK, and that provides all the functionality that we need while keeping things simple, so we will use it throughout the rest of this chapter.

Let's get a taste of javap and bytecode with a very simple Java class, and its attendant bytecode as rendered by javap. The class will have a `public static void main` method that does nothing at all. Given just that, what is the resulting bytecode? What is generated there will be the baseline for everything that follows, and will give us an opportunity to see the basic structure of a class file. This is given in Listing 8-1.

Listing 8-1. A Simple Java Class and Its Bytecode

```
1    // Listing1.java, which is compiled to Listing1.class)
2    public class Listing1 {
3      public static void main(String[] args) {}
4    }
5
6    // Result of executing /usr/bin/javap -v -l -p -s -c Listing1 in the same directory as
     Listing1.class
7    Classfile /Users/RCFischer/wkdir/Books/java8/build/classes/production/ch8/Listing1.
     class
8      Last modified Dec 6, 2014; size 367 bytes
9      MD5 checksum 008abb234928faafc8a836436ea158db
10     Compiled from "Listing1.java"
11   public class Listing1
12     SourceFile: "Listing1.java"
13     minor version: 0
14     major version: 52
15     flags: ACC_PUBLIC, ACC_SUPER
16   Constant pool:
17       #1 = Methodref          #3.#17         //  java/lang/Object."<init>":()V
18       #2 = Class              #18            //  Listing1
19       #3 = Class              #19            //  java/lang/Object
20       #4 = Utf8               <init>
21       #5 = Utf8               ()V
22       #6 = Utf8               Code
23       #7 = Utf8               LineNumberTable
24       #8 = Utf8               LocalVariableTable
25       #9 = Utf8               this
26       #10 = Utf8              LListing1;
27       #11 = Utf8              main
28       #12 = Utf8              ([Ljava/lang/String;)V
29       #13 = Utf8              args
30       #14 = Utf8              [Ljava/lang/String;
31       #15 = Utf8              SourceFile
32       #16 = Utf8              Listing1.java
33       #17 = NameAndType       #4:#5          //  "<init>":()V
34       #18 = Utf8              Listing1
35       #19 = Utf8              java/lang/Object
```

```
36    {
37      public Listing1();
38        descriptor: ()V
39        flags: ACC_PUBLIC
40        LineNumberTable:
41          line 1: 0
42        LocalVariableTable:
43          Start  Length  Slot  Name   Signature
44              0       5     0  this   LListing1;
45        Code:
46          stack=1, locals=1, args_size=1
47            0: aload_0
48            1: invokespecial #1                    // Method java/lang/Object."<init>":()V
49            4: return
50          LineNumberTable:
51            line 1: 0
52          LocalVariableTable:
53            Start  Length  Slot  Name   Signature
54                0       5     0  this   LListing1;
55
56      public static void main(java.lang.String[]);
57        descriptor: ([Ljava/lang/String;)V
58        flags: ACC_PUBLIC, ACC_STATIC
59        LineNumberTable:
60          line 3: 0
61        LocalVariableTable:
62          Start  Length  Slot  Name   Signature
63              0       1     0  args   [Ljava/lang/String;
64        Code:
65          stack=0, locals=1, args_size=1
66            0: return
67          LineNumberTable:
68            line 3: 0
69          LocalVariableTable:
70            Start  Length  Slot  Name   Signature
71                0       1     0  args   [Ljava/lang/String;
72    }
```

That javap result is lengthy compared to the original Java source code: that goes to show just how expressive Java is. It is worth noting at this point that the result of javap is not the same thing as what is in the classfile: Listing1.class is not a compressed version of the same content. Instead, the javap command gives us a human rendition of the information that is in the classfile.

Let's move through things step by step. The first part is the preamble (lines 7-10):

```
Classfile /Users/RCFischer/wkdir/Books/java8/build/classes/production/ch8/Listing1.class
  Last modified Dec 6, 2014; size 367 bytes
  MD5 checksum 008abb234928faafc8a836436ea158db
  Compiled from "Listing1.java"
```

This is information generated by javap to give us information about the class file. It's useful for keeping a record of what you are doing, and helping you catch silly mistakes when you're working with classfile printouts. The first line is the file system information about the file; the next line is a checksum, which is a quick way to see if two class files are equal; the final line tells you what the origin of this classfile is. None of this is about the class in the classfile itself, however. For that, we need to look at the following (lines 11–15):

```
public class Listing1
  SourceFile: "Listing1.java"
  minor version: 0
  major version: 52
  flags: ACC_PUBLIC, ACC_SUPER
```

These lines declare the class. The first line tells us that we are declaring a class (instead of an interface), and what the name and permission level is. The next line tells us where the class comes from, which is usually redundant with the final line of the preamble. The next two lines are the version number, which tells you that the class was compiled with Java bytecode version 52.0 – that is a magic value which corresponds to Java 8.0. The very last lines tell you what the access flags are for the class: ACC_PUBLIC and ACC_SUPER. ACC_PUBLIC means that this class is publicly visible. You can read ACC_SUPER as meaning that the class was compiled post-Java 2: it is mandatory for all contemporary class definitions, and exists purely for backwards compatibility.

Immediately after the class declaration is the constant pool. The constant pool contains all of the constants that are used by the class. This constant pool will include all the constants that you are used to in Java, such as character strings and integer values. It will also include many things that you might not think of as constants, such as class and method names. In our case, the constant pool looks like this (lines 16–35):

```
Constant pool:
   #1 = Methodref        #3.#17        //  java/lang/Object."<init>":()V
   #2 = Class            #18           //  Listing1
   #3 = Class            #19           //  java/lang/Object
   #4 = Utf8             <init>
   #5 = Utf8             ()V
   #6 = Utf8             Code
   #7 = Utf8             LineNumberTable
   #8 = Utf8             LocalVariableTable
   #9 = Utf8             this
  #10 = Utf8             LListing1;
  #11 = Utf8             main
  #12 = Utf8             ([Ljava/lang/String;)V
  #13 = Utf8             args
  #14 = Utf8             [Ljava/lang/String;
  #15 = Utf8             SourceFile
  #16 = Utf8             Listing1.java
  #17 = NameAndType      #4:#5         //  "<init>":()V
  #18 = Utf8             Listing1
  #19 = Utf8             java/lang/Object
```

The numbers on the constant pool entries are how the rest of the bytecode will refer to each constant. For example, if you wanted to refer to the class "Listing1," then you would refer to constant #3. Most of the constant pool is character strings encoded using utf8. Constants #2 and #3 represent Java class names: note that which class name they implement is given by a string constant. So the way you read this is that constant #2 is the class whose name is given by the string at constant #18. Helpfully, javap will provide a comment explaining what the corresponding value is, so you don't have to do that work yourself. Constant #17 is of type NameAndType, which is the name and shape of the method. Like the class names, the particular name and type information is represented by other strings in the constant pool. In this case, the name is "<init>," which is the magic bytecode name for constructors. The method's shape is that it takes no arguments (that's the empty parenthesis, ()) and returns void (V). The last constant in the pool is a method reference, which is going to be a Class combined with a NameAndType. That combination will uniquely define a method to invoke. The value of constant #1 is defining to the Object default constructor method reference –we will see why when we move to the next element of the classfile.

The body of the class is defined within brackets, just like in the Java language. The method names are similar to the Java declaration: in our case, we have public static void main(java.lang.String[]); and public Listing1();. We have two methods in the bytecode, but we only have one method declared in our Java code. What's the second method? The answer is that Java requires each class to have a constructor. If you don't have a constructor, one will be provided to you by the compiler: namely, a default constructor that takes no arguments and allows all the field values to be the default. Since we did not declare a constructor, the compiler gave us one, and that is what "public Listing1();." is. Before we look into its implementation, though, let's take a look at the method we did declare. The main method that we declared in the Java code was empty, but there is a fair bit going on in the bytecode (lines 56–71):

```
public static void main(java.lang.String[]);
  descriptor: ([Ljava/lang/String;)V
  flags: ACC_PUBLIC, ACC_STATIC
  LineNumberTable:
    line 3: 0
  LocalVariableTable:
    Start  Length  Slot  Name  Signature
        0       1     0  args  [Ljava/lang/String;
  Code:
    stack=0, locals=1, args_size=1
       0: return
    LineNumberTable:
      line 3: 0
    LocalVariableTable:
      Start  Length  Slot  Name  Signature
          0       1     0  args  [Ljava/lang/String;
```

After the declaration of the method is the descriptor. This is the official bytecode declaration of the shape of the method. The arguments of the declaration are within parentheses: in this case, it is an array of type java.lang.String. Object types in bytecode are given between the character "L" and the character ";". Packages are delimited by forward slashes instead of periods. Therefore, java.lang.String becomes Ljava.lang.String;. Arrays are specified by an open square brace: "[". Since the main method takes a single array of type string, its argument type is therefore ([Ljava.lang.String;). We again see the "V" dangling at the end to represent the void return type. That gives you the whole descriptor, which is the signature of the method. In programming language geek parlance, the signature of a method describes the method's "shape": the signature describes how the method can fit into the program as a whole, the same way a shape of a puzzle piece determines how the piece fits into the puzzle.

The next line is again the flags. In this case, they correspond to the public and static keywords in Java. Following that, we have a LineNumberTable for the method, which is effectively repeated in the Code section below. This table is how debuggers know what line of code corresponds to what operation. In this case, it is saying that line 3 of the source file is where the method is declared. After the LineNumberTable is the LocalVariableTable, which stores the local variables, and which is also repeated in the Code section. Our

Java code does not declare any local variables, but we have one here in the bytecode: the hint why is given by the name, args. The arguments for a method also count as local variables: they just happen to be local variables that are set when the method is invoked.

The last section is the "Code" section. This is where the body of the method is defined. The numbers are offsets, which tells you how long your method is within bytecode. In our case, the only thing that the method is going to do is return, so there is only the single instruction at index 0: return. The locals value is the number of local variables used by the method, and the args_size is the size of the arguments. This just leaves stack=0 to explain.

Java bytecode is a stack-based language. There are more sophisticated stack-based languages (such as Factor), so do not base your opinion of all stack-based languages on your experience with Java bytecode. Nonetheless, the fact that Java bytecode is a stack-based language means that each instruction acts on a stack. Everything you do in bytecode is either a non-operation ("nop"), pushing elements on a stack, or popping elements off. Therefore, every behavior in Java (e.g., referring to a variable) corresponds to some sequence of stack operations (e.g., pushing the variable's value onto the stack). There can be side effects, most notably in flow control: for instance, when you invoke a method, you are popping elements off the stack to invoke the method, and when the method returns, it may push an element back onto the stack.

In bytecode, each method has to declare the maximum depth of its particular stack. This allows the runtime to optimize allocation for the stack: it can allocate a single block of memory once when it enters the method, instead of potentially needing to allocate more when elements are pushed onto the stack. In the case of our main method, we do not need any space on the stack since we are simply going to return void. Therefore, our bytecode tells the runtime that we need a stack size of 0 by setting stack=0. And that is it for our main method. The constructor (lines 37–49), however, is somewhat more complicated:

```
public Listing1();
  descriptor: ()V
  flags: ACC_PUBLIC
  LineNumberTable:
    line 1: 0
  LocalVariableTable:
    Start  Length  Slot  Name   Signature
        0       5     0  this   LListing1;
  Code:
    stack=1, locals=1, args_size=1
      0: aload_0
      1: invokespecial #1                  // Method java/lang/Object."<init>":()V
      4: return
```

The first thing to note is that the constructor is not a static method: there is no ACC_STATIC flag set. The constructor is an instance method that is invoked on an instance of the class. Since it is an instance method, it has access to the variable, which is declared in the LocalVariableTable. Its type is LListing1;—the two "L" characters at the front is not a typo. Again, the type name is declared between "L" and ";", which gives our initial duplication. The existence of this again gives us our values locals=1 and args_size=1, even though we have no arguments declared in our descriptor. It is also interesting to note that Java does not want you to think of constructors as having a return type, but as far as the bytecode method descriptor is concerned, the constructor returns void.

The maximum stack size for our constructor is 1, and that is because the constructor is going to do something interesting. In the Java language, the first line of the constructor may be a call to this() or super() (possibly with arguments). Those calls delegate to another constructor. In bytecode, the first line of a constructor must be a delegation to another constructor: it is optional in the Java language, but required in the bytecode. Our parent class for Listing1 is the Object class, so the bytecode delegates our constructor to the Object class super constructor. The bytecode accomplishes this by loading the this local variable and then invoking the superclass constructor on it. The command `aload_0` pushes onto the stack the local variable at offset 0 in the local variable table: that is our `this` variable. At that point, we have a stack whose top element is our `this` variable. Constructors are strange kinds of beasts, so you invoke them in bytecode by saying `invokespecial`. You need to tell the runtime what constructor you are invoking, so you call `invokespecial` with a method reference: in our code, the method reference is the `Object` class constructor. With all of that accomplished, we `return`. (Remember, a constructor is a void method according to bytecode.)

At this point, I do not expect that you feel like a bytecode expert. However, you should no longer be overwhelmed or lost when looking at Listing 8-1. You should have a general sense as to how to read a basic class. With that skill, we can move into reading the bytecode that backs lambdas.

Method References in Bytecode

In terms of bytecode, the simplest kind of lambda is the method reference. In Listing 8-2, we will construct a method reference to the static method `Listing2::lambdiseMe`. That method is coerced into a `Supplier<String>`. The result of this relatively short bit of Java is a lot of additional bytecode in the class, and we might start to feel overwhelmed or lost again, but we will take it step by step to see what is going on.

Before we get into the bytecode, let's be clear about what we are doing in Java. We are going to declare a static method, `lambdiseMe`, that takes no arguments and returns a `String` value. We will also declare another static method, `getSupplier`, that takes no arguments and returns a `Supplier<String>`. All `getSupplier` will do is return a reference to `lambdiseMe`. This is simple stuff that we have been doing since Chapter 2. The result is in Listing 8-2. The javap result is a bit too long, so we omitted the constant pool, the default constructor, and some of the other extraneous details.

Listing 8-2. Java Code for a Static Method Reference with Its Bytecode (Abbreviated)

```
1    // Listing2.java, which is compiled to Listing2.class
2    import java.util.function.*;
3
4    public class Listing2 {
5
6      public static String lambdiseMe() {
7        return "Hello, World!";
8      }
9
10     public static Supplier<String> getSupplier() {
11       return Listing2::lambdiseMe;
12     }
13
14   }
15
16   // Abbreviated result of executing /usr/bin/javap -v -l -p -s -c Listing2 in the same
     directory as Listing2.class
17   public class Listing2
18   BootstrapMethods:
19     0: #24 invokestatic java/lang/invoke/LambdaMetafactory.metafactory:(
       Ljava/lang/invoke/MethodHandles$Lookup;
       Ljava/lang/String;
       Ljava/lang/invoke/MethodType;
```

```
        Ljava/lang/invoke/MethodType;
        Ljava/lang/invoke/MethodHandle;
        Ljava/lang/invoke/MethodType;
     )Ljava/lang/invoke/CallSite;
20        Method arguments:
21          #25 ()Ljava/lang/Object;
22          #26 invokestatic Listing2.lambdiseMe:()Ljava/lang/String;
23          #27 ()Ljava/lang/String;
24   {
25   public static java.lang.String lambdiseMe();
26       descriptor: ()Ljava/lang/String;
27       Code:
28         stack=1, locals=0, args_size=0
29            0: ldc            #2                  // String Hello, World!
30            2: areturn
31
32     public static java.util.function.Supplier<java.lang.String> getSupplier();
33       descriptor: ()Ljava/util/function/Supplier;
34       Code:
35         stack=1, locals=0, args_size=0
36            0: invokedynamic #3,  0
               // InvokeDynamic #0:get:()Ljava/util/function/Supplier;
37            5: areturn
38   }
```

The most familiar fragment of the javap results is the lambdiseMe method. It is a static method with no arguments and no locals. This method pushes constant #2 from the constant pool onto the stack using the ldc command. From the comment, we can see that the constant is the String value "Hello, World!" The code then returns the top value of the stack by calling areturn: previously, we always saw void methods, and so they called return instead of areturn. But, as we can see from the descriptor, we are going to return a value of type String, and so we use areturn.

The getSupplier method is of the same basic form of the lambdiseMe method: it executes a command to push an object onto the stack, and then it returns the object on that stack. The difference is the command that pushes the object onto the stack. In lambdiseMe, it is loading a constant. In getSupplier, the value for the stack comes from this strange call, invokedynamic.

The invokedynamic instruction was introduced in Java 7 to support dynamic languages that ran on the JVM, such as JRuby and Groovy. These dynamic languages had a similar problem: for certain common method calls, they could not know exactly what method to call until runtime. No amount of polymorphism helped them out: they simply had to defer the decision about what method to run until the moment the code was executed. The result was that each dynamic language had its own method dispatch structure built on top of Java's own method dispatch structure, and those structures tended to be bad for Java's optimizations. To help them out (and lay the groundwork for lambdas), Java 7 introduced invokedynamic.

The invokedynamic instruction tells Java to wait until runtime, and then resolve the method name when the invokedynamic instruction is first encountered. When the invokedynamic instruction is encountered, it will delegate to another method provided by the classfile, called the "bootstrap method." The bootstrap method will get a bunch of information about the call site, and may also take some extra constants. The bootstrap method will be expected to return the method binding for that location, which is encapsulated in the type java.lang.invoke.CallSite. That CallSite has all the information that the JVM needs to dispatch that method: from that point forward, when that particular invokedynamic instruction is encountered, the JVM will execute the method as specified by the CallSite.

In this case, the instruction executes the Bootstrap Method #0, which is the "0" argument to the invokedynamic instruction. That bootstrap methods have their own pool, and in this case, #0 is the static method metafactory on the class java.lang.invoke.LambdaMetafactory. Every bootstrap method is automatically passed MethodHandles.Lookup (a utility class to look up methods), the String name of the invoked method, and the type the CallSite is expected to provide as a MethodType. In this case, the type that is expected is a Supplier, and we are implementing the get method: that is specified by the other argument to invokedynamic (the #3).

In the bootstrap method pool, though, we see a few other method arguments declared. These are tacked onto the end, and they are the three remaining arguments to the metafactory call. The second argument is the simplest: it is the source of the implementation for the lambda. In this case, it is the static invocation of our lambdiseMe method. The first and last arguments are the implementation signature and runtime type of the method being implemented. The implementation signature is something that takes no arguments and returns an object – ()Ljava/lang/Object; – because that is the signature of Supplier.get() that we are trying to match. However, we also tell the runtime via the third argument that this method will actually always return a String – ()Ljava/lang/String; – which is useful for optimization and casting.

Let's pull it all together. The invokedynamic instruction is encountered for the first time. The metafactory method is called, being passed some default arguments and some custom arguments. The default arguments are the utility for method lookup, the name of the invoked method, and an instruction to return a Supplier. The custom arguments specify that we will implement Supplier.get(), and even though it normally takes no arguments and returns an Object, we will really provide an implementation that takes no arguments and returns a String. Another custom argument specifies that the implementation of that is through statically invoking our lambdiseMe method. This bootstrap method returns the details about the call site, which is invoked to generate the Supplier based on our lambda. Whew!

This is a lot of work on paper, but the shocking part is how fast this is, especially given repeated invocations. The overhead of lambdas compared to anonymous functions is usually too small to be measured, especially on any kind of modern hardware. The Java 8 runtime is tuned well for this kind of work, and it does all this heavy lifting on the first invocation so that later invocations are lightweight and easy to optimize.

Given all this work for a static method, though, what happens when we want to call a method on some bound object, such as our old friend, System.out::println?

Bound Instance Method References in Bytecode

In the previous section, we saw how a static method was turned into a functional interface implementation via a method reference. The static case is the simplest; binding an instance method is trickier. An instance method also has to store its particular instance for later execution, and that instance has to be used to invoke the method.

Throughout this book, we have used System.out::println as our generic instance method reference, and so our current example will be the same. Using the bytecode notation, the shape of System.out::println is (Ljava/lang/String)V – it takes a string and returns void. This is the shape of the Consumer<String> functional interface class, so our example will produce a Consumer<String> based on System.out::println. When we do this, we get the result in Listing 8-3.

Listing 8-3. Java Code for a Bound Instance Method Reference with Its Bytecode (Abbreviated)

```
1    // Listing3.java, which is compiled to Listing3.class
2    import java.util.function.*;
3    public class Listing3 {
4      public Consumer<String> getConsumer() {
5        return System.out::println;
6      }
7    }
8
9    // Abbreviated result of executing /usr/bin/javap -v -l -p -s -c Listing3 in the same
     directory as Listing3.class
10   public class Listing3
11   BootstrapMethods:
12       0: #25 invokestatic java/lang/invoke/LambdaMetafactory.metafactory:(
         Ljava/lang/invoke/MethodHandles$Lookup;
         Ljava/lang/String;
         Ljava/lang/invoke/MethodType;
         Ljava/lang/invoke/MethodType;
         Ljava/lang/invoke/MethodHandle;
         Ljava/lang/invoke/MethodType;
     )Ljava/lang/invoke/CallSite;
13       Method arguments:
14         #26 (Ljava/lang/Object;)V
15         #27 invokevirtual java/io/PrintStream.println:(Ljava/lang/String;)V
16         #28 (Ljava/lang/String;)V
17   {
18   public java.util.function.Consumer<java.lang.String> getConsumer();
19       LocalVariableTable:
20         Start  Length  Slot  Name   Signature
21             0      14     0   this   LListing3;
22       Code:
23         stack=2, locals=1, args_size=1
24           0: getstatic     #2     // Field java/lang/System.out:Ljava/io/PrintStream;
25           3: dup
26           4: invokevirtual #3
             // Method java/lang/Object.getClass:()Ljava/lang/Class;
27           7: pop
28           8: invokedynamic #4,  0 // InvokeDynamic
                                   // #0:accept:(Ljava/io/PrintStream;)Ljava/util/
                                   function/Consumer;
29          13: areturn
30   }
```

If we compare this to the function in 8-2, we see that there is a bit more going on. The first thing is the getstatic call, which loads System.out onto the stack. Eventually, we will pass that instance into our invokedynamic call on instruction 8, which will again go by way of the bootstrap method to produce our Consumer. The bootstrap method is practically identical to what we saw with the static method reference, except that our method is being invoked using invokevirtual instead of invokestatic. Whereas invokestatic makes the static method call, invokevirtual makes an instance method call. So that is our method reference, and the instance to invoke it on is also passed into the bootstrap method. Aside from that difference, this is all very similar to what we saw before. But what is that stuff in instructions 3, 4, and 7?

It is possible that this variable came from some other classloader far away, or that it was somehow gamed into existence. The bootstrap method, however, is going to need access to the class, and is going to need it to be fully formed. To ensure that the class is fully loaded and accessible in the current context, we will call the Object.getClass() method on System.out. The invokevirtual call, however, will consume the top element of the stack as the target, and we want to keep the top element around – it's our reference to System.out. So we first do a dup, which duplicates the top element of the stack. The stack now has two System.out references, and we consume one with invokevirtual to call the Object.getClass() method. We don't want to actually do anything with the class, however, so we can then just pop it off the stack.

This class maneuver is the kind of bookkeeping that you do not have to deal with in the world of Java, and which the compiler provides to you free of charge. It also demonstrates the subtlety and complexity of bootstrapping and method handle lookups, which it is very easy to get wrong. So please love and appreciate your compiler!

Free Instance Method References in Bytecode

There is one last kind of method reference: the free instance method reference. This is the case when we pass in a type and an instance method to the method reference, and it creates a method that accepts that type and calls the given instance method. This is somewhat like the bound method reference, in that it has to track what type is being called. However, we do not have a particular instance that is being called in this case, so it can't act like the bound instance method reference. How does it work?

To demonstrate this, we will create a method that will return the BigInteger::toString free instance method reference. This free instance method reference requests a BigInteger to call, and returns a String. The shape of this, therefore, is Function<BigInteger,String>. The resulting method and its abbreviated bytecode is in Listing 8-4.

Listing 8-4. Java Code for a Free Instance Method Reference with Its Bytecode (Abbreviated)

```
1     // Listing4.java, which is compiled to Listing4.class
2     import java.math.BigInteger;
3     import java.util.function.*;
4
5     public class Listing4 {
6       public static Function<BigInteger, String> getFunction() {
7         return BigInteger::toString;
8       }
9     }
10
11    // Abbreviated result of executing /usr/bin/javap -v -l -p -s -c Listing4 in the same
      directory as Listing4.class
12    public class Listing4
13    BootstrapMethods:
14       0: #25 invokestatic java/lang/invoke/LambdaMetafactory.metafactory:(
         Ljava/lang/invoke/MethodHandles$Lookup;
         Ljava/lang/String;
         Ljava/lang/invoke/MethodType;
         Ljava/lang/invoke/MethodType;
         Ljava/lang/invoke/MethodHandle;
         Ljava/lang/invoke/MethodType;
      )Ljava/lang/invoke/CallSite;
```

```
15          Method arguments:
16              #21 (Ljava/lang/Object;)Ljava/lang/Object;
17              #22 invokevirtual java/math/BigInteger.toString:()Ljava/lang/String;
18              #23 (Ljava/math/BigInteger;)Ljava/lang/String;
19   {
20     public static java.util.function.Function<java.math.BigInteger, java.lang.String>
       getFunction();
21     Code:
22          stack=1, locals=0, args_size=0
23          0: invokedynamic #2,  0
                // InvokeDynamic #0:apply:()Ljava/util/function/Function;
24          5: areturn
25   }
```

It may seem like the free instance method is the strangest of all three types of method references, but the actual implementation is just as simple as the static method reference! Just like in Listing 8-2, we see a single invokedynamic call followed by a return. The bootstrap method is also the same. The only difference is that the method handle passed into the bootstrap uses invokevirtual instead of invokestatic. This goes to show that the invokevirtual and the invokestatic calls are not directly invoked, but are instead implementation details about the functional interface itself. So there is no difference between creating a static and a free instance method, except in the way the implementation calls the methods.

Inline Lambda Definitions and Lambda Lifting

The last kind of lambda that you can have is a lambda with an inline definition. We are not talking about a reference to an existing method here, but instead defining an entirely new unit of functionality right inline. You may consider code like this:

```
public Supplier<String> getSupplier() {
  return () -> "Hello, World!";
}
```

What the compiler will do in this case is create a method for you with that implementation. That is called a "synthetic method." This will be a static method that takes no arguments and returns the string, "Hello, World!" Once that is created, the compiler has now reduced the problem of the inline lambda into the static method reference problem that we saw before. It is a quite clever solution, and ultimately quite trivial an implementation – which means it is boring for us.

The more interesting case is when you have variables in the mix. Let's create a method that calls an instance method (requiring access to this) along with a local variable in the scope. After all, these lambdas are closures: they enclose their scope. This kind of stuff is their job! How is the compiler going to deal with that complexity? The answer is in Listing 8-5.

Listing 8-5. Java Code for an Inline Lambda with Its Bytecode (Abbreviated)

```
1    // Listing5.java, which is compiled to Listing5.class
2    import java.util.function.*;
3
4    public class Listing5 {
5
6      public String provideMessage(String message) {
7        return message;
8      }
9
10     public Supplier<String> getSupplier(String message) {
11       return () -> this.provideMessage(message);
12     }
13
14   }
15
16   // Abbreviated result of executing /usr/bin/javap -v -l -p -s -c Listing5 in the same
     directory as Listing5.class
17   public class Listing5
18   BootstrapMethods:
19       0: #25 invokestatic java/lang/invoke/LambdaMetafactory.metafactory:(
         Ljava/lang/invoke/MethodHandles$Lookup;
         Ljava/lang/String;
         Ljava/lang/invoke/MethodType;
         Ljava/lang/invoke/MethodType;
         Ljava/lang/invoke/MethodHandle;
         Ljava/lang/invoke/MethodType;
     )Ljava/lang/invoke/CallSite;
20         Method arguments:
21           #27 ()Ljava/lang/Object;
22           #28 invokespecial Listing5.lambda$getSupplier$0:(Ljava/lang/String;)Ljava/lang/
             String;
23           #29 ()Ljava/lang/String;
24   {
25     public Listing5();
26
27     public java.lang.String provideMessage(java.lang.String);
28       Code:
29         stack=1, locals=2, args_size=2
30           0: aload_1
31           1: areturn
32
33     public java.util.function.Supplier<java.lang.String> getSupplier(java.lang.String);
34       Code:
35         stack=2, locals=2, args_size=2
36           0: aload_0
37           1: aload_1
38           2: invokedynamic #2,  0            // InvokeDynamic
                                                 // #0:get:(LListing5;Ljava/lang/String;)
                                                 Ljava/util/function/Supplier;
```

```
39              7: areturn
40
41     private java.lang.String lambda$getSupplier$0(java.lang.String);
42       flags: ACC_PRIVATE, ACC_SYNTHETIC
43       Code:
44         stack=2, locals=2, args_size=2
45            0: aload_0
46            1: aload_1
47            2: invokevirtual #3
               // Method provideMessage:(Ljava/lang/String;)Ljava/lang/String;
48            5: areturn
49   }
```

Now things have gotten really quite strange. We see the example of the synthetic method with the strange name: lambda$getSupplier$0(java.lang.String);. That is an instance method that takes a String, and calls provideMessage on that string using the instance: it loads aload_0, which is this, and then aload_1, which is the argument, and then does an invokevirtual. Our getSupplier method does something similar: it loads the message and this, and then does our familiar invokedynamic call to generate the supplier.

Note that we are passing in two arguments in our signature to invokedynamic now: all the variables that we need to reference inside our lambda implementation become arguments to invokedynamic. This is called "lambda lifting": we lift the bound variables out of the lambda and make them arguments to instantiating it. The signal that we have performed lambda lifting is the use of invokespecial as our means of method invocation: we saw it used before to signal a constructor, but now we are using it as a signal to the bootstrap method that we are having to construct a new instance with the lifted arguments.

The important part to realize is that declaring a lambda that uses variables is a lot like declaring a new type that refers to those variables: we will end up instantiating a new instance that will hold onto those variables, and it will end up referring to those member fields when it executes. Therefore, defining a lambda inline and defining your own anonymous inner class have practically identical performance characteristics. Use whichever approach is more natural for the space you are in.

Conclusion

Lambdas are extremely powerful, but under the hood, they are conceptually simple: the Java SDK has a method which will take in your lambda and return an instance of whatever type your lambda is targeting. It performs that binding just once using the invokedynamic bytecode instruction, and after the first execution, it is equivalent to instantiating the interface implementation directly. If you define a lambda inline, then you are going to get a synthetic method, but everything else is practically the same. There is a lot of noise in the bytecode and some careful bookkeeping to make this all happen right, but the concept of the implementation is actually rather simple. Most importantly, there is nothing innate in this implementation that makes lambdas slow or heavyweight compared to other ways to solve the same problem: you are never going to see significant improvements by rewriting lambdas into something else. The implementation is smarter than that!

■ ■ ■

A Tour of Paradigms

Many books, articles, and conversations will wax poetic about programming language paradigms, comparing and contrasting "imperative," "object-oriented," and "functional" without explaining what they are. Worse, when people go to explain these particular styles, the result is often rather vague. This appendix will provide an overview of the three dominant paradigms in post-functional programming by implementing the same functionality three different ways: we will use a database set-up process as a common problem, and show how you would solve that problem in each of the different paradigms. All of this will be done directly from within Java, so you can see how Java looks when forced to be strongly in one single paradigm. At the end of the chapter, we will highlight some additional programming paradigms and styles so that you are at least familiar with the terms.

The database that we will be setting up is the database we used in chapter 5. This is a collection of the words used in all the works of Shakespeare, indexed by line. The database looks like Figure A-1. The data comes from the Project Gutenberg text at http://www.gutenberg.org/ebooks/100. To create this database, we will have to perform the following steps:

1. Create the schema, including the tables.

2. Parse and insert the works of Shakespeare file.

   a. Empty lines and comments should be skipped.

   b. Text breaks (i.e., where a new text begins) need to be recognized, and a text entry created.

   c. Each line needs to be parsed, and a line entry created.

   d. Each word in the line needs to be parsed.

      i. If the word does not previously exist, a word entry needs to be created.

      ii. A line_word entry needs to be created.

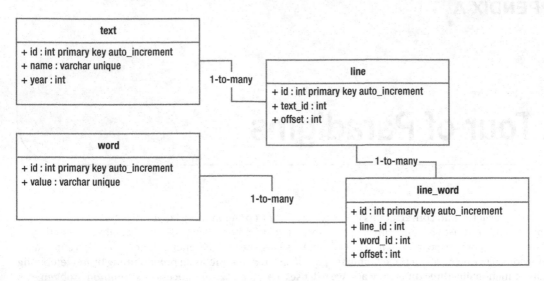

Figure A-1. *The Database Layout*

Most of the text breaks look like the sample given in Figure A-2: it is the date of publication, the title, and then "by William Shakespeare." However, the sonnets are numbered, and so they follow a slightly different format. This format is shown in Figure A-3. "THE SONNETS" is the title, and when we see that title, we need to start looking for lines that are only numbers – those lines denote the start of a new sonnet. So parsing texts is slightly different for the Sonnets than for everything else, which adds a wrinkle of complexity.

1603

ALLS WELL THAT ENDS WELL

by William Shakespeare

Dramatis Personae

 KING OF FRANCE

 THE DUKE OF FLORENCE

 BERTRAM, Count of Rousillon

 LAFEU, an old lord

Figure A-2. *A Sample Text Start*

THE SONNETS

by William Shakespeare

1

From fairest creatures we desire increase,

That thereby beauty's rose might never die,

But as the riper should by time decease,

His tender heir might bear his memory:

But thou contracted to thine own bright eyes,

Feed'st thy light's flame with self-substantial fuel,

Making a famine where abundance lies,

Thy self thy foe, to thy sweet self too cruel:

Thou that art now the world's fresh ornament,

And only herald to the gaudy spring,

Within thine own bud buriest thy content,

And tender churl mak'st waste in niggarding:

    Pity the world, or else this glutton be,

    To eat the world's due, by the grave and thee.

2

When forty winters shall besiege thy brow,

And dig deep trenches in thy beauty's field,

Thy youth's proud livery so gazed on now,

Will be a tattered weed of small worth held:

Then being asked, where all thy beauty lies,

Where all the treasure of thy lusty days;

To say within thine own deep sunken eyes,

Were an all-eating shame, and thriftless praise.

How much more praise deserved thy beauty's use,

If thou couldst answer 'This fair child of mine

Shall sum my count, and make my old excuse'

Proving his beauty by succession thine.

    This were to be new made when thou art old,

    And see thy blood warm when thou feel'st it cold.

Figure A-3. *Sonnets Start*

155

This is not a hugely difficult problem, but it is complex enough that we can see how different paradigms approach the problems in different ways. The paradigms are all theoretically equivalent: that is, there is no problem that one paradigm can solve that another can't solve. However, each paradigm is best suited to address particular kinds of problems. It is easy to see these differences when you see the paradigms at work.

Imperative Programming Paradigm

The first computer programming languages were assembly languages. These are strange and low-level beasts, and are arguably a paradigm unto themselves. Once computer programmers began to work in higher levels of abstractions, the first batch of languages they invented were imperative. The word "imperative" here comes from the human language structure: in the sentence, "Pick up that garbage," the command, "Pick up," is the imperative. Imperatives are commands to perform some action. An imperative programming language is a language that executes a system of instructions. If that sounds like a description of all programming languages, it is because almost all the most popular programming languages are of this type, so you can go through your entire career working in imperative (or near-imperative) code.

Java is fundamentally object oriented, but a lot of Java code can look quite imperative. Imperative programming is a natural way for people to think about problems: even the pseudocode given in the introduction was implicitly imperative. Because it is so natural, it is easy for a programmer to go from a gut understanding of how to solve the problem into a series of instructions, entirely bypassing the design phase. The result is imperative code. This approach works very well for simple scripts, especially when those scripts are mimicking the interaction of a human being. This is why imperative languages such as perl, bash, and Power Shell dominate shell scripting.

You can recognize imperative code in Java by looking at the methods. The dead giveaway is if the codebase is dominated by static methods: if so, chances are you are seeing very imperative code. Imperative code also lends itself to long methods with many arguments, and those methods will tend to call out to other long methods with many arguments. What is going on is that the entire state of the application is being passed around, including various signals for exceptional conditions. Everything needs to know everything about everything in an imperative language.

For the imperative implementation, we will start by executing the schema creation. When that is done, we will prepare all the statements that we will use throughout our execution. When that is done, we will load the text stream. Then, for each line in the text stream, we will drop into a big if-else block. That block will be responsible for determining where we are at in the processing, and how to process the current line. If we are in the sonnets and the line is just a digit, we will create the new text in the database representing our new sonnet. Otherwise, if the line is a year, that is signifying a start of a new text, and we will check to see if we are in the sonnets, and we will handle things appropriately. Otherwise, if we are in a comment, we will scroll to a comment. Otherwise, if it's the end, we'll note that we are definitely no longer in the sonnets. Otherwise, we will break the line up into words and store each of the words into the database. The code for this is given in Listing A-1.

Listing A-1. Imperative Database Loading

```java
import java.io.BufferedReader;
import java.io.IOException;
import java.io.InputStream;
import java.io.InputStreamReader;
import java.sql.*;
import java.util.*;
import java.util.concurrent.*;
import java.util.function.*;
import java.util.regex.*;
```

```java
public class Database {

  private static final String SOURCE = "shakespeare.txt";
  private static final String SCHEMA = "shakespeare";
  private static final Predicate<String> IS_WHITESPACE =
    Pattern.compile("^\\s*$").asPredicate();
  private static final Predicate<String> IS_YEAR =
    Pattern.compile("^1(5|6)\\d\\d$").asPredicate();
  private static final Predicate<String> IS_COMMENT_START =
    Pattern.compile("^<<").asPredicate();
  private static final Predicate<String> IS_COMMENT_END =
    Pattern.compile(">>$").asPredicate();
  private static final Predicate<String> IS_THE_END =
    Pattern.compile("^THE\\s+END$").asPredicate();
  private static final Predicate<String> IS_DIGITS =
    Pattern.compile("^\\d+$").asPredicate();
  private static final Predicate<String> IS_AUTHOR =
    Pattern.compile("^by\\s+William\\s+Shakespeare$").asPredicate();
  private static final String SONNETS_TITLE = "THE SONNETS";
  private static final Pattern BAD_CHARS =
    Pattern.compile("\uFEFF|\\p{Cntrl}"); // BOMs and control characters

  public static Connection getConnection() throws SQLException {
    return DriverManager.getConnection(
      "jdbc:h2:mem:shakespeare;INIT=CREATE SCHEMA IF NOT EXISTS " +
      SCHEMA + "\\; " +
      "SET SCHEMA " + SCHEMA + ";DB_CLOSE_DELAY=-1", "sa", ""
    );
  }

  /**
   * Creates the database by parsing {@link #SOURCE} and populating
   * its contents into the database connected to via the
   * {@link #getConnection()} method.
   */
  public static void createDatabase() throws Exception {
    final Map<String, Integer> wordMap = new HashMap<>();
    final ExecutorService executor = Executors.newCachedThreadPool();
    try (Connection conn = getConnection()) {
      Statement stmt = conn.createStatement();
      stmt.execute("DROP SCHEMA " + SCHEMA);
      stmt.execute("CREATE SCHEMA " + SCHEMA);
      stmt.execute("SET SCHEMA " + SCHEMA);
      stmt.execute("CREATE TABLE \"text\" (" +
        "id INT PRIMARY KEY AUTO_INCREMENT, name VARCHAR UNIQUE, year INT)");
      stmt.execute("CREATE TABLE line (" +
        "id INT PRIMARY KEY AUTO_INCREMENT, text_id INT, \"offset\" INT)");
      stmt.execute("CREATE TABLE word (" +
        "id INT PRIMARY KEY AUTO_INCREMENT, \"value\" VARCHAR UNIQUE)");
```

```
    stmt.execute("CREATE TABLE line_word (" +
      "id INT PRIMARY KEY AUTO_INCREMENT, line_id INT, word_id INT, " +
      "\"offset\" INT)"
    );

    PreparedStatement createBook = conn.prepareStatement(
      "INSERT INTO \"text\" (name, year) VALUES (?,?)",
        Statement.RETURN_GENERATED_KEYS
    );
    PreparedStatement createLine = conn.prepareStatement(
      "INSERT INTO line (text_id, \"offset\") VALUES (?,?)",
        Statement.RETURN_GENERATED_KEYS
    );
    PreparedStatement createWord = conn.prepareStatement(
      "INSERT INTO word (\"value\") VALUES (?)",
        Statement.RETURN_GENERATED_KEYS
    );
    PreparedStatement createLineWord = conn.prepareStatement(
        "INSERT INTO line_word " +
          " (line_id, word_id, \"offset\") " +
          " VALUES (?,?,?)",
        Statement.NO_GENERATED_KEYS
    );

    try (InputStream stream =
      Database.class.getClassLoader().getResourceAsStream(SOURCE)
    ) {
      assert stream != null : "No resource found at: " + SOURCE;
      BufferedReader reader = new BufferedReader(
        new InputStreamReader(stream, "UTF-8"));
      String line;
      int textId = 0;
      int lineOffset = 0;
      boolean inTheSonnets = false;
      while ((line = nextLine(reader)) != null) {
        if (inTheSonnets && IS_DIGITS.test(line)) {
          textId = doCreateBook(createBook, "Sonnet #" + line,
            1609, executor);
          lineOffset = 0;
        } else if (IS_YEAR.test(line)) {
          String year = line;
          String title = nextLine(reader);
          String author = nextLine(reader);
          assert IS_AUTHOR.test(author) : (title + " " + year +
            " did not provide the right author: " + author);

          inTheSonnets = SONNETS_TITLE.equalsIgnoreCase(title);
```

```java
    if (!inTheSonnets) {
      textId = doCreateBook(createBook, title,
        Integer.parseInt(year), executor);
      lineOffset = 0;
    }
} else if (IS_COMMENT_START.test(line)) {
  while (
    (line = nextLine(reader)) != null &&
    !IS_COMMENT_END.test(line)
  ) {
    continue;
  }
  assert line != null : "No ending comment found";
} else if (IS_THE_END.test(line)) {
  inTheSonnets = false;
} else {
  assert (textId != 0) : "Processing, but no title provided";
  lineOffset += 1;
  createLine.setInt(1, textId);
  createLine.setInt(2, lineOffset);
  boolean createdLine = createLine.executeUpdate() == 1;
  assert createdLine : "Could not create line";
  ResultSet rs = createLine.getGeneratedKeys();
  boolean hasNext = rs.next();
  assert hasNext :
    "No result when getting generated keys for for line " +
    textId + "-" + lineOffset;
  int lineId = rs.getInt(1);
  rs.close();

  String[] words = line.split("\\s+");
  for (int i = 0; i < words.length; i++) {
    int wordOffset = i + 1;
    String word = words[i];
    word = word.replaceAll("(?!')\\p{Punct}", "");

    final int wordId;
    if (wordMap.containsKey(word)) {
      wordId = wordMap.get(word);
    } else {
      createWord.setString(1, word);
      boolean createdWord = createWord.executeUpdate() == 1;
      assert createdWord : "Could not create word: " + word;
      rs = createWord.getGeneratedKeys();
      hasNext = rs.next();
      assert hasNext : "Created word but still could not find it!";
```

```
                String newWord = word;
                executor.submit(() ->
                  System.out.println("New word: " + newWord));
                wordId = rs.getInt(1);
                rs.close();
                wordMap.put(word, wordId);
              }
            createLineWord.setInt(1, lineId);
            createLineWord.setInt(2, wordId);
            createLineWord.setInt(3, wordOffset);
            boolean createdLineWord = createLineWord.executeUpdate() == 1;
            assert createdLineWord : "Could not create line-word";
          }
        }
      }
    }
  } finally {
    executor.shutdown();
    executor.awaitTermination(1L, TimeUnit.MINUTES);
  }
}

/**
 * Returns the next
 */
public static String nextLine(BufferedReader reader) throws IOException {
  String line;
  while ((line = reader.readLine()) != null) {
    line = BAD_CHARS.matcher(line).replaceAll("");
    line = line.trim();
    if (line.isEmpty() || IS_WHITESPACE.test(line)) {
      continue;
    } else {
      break;
    }
  }
  return line;
}


private static int doCreateBook(
    PreparedStatement createBook, String title, int year,
    ExecutorService executor
) throws SQLException {
  createBook.setString(1, title);
  createBook.setInt(2, year);
  boolean createdBook = createBook.executeUpdate() == 1;
  assert createdBook : "Could not create book";
  ResultSet rs = createBook.getGeneratedKeys();
  boolean hasNext = rs.next();
```

```
    assert hasNext : "No result when getting generated keys for " + title;
    int textId = rs.getInt(1);
    rs.close();

    executor.submit(() -> System.out.println(title));

    return textId;
  }

  public static void main(String[] args) throws Exception {
    createDatabase();
  }

}
```

This code is accomplishing a relatively simple task, but it's already becoming impossible to follow. This reveals the problem with imperative code: it has limited semantic structure. A lot is happening, but not a lot is communicated to the reader about why those things are happening. Instead, the script's gritty details are entirely exposed in a mostly unstructured stream of instructions.

Despite the obvious drawbacks of imperative programming, there are still a number of places where it is very useful. Because imperative code is so quickly written, it works well for very short bits of code with a clear and simple purpose. Unit tests, for instances, are almost universally imperative in Java. Most method bodies in Java are imperative, as well, which is part of the motivation for keeping them very short. Other languages and contexts also make the imperative paradigm a more natural fit, such as bash or perl for system administration scripts. In general, if you can keep the whole thing in your head at the same time without any confusion, then the imperative style is a nice way to go.

Object-Oriented Programming Paradigm

The imperative programming paradigm lead to many struggles with maintainability, composability, and reusability. Out of these struggles came a refinement of that paradigm called the object-oriented paradigm. Practically from its inception, Java was the poster child for object-oriented programming. In imperative programming, your application is a series of instructions. In object-oriented programming, your application is still a series of instructions, but the application can be quite clever in deciding which instructions to call. The application has many containers for a set of instructions – objects – and the programmer specifies at runtime which container's instruction to call. Within an object-oriented paradigm, an imperative program can be thought of as a program with one global object, and all the methods are on that single object.

Object-oriented programming is a derivative of imperative, but brings with it many advantages. The biggest advantages are that you can encapsulate state: no longer does everything need to know everything about everything. Instead, the developer can capture all that relevant information inside of a single object, and expose instructions that use that state without exposing that state. The other advantages of object-oriented programming derive from this encapsulation stunt: for instance, I can specify a contract about the instructions that you have to implement, and then you can provide any implementation that you like to satisfy that contract.

Even though Java is an object-oriented programming language at its heart, not all Java code is object oriented. You will recognize object-oriented Java code by a proliferation of small, extensible types that are composed together to build up more advanced objects. Methods will be a thin wrapper around the object's properties, with minimal business logic attached to delegation. In object-oriented programming, every class is like a lazy manager: it delegates work to its constituents as quickly as possible.

To implement our object-oriented solution, we will decompose the problem into objects, each of which do a tiny bit of work and delegate to another object. So we will start with a ShakespeareLineIterator that will iterate over the lines of the texts. That will get passed to a ShakespeareAnthologyParser, which is responsible for breaking the iterated lines into texts. Each text will get passed to a ShakespeareTextParser, which is responsible for parsing the texts. It will have a method that will return a collection of ShakespeareText instances. Those ShakespeareText instances will each provide their title, and a series of ShakespeareLine instances. Each of those lines will contain a series of ShakespeareWord instances. The code for these classes is given in Listing A-2.

Listing A-2. Object-Oriented Text Parsing

```
### ShakespeareLineIterator.java
import java.io.*;
import java.util.*;
import java.util.function.*;
import java.util.regex.*;

/**
 * Iterates through the Shakespeare anthology, providing the lines of
 * the anthology.
 */
public class ShakespeareLineIterator implements Iterator<String> {

  private static final String SOURCE = "shakespeare.txt";
  private static final Predicate<String> IS_WHITESPACE =
    Pattern.compile("^\\s*$").asPredicate();
  private static final Pattern BAD_CHARS =
    Pattern.compile("\uFEFF|\\p{Cntrl}"); // BOMs and control characters
  private static final Predicate<String> IS_COMMENT_START =
    Pattern.compile("^<<").asPredicate();
  private static final Predicate<String> IS_COMMENT_END =
    Pattern.compile(">>$").asPredicate();

  private final BufferedReader reader;
  private volatile boolean closed = false;
  private volatile String nextElement = null;
  private volatile IOException exception = null;

  /**
   * Constructs an instance of the class which draws from the packaged
   * complete works of Shakespeare text.
   *
   * @throws IOException If there is an exception getting access to
   *                     the resource.
   */
  public ShakespeareLineIterator() throws IOException {
    InputStream inputStream =
      ShakespeareLineIterator.class
        .getClassLoader()
        .getResourceAsStream(SOURCE);
```

```
    this.reader =
      new BufferedReader(
        new InputStreamReader(
          inputStream, "UTF-8"
        )
      );
}

private void explodeIfException() {
  if (exception != null) {
    throw new UncheckedIOException("error reading the stream", exception);
  }
}

/**
 * Returns the next line of the text, filtering out whitespace, bad
 * characters, comments, etc.
 * Assigns {@link #nextElement} to the next line, or to {@code null} if
 * there are no lines remaining.
 */
private String nextLine() {
  explodeIfException();
  if (closed) return nextElement = null;
  try {
    String line;
    while ((line = reader.readLine()) != null) {
      line = BAD_CHARS.matcher(line).replaceAll("");
      line = line.trim();
      if (line.isEmpty() || IS_WHITESPACE.test(line)) {
        continue;
      } else {
        break;
      }
    }

    if (line != null && IS_COMMENT_START.test(line)) {
      while ((line = reader.readLine()) != null) {
        if (IS_COMMENT_END.test(line)) break;
      }
      if (line != null) return nextLine();
    }

    if (line == null) {
      reader.close();
      closed = true;
    }
```

```
      return nextElement = line;
    } catch (IOException ioe) {
      this.exception = ioe;
      explodeIfException();
      throw new IllegalStateException("This code should never be reached!");
    }
  }

  /**
   * Returns {@code true} if the iteration has more elements.
   * (In other words, returns {@code true} if {@link #next} would
   * return an element rather than throwing an exception.)
   *
   * @return {@code true} if the iteration has more elements
   */
  @Override
  public boolean hasNext() {
    explodeIfException();
    if (nextElement != null) return true;
    if (closed) return false;
    if (nextLine() != null) return true;
    return false;
  }

  /**
   * Returns the next element in the iteration.
   *
   * @return the next element in the iteration
   * @throws java.util.NoSuchElementException if the iteration has no
   *                                          more elements
   */
  @Override
  public String next() {
    explodeIfException();
    if (nextElement != null || nextLine() != null) {
      String toReturn = nextElement;
      nextElement = null;
      return toReturn;
    }
    throw new NoSuchElementException("No more lines to be read!");
  }

  /**
   * Provides the element that will be returned by {@link #next()}
   * without progressing the iterator.
   *
   * @return What will be the next element, or {@code null} if there is
   *         no next element.
   */
```

```java
  public String peek() {
    explodeIfException();
    if (nextElement != null) return nextElement;
    if (closed) return null;
    return nextLine();
  }
}

### ShakespeareAnthologyParser.java
import java.io.IOException;
import java.util.*;
import java.util.function.*;
import java.util.regex.*;

/**
 * Responsible for parsing a Shakespeare anthology into texts.
 */
public class ShakespeareAnthologyParser {

  private static final Predicate<String> IS_YEAR =
    Pattern.compile("^1(5|6)\\d\\d$").asPredicate();
  private static final Predicate<String> IS_AUTHOR =
    Pattern.compile("^by\\s+William\\s+Shakespeare$").asPredicate();
  private static final Predicate<String> IS_THE_END =
    Pattern.compile("^THE\\s+END$").asPredicate();
  private static final Predicate<String> IS_DIGITS =
    Pattern.compile("^\\d+$").asPredicate();
  private static final String SONNETS_TITLE = "THE SONNETS";

  /**
   * Parses the texts based on the in-memory Shakespeare anthology.
   *
   * @return The parsed texts
   * @throws IOException If an exception occurs in reading the texts
   */
  public Collection<ShakespeareText> parseTexts() throws IOException {
    List<ShakespeareText> texts = new ArrayList<>();
    ShakespeareLineIterator lines = new ShakespeareLineIterator();
    while (lines.hasNext()) {
      int year = parseYear(lines);
      String title = parseTitle(lines);
      parseAuthor(lines);
      if (SONNETS_TITLE.equalsIgnoreCase(title)) {
        texts.addAll(parseSonnets(lines));
      } else {
        texts.add(parseText(title, year, lines));
      }
    }
    return texts;
  }
```

```java
  private ShakespeareText parseText(
    final String title, final int year,
    final ShakespeareLineIterator lines
  ) {
    List<ShakespeareLine> parsedLines = new ArrayList<>();
    int lineNumber = 0;
    String line;
    while (lines.hasNext() && !IS_THE_END.test(line = lines.next())) {
      lineNumber += 1;
      parsedLines.add(new ShakespeareLine(lineNumber, line));
    }
    return new ShakespeareText(title, year, parsedLines);
  }

  private Collection<ShakespeareSonnet> parseSonnets(
    final ShakespeareLineIterator lines
  ) {
    List<ShakespeareSonnet> sonnets = new ArrayList<>();
    while (lines.hasNext() && !IS_THE_END.test(lines.peek())) {
      sonnets.add(parseSonnet(lines));
    }
    if (lines.hasNext()) lines.next(); // Move past THE END
    return sonnets;
  }

  private ShakespeareSonnet parseSonnet(final ShakespeareLineIterator lines) {
    List<ShakespeareLine> parsedLines = new ArrayList<>();
    int number = parseSonnetNumber(lines);
    int lineNumber = 0;
    while (
      lines.hasNext() &&
      !IS_DIGITS.test(lines.peek()) &&
      !IS_THE_END.test(lines.peek())
    ) {
      lineNumber += 1;
      parsedLines.add(new ShakespeareLine(lineNumber, lines.next()));
    }
    return new ShakespeareSonnet(number, parsedLines);
  }

  private static int parseSonnetNumber(ShakespeareLineIterator lines) {
    String number = lines.next();
    boolean isNumber = IS_DIGITS.test(number);
    assert isNumber : "Expected a sonnet number, but got: " + number;
    return Integer.parseInt(number);
  }

  private static String parseTitle(ShakespeareLineIterator lines) {
    String title = lines.next();
    boolean isTitle = title != null && !title.isEmpty();
    isTitle = isTitle && !IS_AUTHOR.test(title);
```

```
      isTitle = isTitle && !IS_THE_END.test(title);
      isTitle = isTitle && !IS_YEAR.test(title);
      assert isTitle : "Expected a title, but got: " + title;
      return title;
    }

    private static String parseAuthor(ShakespeareLineIterator lines) {
      String author = lines.next();
      boolean isAuthor = IS_AUTHOR.test(author);
      assert isAuthor : "Expected the author, but got: " + author;
      return author;
    }


    private static int parseYear(ShakespeareLineIterator lines) {
      String year = lines.next();
      boolean isYear = IS_YEAR.test(year);
      assert isYear : "Expected the year, but got: " + year;
      return Integer.parseInt(year);
    }

}
```

ShakespeareText.java
```
import java.util.*;

/**
 * The object representing one of Shakespeare's texts.
 */
public class ShakespeareText {

  private final String name;
  private final int year;
  private final List<ShakespeareLine> lines;

  public ShakespeareText(String name, int year, List<ShakespeareLine> lines) {
    Objects.requireNonNull(name, "name of the text");
    this.name = name;

    if (year < 1500 || year > 1699) {
      throw new IllegalArgumentException(
        "Egregiously wrong year for " + name + ": " + year
      );
    }
    this.year = year;

    Objects.requireNonNull(lines, "lines");
    if (lines.isEmpty()) {
      throw new IllegalArgumentException("Provided empty lines for " + name);
    }
    this.lines = lines;
  }
```

```java
  public String getName() {
    return name;
  }

  public int getYear() {
    return year;
  }

  public List<ShakespeareLine> getLines() {
    return lines;
  }
}
```

ShakespeareSonnet.java
```java
import java.util.*;

/**
 * Special case of a {@link ShakespeareText} containing the
 * specific information for the sonnets.
 */
public class ShakespeareSonnet extends ShakespeareText {

  public ShakespeareSonnet(int number, List<ShakespeareLine> lines) {
    super("Sonnet #" + number, 1609, lines);
    if (number < 1 || number > 175) {
      throw new IllegalArgumentException(
        "Egregiously wrong number for the sonnet: " + number
      );
    }
  }
}
```

ShakespeareLine.java
```java
import java.util.*;

/**
 * Created by RCFischer on 11/11/14.
 */
public class ShakespeareLine {

  private final int position;
  private final String[] words;

  public ShakespeareLine(final int textPosition, final String line) {
    Objects.requireNonNull(line, "line");
    words = line.split("\\s+");
```

```java
    if(textPosition < 1) {
      throw new IllegalArgumentException(
        "Invalid text position: " + textPosition
      );
    }
    this.position = textPosition;
  }

  public int getTextPosition() {
    return position;
  }

  public List<ShakespeareWord> getWords() {
    List<ShakespeareWord> swords = new ArrayList<>();
    for(int i = 0; i < words.length; i++) {
      swords.add(new ShakespeareWord(i+1, words[i]));
    }
    return swords;
  }

}

### ShakespeareWord.java
import java.util.*;

/**
 * Represents a word positioned within a line of Shakespeare.
 */
public class ShakespeareWord {

  private final int linePosition;
  private final String word;

  public ShakespeareWord(final int linePosition, final String word) {
    if (linePosition < 1) {
      throw new IllegalArgumentException("Bad line position: " + linePosition);
    }
    this.linePosition = linePosition;
    Objects.requireNonNull(word, "word");
    this.word = word;
  }

  public int getLinePosition() {
    return linePosition;
  }

  public String getWord() {
    return word;
  }
}
```

At this point, we have still only parsed the content. We still have to load it to the database. To do this, we will have a TextDatabase. It will have a method that will configure the database schema and another that will load the database given a collection of ShakespeareText. This, of course, will delegate immediately to a TextDatabaseTextLoader instance, which is responsible for loading a text. It will delegate to a TextDatabaseLineLoader instance, which is responsible for loading a line. It, in turn, will delegate to a TextDabaseWordLoader instance, which is responsible for loading the word. And then it will all be loaded! The code for all these classes (along with a Main class to test it) is given in Listing A-3.

Listing A-3. Object-Oriented Database Loading

```
### Main.java
import java.sql.Connection;
import java.sql.ResultSet;
import java.sql.SQLException;
import java.sql.Statement;
import java.util.*;

public class Main {

  public static void printDatabaseSizing(Connection conn) throws SQLException {
    System.out.println("SIZES");
    System.out.println("-----");
    Statement stmt = conn.createStatement();
    for (String table : new String[]{"\"text\"", "line", "word", "line_word"})
    {
      try (ResultSet rs = stmt.executeQuery("SELECT COUNT(*) FROM " + table)) {
        boolean hasNext = rs.next();
        assert hasNext : "No result in count from table " + table;
        System.out.println(table + " => " + rs.getInt(1));
      }
    }
  }

  public static ResultSet queryResults(Connection conn) throws SQLException {
    return conn.createStatement().executeQuery(
        "SELECT t.name, l.\"offset\", w.\"value\", lw.\"offset\" " +
          "FROM \"text\" t, word w " +
          "INNER JOIN line l ON (t.id = l.text_id) " +
          "INNER JOIN line_word lw ON (" +
            "lw.line_id = l.id AND lw.word_id = w.id" +
          ")"
    );
  }

  public static void printWordUsages(Connection conn) throws SQLException {
    int lineNumber = 0;
    try (ResultSet rs = queryResults(conn)) {
      String lastText = null;
      int lastLine = -1;
```

```java
      while (rs.next()) {
        if (lineNumber % 20 == 0) {
          System.out.println("text\tline-offset\tword\tword-offset");
          System.out.println("----\t-----------\t----\t-----------");
        }
        lineNumber += 1;
        String text = rs.getString(1);
        if (!text.equals(lastText)) {
          lastText = text;
        }
        int lineOffset = rs.getInt(2);
        String word = rs.getString(3);
        int wordOffset = rs.getInt(4);
        if (lineOffset != lastLine) {
          lastLine = lineOffset;
        }
        System.out.println(
          String.format("%s\t%d\t%s\t%d", text, lineOffset, word, wordOffset));
      }
    }
  }


  public static void main(String[] args) throws Exception {
    ShakespeareAnthologyParser textParser = new ShakespeareAnthologyParser();
    Collection<ShakespeareText> texts = textParser.parseTexts();

    TextDatabase db = new TextDatabase("shakespeare");
    db.createDatabase();
    db.insertTexts(texts);

    printWordUsages(db.getConnection());
    printDatabaseSizing(db.getConnection());
  }
}

### TextDatabase.java
import java.sql.Connection;
import java.sql.DriverManager;
import java.sql.SQLException;
import java.sql.Statement;
import java.util.*;

/**
 * Represents the database for holding texts, their lines, and words.
 */
public class TextDatabase {

  private final String schema;
```

```java
/**
 * Defines a given text base which will operate on the given schema.
 *
 * @param schema The schema to operate on; may not be {@code null}.
 */
public TextDatabase(String schema) {
  Objects.requireNonNull(schema, "schema name");
  this.schema = schema;
}


/**
 * Provides a new connection to the text database.
 */
public Connection getConnection() throws SQLException {
  return DriverManager.getConnection(
    "jdbc:h2:mem:shakespeare;INIT=CREATE SCHEMA IF NOT EXISTS " +
      schema + "\\; " +
      "SET SCHEMA " + schema + ";DB_CLOSE_DELAY=-1",
    "sa", ""
  );
}


/**
 * Creates the database, removing the schema if it previously existed.
 */
public void createDatabase() throws SQLException {
  try (Connection conn = getConnection()) {
    try (Statement stmt = conn.createStatement()) {
      stmt.execute("DROP SCHEMA " + schema);
      stmt.execute("CREATE SCHEMA " + schema);
      stmt.execute("SET SCHEMA " + schema);
    }
    TextDatabaseTextLoader.createTables(conn);
  }
}

public void insertTexts(Collection<ShakespeareText> texts)
  throws SQLException
{
  try (Connection conn = getConnection()) {
    try (
      TextDatabaseTextLoader textLoader = new TextDatabaseTextLoader(conn)
    ) {
      for (ShakespeareText text : texts) {
        textLoader.insertText(text);
      }
    }
  }
}

}
```

```
### TextDatabaseTextLoader.java
import java.sql.*;
import java.util.*;

/**
 * Responsible for loading a text.
 */
public class TextDatabaseTextLoader implements AutoCloseable {

  private final PreparedStatement createBook;
  private final TextDatabaseLineLoader lineLoader;

  public TextDatabaseTextLoader(Connection conn) throws SQLException {
    Objects.requireNonNull(conn, "connection for loading texts");
    createBook = conn.prepareStatement(
      "INSERT INTO \"text\" (name, year) VALUES (?,?)",
      Statement.RETURN_GENERATED_KEYS
    );
    lineLoader = new TextDatabaseLineLoader(conn);
  }

  /**
   * Creates the tables used for populating the text.
   *
   * @param conn The connection to use; never {@code null}
   */
  public static void createTables(final Connection conn) throws SQLException {
    Objects.requireNonNull(conn, "connection");
    try (Statement stmt = conn.createStatement()) {
      stmt.execute(
        "CREATE TABLE \"text\" " +
        "(id INT PRIMARY KEY AUTO_INCREMENT, name VARCHAR UNIQUE, year INT)"
      );
    }
    TextDatabaseLineLoader.createTables(conn);
  }

  public void insertText(ShakespeareText text) throws SQLException {
    int textId = insertTextRecord(text.getName(), text.getYear());
    for (ShakespeareLine line : text.getLines()) {
      lineLoader.insertLine(textId, line);
    }
  }

  private int insertTextRecord(String title, int year) throws SQLException {
    createBook.setString(1, title);
    createBook.setInt(2, year);
    boolean createdBook = createBook.executeUpdate() == 1;
    assert createdBook : "Could not create book";
```

```
      try (ResultSet rs = createBook.getGeneratedKeys()) {
        boolean hasNext = rs.next();
        assert hasNext : "No result when getting generated keys for " + title;
        return rs.getInt(1);
      }
    }

    public void close() throws SQLException {
      createBook.close();
      lineLoader.close();
    }

}

### TextDatabaseLineLoader.java
import java.sql.*;
import java.util.*;

/**
 * Responsible for loading lines into the database.
 */
public class TextDatabaseLineLoader implements AutoCloseable {

  private final PreparedStatement createLine;
  private final TextDatabaseWordLoader wordLoader;

  public TextDatabaseLineLoader(final Connection conn) throws SQLException {
    Objects.requireNonNull(conn, "connection");
    createLine = conn.prepareStatement(
      "INSERT INTO line (text_id, \"offset\") VALUES (?,?)",
      Statement.RETURN_GENERATED_KEYS
    );
    wordLoader = new TextDatabaseWordLoader(conn);
  }

  public static void createTables(final Connection conn) throws SQLException {
    try (Statement stmt = conn.createStatement()) {
      stmt.execute("CREATE TABLE line " +
        "(id INT PRIMARY KEY AUTO_INCREMENT, text_id INT, \"offset\" INT)"
      );
    }
    TextDatabaseWordLoader.createTables(conn);
  }

  public void insertLine(int textId, ShakespeareLine line)
    throws SQLException
  {
    int lineId = insertLineRecord(textId, line.getTextPosition());
    for (ShakespeareWord word : line.getWords()) {
      wordLoader.insertWord(lineId, word);
    }
  }
```

```java
  private int insertLineRecord(final int textId, final int textPosition)
    throws SQLException
  {
    createLine.setInt(1, textId);
    createLine.setInt(2, textPosition);
    boolean createdLine = createLine.executeUpdate() == 1;
    assert createdLine : "Could not create line";
    try (ResultSet rs = createLine.getGeneratedKeys()) {
      boolean hasNext = rs.next();
      assert hasNext :
        "No result when getting generated keys for line in text id " +
        textId + ", " + "offset " + textPosition;
      return rs.getInt(1);
    }
  }

  public void close() throws SQLException {
    createLine.close();
    wordLoader.close();
  }
}

### TextDatabaseWordLoader.java
import java.sql.*;
import java.util.*;

/**
 * Responsible for loading words into the database
 */
public class TextDatabaseWordLoader implements AutoCloseable {

  private final PreparedStatement createWord;
  private final PreparedStatement createLineWord;
  private final Map<String, Integer> wordIds = new HashMap<>();

  public TextDatabaseWordLoader(final Connection conn) throws SQLException {
    Objects.requireNonNull(conn, "connection");
    createWord = conn.prepareStatement(
     "INSERT INTO word (\"value\") VALUES (?)",
     Statement.RETURN_GENERATED_KEYS
    );
    createLineWord = conn.prepareStatement(
        "INSERT INTO line_word " +
            " (line_id, word_id, \"offset\") " +
            " VALUES (?,?,?)",
        Statement.NO_GENERATED_KEYS
    );
  }
```

```java
  public static void createTables(final Connection conn) throws SQLException {
    try (Statement stmt = conn.createStatement()) {
      stmt.execute("CREATE TABLE word " +
        "(id INT PRIMARY KEY AUTO_INCREMENT, \"value\" VARCHAR UNIQUE)"
      );
      stmt.execute("CREATE TABLE line_word " +
        "(id INT PRIMARY KEY AUTO_INCREMENT, line_id INT, word_id INT, " +
        "\"offset\" INT)"
      );
    }
  }

  public void insertWord(final int lineId, final ShakespeareWord word)
    throws SQLException
  {
    int wordId = determineWordId(word.getWord());
    createLineWord.setInt(1, lineId);
    createLineWord.setInt(2, wordId);
    createLineWord.setInt(3, word.getLinePosition());
    boolean createdLineWord = createLineWord.executeUpdate() == 1;
    assert createdLineWord : "Could not create line-word";
  }

  private int determineWordId(String word) throws SQLException {
    if(wordIds.containsKey(word)) {
      return wordIds.get(word);
    } else {
      int wordId = insertWordRecord(word);
      wordIds.put(word, wordId);
      return wordId;
    }
  }

  private int insertWordRecord(String word) throws SQLException {
    createWord.setString(1, word);
    boolean createdWord = createWord.executeUpdate() == 1;
    assert createdWord : "Could not create word: " + word;
    try(ResultSet rs = createWord.getGeneratedKeys()) {
      boolean hasWord = rs.next();
      assert hasWord : "Created word but still could not find it!";
      return rs.getInt(1);
    }
  }

  public void close() throws SQLException {
    createWord.close();
    createLineWord.close();
  }

}
```

The primary difficulty with object-oriented programming should be readily apparent: our task takes a lot of code in this paradigm, and there are a lot of interoperating parts. In the imperative code, we lost the forest in the trees: implementation details became confusing and interfered with seeing the big picture. Object-oriented programming intends to solve this problem by cleaning up the trees. The implementation details are a lot cleaner, but it is still easy to get lost. It is a common experience for a new developer to enter onto an object-oriented project and be at a loss for how the system works, especially if the system does not have an obvious entry point (such as a main method). The problem is that it is hard to follow the flow of the application: it is hard to understand how these parts all interact during the execution of the system. For instance, the word loader takes a line id, but if you were new to the system, it could easily be unclear what that line id was or how it was calculated.

This is not to say that object-oriented programming is bad. If you need a highly modular, highly decoupled system, it is the perfect paradigm. Tools like interfaces and abstract base classes allow you to provide clear contracts while still being nice to your consumers. It is also an excellent approach if you need a highly testable system: it is not a coincidence that practices such as test-driven development arose out of object-oriented languages. The testability advantage comes from the fact that functionality is entirely contained within a single object, so it is possible to treat that object as its own independent microcosm of reality. The object-oriented model also fits with concurrent execution much better than imperative or some other paradigms, since the clearer separation of concerns make for clear breakpoints. Borrowing key practices from functional programming makes object-oriented concurrency even nicer: it was this discovery that created the post-functional paradigm.

Post-Functional Programming Paradigm

Object-oriented programming was heralded as a major revolution in programming, and it did do a lot to improve the maintainability and reusability of large codebases. However, mutability became a major problem in object-oriented programming. Another common problem came from mixing data and flow: underlying the object-oriented paradigm is still the imperative paradigm, but the encapsulation of data also led to obscuring the logic that acted on that data. Both of these problems are addressed by changing the underlying model of execution from imperative to functional: that is, instead of thinking of executing a series of steps, you think about applying transformations and mappings. This gave rise to the post-functional programming paradigm.

Post-functional programming makes it much easier to reason about your object-oriented application. By strongly limiting mutability and focusing on composing small transformations, we can minimize the drawbacks in object-oriented programming while still leveraging its advantages. Technically, the post-functional paradigm gets away from the imperative paradigm, so the programmer worries about what to implement and not how it is executed. This results in more semantically meaningful code, but also frees the runtime to decide the best way to execute the transformations. The result is improved performance for little to no cost, especially when executing in a concurrent environment.

If you have read this book, then you should hopefully be able to spot post-functional code in Java. The ubiquitous use of streams and lambdas is the obvious sign. The use of the `final` keyword is another major hint, especially if that keyword is occurring in a large number of very small classes, each of which does a very limited and very precise transformation on data. Before Java 8, the key sign for post-functional Java code was collection comprehensions: methods that took in a collection and performed some user-specified operation on it.

To implement our post-functional solution, we will start by constructing our schema by executing each string in a stream of DDL statements. This will get our database into the proper format. We will then get the anthology text as a stream, and filter out the undesirable elements from that stream. Now we have a clean stream and a database initialized, so our goal will be to produce a stream of data to insert into the database. The intermediate form will be a stream of lines coming from the input. So we will go from a stream of Strings to a stream of parsed lines to a stream of words to insert into the database. That final form can then be inserted into the database. The code for this is given in Listing A-4.

Listing A-4. Post-Functional Database Loading

```
### Main.java
import java.sql.*;
import java.util.*;

public class Main {

  public static void printDatabaseSizing(Database database)
    throws SQLException
  {
    System.out.println("SIZES");
    System.out.println("-----");
    try (Connection conn = database.getConnection()) {
      Statement stmt = conn.createStatement();
      for (String table : new String[]{
        "\"text\"", "line", "word", "line_word"
      }) {
        try (ResultSet rs = stmt.executeQuery(
                           "SELECT COUNT(*) FROM " + table)
        ) {
          boolean hasNext = rs.next();
          assert hasNext : "No result in count from table " + table;
          System.out.println(table + " => " + rs.getInt(1));
        }
      }
    }
  }

  public static ResultSet queryResults(Connection conn) throws SQLException {
    return conn.createStatement().executeQuery(
        "SELECT t.name, l.\"offset\", w.\"value\", lw.\"offset\" " +
          "FROM \"text\" t, word w " +
          "INNER JOIN line l ON (t.id = l.text_id) " +
          "INNER JOIN line_word lw ON " +
          " (lw.line_id = l.id AND lw.word_id = w.id)"
    );
  }

  public static void printWordUsages(Database database) throws SQLException {
    int lineNumber = 0;
    try (Connection conn = database.getConnection()) {
      try (ResultSet rs = queryResults(conn)) {
        String lastText = null;
        int lastLine = -1;
        while (rs.next()) {
          if (lineNumber % 20 == 0) {
            System.out.println("text\tline-offset\tword\tword-offset");
            System.out.println("----\t-----------\t----\t-----------");
          }
```

```
        lineNumber += 1;
        String text = rs.getString(1);
        if (!text.equals(lastText)) {
          lastText = text;
        }
        int lineOffset = rs.getInt(2);
        String word = rs.getString(3);
        int wordOffset = rs.getInt(4);
        if (lineOffset != lastLine) {
          lastLine = lineOffset;
        }
        System.out.println(String.format(
          "%s\t%d\t%s\t%d", text, lineOffset, word, wordOffset));
      }
    }
  }
}

  public static void main(String[] args) throws Exception {
    Database database = new Database();
    database.initializeDb();

    new ShakespeareTextSource().getStream().sequential()
        .map(new TextMapper())
        .filter(Optional::isPresent).map(Optional::get)
        // In a longer example, this next line might be broken out into
        // distinct intermediate forms for providing text id, line id,
        // and word id.
        .map(new DatabaseLineMapper(database))
        .forEach(database::insertLine);

    printWordUsages(database);
    printDatabaseSizing(database);
  }

}

### Database.java
import java.sql.*;
import java.util.*;
import java.util.function.*;

/**
 * Represents that database holding the text information
 */
public class Database {

  private static final String SCHEMA = "shakespeare";
```

```java
public Connection getConnection() throws SQLException {
  return DriverManager.getConnection(
    "jdbc:h2:mem:shakespeare;INIT=CREATE SCHEMA IF NOT EXISTS " + SCHEMA
    + "\\; SET SCHEMA " + SCHEMA + ";DB_CLOSE_DELAY=-1", "sa", ""
  );
}

public void initializeDb() throws SQLException {
  try (Connection c = getConnection()) {
    try (Statement stmt = c.createStatement()) {
      BiFunction<SQLException, String, SQLException> exec = (ex, s) -> {
        // If there is an exception, return it (punt)
        if (ex != null) return ex;

        // Execute this command
        try {
          stmt.execute(s);
          return null;
        } catch (SQLException e) {
          return e;
        }
      };

      // How to manage multiple exceptions
      BinaryOperator<SQLException> pickNonnull = (e1, e2) -> {
        if (e1 == null) return e2;
        if (e2 == null) return e1;
        e1.addSuppressed(e2);
        return e1;
      };

      // Execute the statements
      SQLException e = Arrays.asList(
          "DROP SCHEMA " + SCHEMA,
          "CREATE SCHEMA " + SCHEMA,
          "SET SCHEMA " + SCHEMA,
          "CREATE TABLE \"text\" " +
            " (id INT PRIMARY KEY AUTO_INCREMENT, name VARCHAR UNIQUE, " +
            " year INT)",
          "CREATE TABLE line " +
            "(id INT PRIMARY KEY AUTO_INCREMENT, text_id INT, " +
            " \"offset\" INT)",
          "CREATE TABLE word " +
            "(id INT PRIMARY KEY AUTO_INCREMENT, " +
            " \"value\" VARCHAR UNIQUE)",
          "CREATE TABLE line_word " +
            " (id INT PRIMARY KEY AUTO_INCREMENT, line_id INT, " +
            " word_id INT, \"offset\" INT)"
      ).stream().reduce(null, exec, pickNonnull);
```

```
        // If we got an exception, explode with it
        if (e != null) throw e;
      }
    }
  }

  /**
   * Inserts a database line into the database.
   *
   * @param databaseLine The line to insert; never {@code null}.
   */
  public void insertLine(final DatabaseLine databaseLine) {
    Objects.requireNonNull(databaseLine, "database line");
    try (Connection conn = getConnection()) {
      PreparedStatement createLineWord = conn.prepareStatement(
          "INSERT INTO line_word " +
            " (line_id, word_id, \"offset\") " +
            " VALUES (?,?,?)",
          Statement.NO_GENERATED_KEYS
      );

      createLineWord.setInt(1, databaseLine.getLineId());

      int[] words = databaseLine.getWords();
      for (int i = 0; i < words.length; i++) {
        createLineWord.setInt(2, words[i]);
        createLineWord.setInt(3, i + 1);
        boolean createdLineWord = createLineWord.executeUpdate() == 1;
        assert createdLineWord : "Could not create line-word";
      }
    } catch (SQLException sqle) {
      throw new RuntimeException("error while inserting database line", sqle);
    }
  }
}

### ShakespeareTextSource.java
import java.io.BufferedReader;
import java.io.IOException;
import java.io.InputStream;
import java.io.InputStreamReader;
import java.util.concurrent.atomic.*;
import java.util.function.*;
import java.util.regex.*;
import java.util.stream.*;
```

```
/**
 * Source for a Shakespeare Text
 */
public class ShakespeareTextSource {

  private static final String SOURCE = "shakespeare.txt";

  /**
   * Provides a reader of the in-memory anthology. No filtering is performed
   * on this reader.
   *
   * @return A reader of the in-memory anthology; never {@code null}
   * @throws IOException If there is an exception retrieving the
   *                     in-memory anthology
   */
  public BufferedReader getReader() throws IOException {
    InputStream inputStream =
      this.getClass()
      .getClassLoader()
      .getResourceAsStream(SOURCE);
    return new BufferedReader(new InputStreamReader(inputStream, "UTF-8"));
  }

  private static UnaryOperator<String> filterBadChars() {
    Pattern BAD_CHARS =
      Pattern.compile("\uFEFF|\\p{Cntrl}"); // BOMs and control characters
    return string -> BAD_CHARS.matcher(string).replaceAll("");
  }

  private static Predicate<String> notInComment() {
    final Predicate<String> IS_COMMENT_START =
      Pattern.compile("^<<").asPredicate();
    final Predicate<String> IS_COMMENT_END =
      Pattern.compile(">>$").asPredicate();

    final AtomicBoolean inComment = new AtomicBoolean(false);
    return line -> {
      if (IS_COMMENT_START.test(line)) {
        inComment.set(true);
        return false;
      } else if (inComment.get() && IS_COMMENT_END.test(line)) {
        inComment.set(false);
        return false;
      } else {
        return !inComment.get();
      }
    };
  }
```

```java
  private static Predicate<String> notEmptyOrWhitespace() {
    return Pattern.compile("^\\s*$").asPredicate().negate();
  }

  /**
   * Provides a sequential stream of the text source. The stream is filtered
   * of bad characters, whitespace lines, and comments. Each line is also
   * trimmed.
   *
   * @return A stream, which must be processed sequentially
   * @throws IOException If there is an exception getting the resource
   */
  public Stream<String> getStream() throws IOException {
    return getReader().lines()
        .sequential()
        .map(filterBadChars())
        .map(String::trim)
        .filter(notEmptyOrWhitespace())
        .filter(notInComment())
        ;

  }

}

### TextLine.java
import java.util.*;

/**
 * A method representing a line in a text
 */
public class TextLine {

  private final String title;
  private final int lineNumber;
  private final String line;
  private final int year;

  public TextLine(
    final String title, final int year,
    final int lineNumber, final String line
  ) {
    Objects.requireNonNull(title, "title");
    this.title = title;

    if (lineNumber < 1) {
      throw new IllegalArgumentException(
        "Line offset must be positive, but was " + lineNumber);
    }
    this.lineNumber = lineNumber;
```

```java
    Objects.requireNonNull(line, "line");
    if (line.isEmpty()) {
      throw new IllegalArgumentException(
        "line is empty for " + title + ", line number " + lineNumber);
    }
    this.line = line;

    if (year < 1500 || year > 1699) {
      throw new IllegalArgumentException("year is egregiously off: " + year);
    }
    this.year = year;
  }

  public String getTitle() {
    return title;
  }

  public int getLineNumber() {
    return lineNumber;
  }

  public String getLine() {
    return line;
  }

  public int getYear() {
    return year;
  }

  public List<String> getWords() {
    return Arrays.asList(line.split("\\s+"));
  }
}
```

TextMapper.java

```java
import java.util.*;
import java.util.function.*;
import java.util.regex.*;

/**
 * A mapper that presumes a sequential execution through the anthology of text.
 */
public class TextMapper implements java.util.function.Function<String, Optional<TextLine>> {

  private volatile String currentTitle;
  private volatile int currentYear;
  private volatile int currentOffset = 0;
  private volatile boolean inSonnets = false;
```

```
private static final Optional<TextLine> SKIP_THIS_LINE = Optional.empty();
private static final Predicate<String> IS_YEAR =
  Pattern.compile("^1(5|6)\\d\\d$").asPredicate();
private static final Predicate<String> IS_AUTHOR =
  Pattern.compile("^by\\s+William\\s+Shakespeare$").asPredicate();
private static final Predicate<String> IS_DIGITS =
  Pattern.compile("^\\d+$").asPredicate();
private static final Predicate<String> IS_THE_END =
  Pattern.compile("^THE\\s+END$").asPredicate();
private static final String SONNETS_TITLE = "THE SONNETS";

/**
 * Creates a text line, or {@link java.util.Optional#empty()} if the
 * string does not correspond to a line.
 *
 * @param s the function argument
 * @return the function result
 */
@Override
public Optional<TextLine> apply(final String s) {
  if (s == null || s.isEmpty()) return SKIP_THIS_LINE;

  // Skip author lines
  if (IS_AUTHOR.test(s)) return SKIP_THIS_LINE;

  // Skip THE END lines, and note that it's the end of the text
  if (IS_THE_END.test(s)) {
    currentOffset = Integer.MIN_VALUE;
    currentTitle = null;
    inSonnets = false;
    return SKIP_THIS_LINE;
  }

  // If this is the year, the next line should be the title
  if (IS_YEAR.test(s)) {
    currentYear = Integer.parseInt(s);
    currentTitle = null;
    return SKIP_THIS_LINE;
  }

  // If we are looking for the title, we just found it!
  if (currentTitle == null || (inSonnets && IS_DIGITS.test(s))) {
    if (inSonnets) {
      currentTitle = "Sonnet #" + s;
    } else {
      currentTitle = s;
      inSonnets = SONNETS_TITLE.equalsIgnoreCase(s);
    }
    currentOffset = 0;
    return SKIP_THIS_LINE;
  }
```

185

```java
    // Just a normal line
    currentOffset += 1;
    return Optional.of(
      new TextLine(currentTitle, currentYear, currentOffset, s)
    );
  }
}
```

DatabaseLineMapper.java
```java
import java.sql.*;
import java.util.*;
import java.util.concurrent.*;
import java.util.function.*;

/**
 * Responsible for mapping text lines into database lines.
 */
public class DatabaseLineMapper implements Function<TextLine, DatabaseLine> {

  private final ConcurrentMap<String, Integer> textIds =
    new ConcurrentHashMap<>();
  private final ConcurrentMap<Integer, ConcurrentMap<Integer, Integer>>
    textLineIds = new ConcurrentHashMap<>();
  private final ConcurrentMap<String, Integer> wordIds =
    new ConcurrentHashMap<>();
  private final Database database;

  public DatabaseLineMapper(Database database) throws SQLException {
    Objects.requireNonNull(database, "database");
    this.database = database;
  }

  private int computeTextId(String title, int year) {
    try (Connection conn = database.getConnection()) {
      PreparedStatement createBook = conn.prepareStatement(
        "INSERT INTO \"text\" (name, year) VALUES (?,?)",
        Statement.RETURN_GENERATED_KEYS
      );
      createBook.setString(1, title);
      createBook.setInt(2, year);
      boolean createdBook = createBook.executeUpdate() == 1;
      assert createdBook : "Could not create book";
      try (ResultSet rs = createBook.getGeneratedKeys()) {
        boolean hasNext = rs.next();
        assert hasNext : "No result when getting generated keys for " + title;
        return rs.getInt(1);
      }
    } catch (SQLException e) {
      throw new RuntimeException(
        "error while computing text id for: " + title, e);
    }
  }
}
```

```java
private int computeLineId(final int textId, final int lineNumber) {
  try (Connection conn = database.getConnection()) {
    PreparedStatement createLine = conn.prepareStatement(
      "INSERT INTO line (text_id, \"offset\") VALUES (?,?)",
      Statement.RETURN_GENERATED_KEYS
    );
    createLine.setInt(1, textId);
    createLine.setInt(2, lineNumber);
    boolean createdLine = createLine.executeUpdate() == 1;
    assert createdLine : "Could not create line";
    try (ResultSet rs = createLine.getGeneratedKeys()) {
      boolean hasNext = rs.next();
      assert hasNext :
        "No result when getting generated keys for for line " + textId +
        "-" + lineNumber;
      return rs.getInt(1);
    }
  } catch (SQLException e) {
    throw new RuntimeException("error while computing line id for: "
      + textId + " - " + lineNumber, e);
  }
}

private int computeWordId(final String word) {
  try (Connection conn = database.getConnection()) {
    PreparedStatement createWord = conn.prepareStatement(
      "INSERT INTO word (\"value\") VALUES (?)",
      Statement.RETURN_GENERATED_KEYS
    );
    createWord.setString(1, word);
    boolean createdWord = createWord.executeUpdate() == 1;
    assert createdWord : "Could not create word: " + word;
    try (ResultSet rs = createWord.getGeneratedKeys()) {
      boolean hasNext = rs.next();
      assert hasNext : "Created word but still could not find it!";
      return rs.getInt(1);
    }
  } catch (SQLException e) {
    throw new RuntimeException(
      "error while computing word id for: " + word, e);
  }
}

/**
 * Applies this function to the given argument.
 *
 * @param textLine the function argument
 * @return the function result
 */
```

```
  @Override
  public DatabaseLine apply(final TextLine textLine) {
    // Get the text id
    int textId = lookupTextId(textLine);

    // Get the line id
    int lineId = lookupLineId(textId, textLine);

    // Get the word ids
    int[] words = textLine.getWords().parallelStream()
        .mapToInt(this::lookupWord)
        .toArray();

    return new DatabaseLine(lineId, words);
  }

  private int lookupWord(final String word) {
    return wordIds.computeIfAbsent(word, this::computeWordId);
  }

  private int lookupLineId(int textId, final TextLine textLine) {
    ConcurrentMap<Integer, Integer> lineIds =
      textLineIds.computeIfAbsent(textId, i -> new ConcurrentHashMap());
    return lineIds.computeIfAbsent(
      textLine.getLineNumber(),
      i -> this.computeLineId(textId, i)
    );
  }

  private int lookupTextId(final TextLine textLine) {
    return textIds.computeIfAbsent(
      textLine.getTitle(),
      s -> this.computeTextId(s, textLine.getYear())
    );
  }

}

### DatabaseLine.java
import java.util.*;

/**
 * A line of a text as understood by the database.
 */
public class DatabaseLine {
  private final int lineId;
  private final int[] words;
```

```
public DatabaseLine(final int lineId, final int[] words) {
  this.lineId = lineId;
  Objects.requireNonNull(words, "words");
  if (words.length == 0) {
    throw new IllegalArgumentException("no words in this line!");
  }
  this.words = words;
}

public int getLineId() {
  return lineId;
}

public int[] getWords() {
  return words;
}
}
```

This code accomplishes the same thing as the pure object-oriented solution, but with significantly less code and a clearer flow of processing. If you wanted to insert additional processing at some point (such as having distinct steps for looking up the text id, line id, and word id), then it is obvious where you would insert that. And the combination of object oriented and more functional models makes for more concise, readable code.

A more advanced, more parallel-friendly version of this processing could produce the texts as an object with a title, year, and a stream of lines with their offset. That object could them be mapped to a text id, and its stream of lines could be mapped in parallel into line ids, word ids, and then into the database. This would be a two-stage approach: the first stage would parse the anthology's lines into a stream of these text objects, and then the second stage would process each of these text objects and their stream of lines. That would be the natural evolution of this approach, should you need it.

There are two major drawbacks to the post-functional approach, and they both come from the fact that you have to think in terms of types, mappings between types, and hook functions like .map and .filter. The first difficulty is that this simply requires a more abstract and higher order of thinking, so you spend more time doodling on paper than writing code. There are some developers who find this very unpalatable, because they just want to keep cranking out code at the speed of thought. Another difficulty with this approach occurs when the solution does not lend itself to an element-wise solution, such as our rule about the year signaling the title. In that case, we force a sequential execution and have to work with mutable state, which reintroduces some of the issues endemic to object-oriented code.

On the other hand, if you want to write a concurrent program with a clear flow of execution that still gets the primary benefits of object-oriented code, then the post-functional paradigm is what you want. As long as your application – or even your segment of an application – has a clear flow and a clear mapping between the steps in the flow, then this is a great paradigm to use. That occurs very often, which is why the introduction of lambdas and post-functional programming in Java is so exciting. It's why this book exists.

Other Programming Paradigms

Those three paradigms – imperative, object-oriented, and post-functional – are the three that Java 8 supports nicely. However, there are many other programming paradigms out there, and it is important to know about some of the dominant ones. Learning new paradigms helps you think about problems in different ways, which means that you are better at solving your problems. Even more, however, knowing about other paradigms allows you to have conversations with developers coming from different contexts, which is how you will avoid intellectual and professional stagnation. There is a kind of stagnation that can creep into a programmer's life after a few years: familiarity and relative satisfaction with a particular set of tools can lead to the mistaken impression that those tools (and derivations from them) define the universe. If you are starting to think that way, here are some ways to shake yourself loose of that trap.

Logical/Mathematical

Most of the references to "functional programming" are referring to this paradigm. In this paradigm, the program is a set of mathematical functions, and the programmer's job is to define and manipulate the functions themselves. The data that is moving through the application is largely irrelevant: the functions are defined based on the types and shapes of that data. The particular implementation details of how these functions are applied are left to the runtime or compiler. I was introduced to the logical/mathematical paradigm through the programming language OCaml, which is a derivative of MetaLanguage (ML). If you want to see how well this approach works with concurrency, see the programming language JoCaml, which is the join calculus (i.e., fork/join) mixed with OCaml. Haskell is probably the current poster child for this paradigm, and there is a strong case to be made for Erlang, too. This paradigm also includes Mathematica and other "computer algebra systems," as well as Coq and other "interactive theorem provers."

This paradigm works very well when I/O is incidental to the work being done, and so it can be quickly abstracted out of existence. If most of your time is spent in doing heavy lifting with data defined and manipulated purely internally, then this paradigm works very well for ensuring that your code is executed quickly and safely.

Homoiconic

This is considered another form of functional programming, although it is very different from the logical/mathematical paradigm. Instead, the homoiconic paradigm draws from the mathematics of computability theory. (For the mathematically inclined, homoiconic programming is the lambda calculus as a programming language.) In the case of a homoiconic programming language, the program processs itself, performing mechanical reductions on the application until there is nothing left except the answer.

This is a very strange concept for people to wrap their head around, but it is easy to see it in action. To see it in action, start by assuming that I define this transformation:

```
For All x, Replace sq(x) With x*x.
```

Note that I am not defining a function or any kind of semantics: this is not a definition of a function. I am saying that when a particular set of characters is encountered within the program, we should replace them with a different set of characters. Now let's say that I define another couple of transformations:

```
For All f x y z, Replace map(f (x y z)) With (f(x) f(y) f(z)).
For All x y z, Replace sum(x y z) With x+y+z.
```

Again, this is a straight text replacement rule. When you see that funny "map" word followed by some parenthesis, replace it and its parenthesis with a specific set of characters. Similarly, when you see that funny "sum" word followed by some parenthesis, replace it and its parenthesis with another specific set of characters. Given that, we can have this simple program.

```
INITIAL PROGRAM > sum(map(sq (1 2 3)))
REDUCTION 1 > sum(sq(1) sq(2) sq(3))
REDUCTION 2 > sum(1*1 2*2 3*3)
REDUCTION 3 > sum(1   4   9 )
REDUCTION 4 > 1+4+9
REDUCTION 5 > 14
```

The only "execution" happening here are the arithmetic operations. Everything else in here is a simple text transformation. It may seem very strange to you, but this is actually an incredibly powerful way of doing programming. The undeniably dominant homoiconic programming language is Lisp. Macro-based languages such as (La)TeX and some pre-processors are also in this paradigm. In these languages, their power comes from the flexibility of these text transformations and the ability to redefine and manipulate them. This makes code very easy to manipulate: Lisp and (La)TeX had monkey-patching long before Ruby provided open classes and JavaScript let you define undefined. In homoiconic programs, it is no big deal if you want to redefine or manipulate any given macro. This makes homoiconic programming languages especially useful for building tools and interfaces for developers, who are prone to want to make those kinds of changes and are willing to deal with the consequences when things fail.

Declarative

This paradigm gets a lot of flak and is often dismissed, but it is also probably the most widely adopted and used programming paradigm of them all. When you hear someone say that HTML or CSS "aren't really programming languages," it is because they are dismissing the declarative paradigm. In the declarative paradigm, the programmer simply declares things as existing, and it is up the the consumer of the program to figure out what to do with it. UI programming languages are overwhelmingly declarative, as are configuration files (e.g., Spring context files), and the build scripts for good build tools. If you were around for the Aspect Oriented Programming flare-up around the turn of the 21st century, then you probably recognize Aspect Oriented Programming as a kind of declarative programming. The more contemporary interest in "optional type systems" and "annotation-driven configuration" in Java are efforts to draw the declarative paradigm more into Java.

The declarative paradigm is good for any case where you want to just create and configure many components. These components may be interrelated, or may be distinct; in any case, the components are simply declared into being. Any customization or logic for the components should be limited to configuring attributes. It is usually possible to sneak in snippets of code here or there, or to use events, callbacks, or hooks, but those are escape hatches into other paradigms, usually the imperative or reactive paradigms.

Reactive

In the reactive paradigm, the program reliquishes the driver's seat. Instead of there being a flow through the application or a function being executed, the program instead consists of event handlers. When a certain criterion is met, the event handler for that criterion is executed. Reactive programming is getting a lot of attention currently, which is drawing more attention to programming languages such as Erlang and libraries such as Akka and RxJava. The reactive programming paradigm is also common on front-end JavaScript, although it is sometimes harder to recognize there.

The advantage of reactive programming is that you do not have to worry about execution at all, which removes an entire place where bugs can arise. Furthermore, the runtime can make wild optimizations because it is given extreme freedom in determining how to execute the code. One example of this is that it is (conceptually) easy to distribute a reactive programming through a variety of other machines, which makes it very cloud friendly.

Stack-Based (Concatenative)

In a way, the stack-based paradigm is a kind of imperative. Stack-based programming is a series of instructions that are executed in order. However, the instructions all manipulate a stack: the whole program is simply manipulating the stack. This stack contains both commands and data are pushed and popped, and in this way, this makes stack-based programming more akin to homoiconic programming than traditional imperative programming. The most interesting stack-based programming language that I have encountered is Factor, which seems to be (regretably) struggling. The Java Virtual Machine bytecode is itself a stack-based programming language, as well, which makes the stack-based paradigm arguably the "native" or "natural" paradigm for the JVM ecosystem.

Post-Modern

There have been a number of efforts to create meta-commentaries and explorations of the boundaries of programming languages, which I will lump together under the heading of "post-modern." Larry Wall, the inventor of the perl programming language, famously referred to perl as "post-modern," by which he meant that you can use it in a variety of different paradigms. There have been a few other languages that have endeavored to allow you to code in any paradigm that you would like: on the JVM, Scala is of this type. It is certainly post-functional, but it also wants to allow you to code in a declarative style (see ScalaCheck), and has a number of advanced features whose primary purpose is to support "internal Domain Specific Languages" and alternative (dot-less) styles.

Beyond this strain of hyper-flexed post-modern languages, there is also the Dadaist strain of post-modern programming languages: languages that are self-referentially mock the concept of a programming language. A perfect example of these languages is Whitespace. In Whitespace, only whitespace is significant: anything that is not whitespace is treated as a comment and ignored by the compiler. The whole language is spaces, tabs, carriage returns, and other whitespace characters. Another example is Brainf#ck, which was intended to be a fully capable language with the smallest possible compiler: the result is practically impossible to use for nontrivial development. It has a, derivative, Ook!, which claims to be a programming language for orangutans.

Paradigms, Style, and Post-Functional Programming

Learning a programming language is not easy. It is almost like a hazing ritual, especially for the more esoteric programming languages. Deeply understanding a new programming language paradigm is quite literally a transformative experience. This means that people who engage in learning a new language and a new paradigm are both deeply invested and profoundly shaped by that experience. Unfortuantely, the tendency of some people – usually young men, and notably including your humble author in an earlier life – is to then form tribes and elitism around this hard-won and transformative knowledge. From experience, it is easy to do this, even inadvertantly. And, just as much from experience, let me tell you: it is a bad way to go.

It is important to remember that these tools are simply that: tools. There are times when you want one tool, and there are times when you want another. Sometimes you want a nail gun, and sometimes you want a claw hammer. The better part of wisdom is knowing when to apply each tool. Introducing post-functional programming in Java 8 is like introducing the nail gun into a world of claw hammers: for a lot of tasks, post-functional will be more efficient and do a better job. There are, however, still times when you want to use object-oriented programming: in our analogy, there are still times when you want to use the claw hammer.

You will have your own style, your own preferences, and your own sense of what is the "natural solution." Other people have their own style, preferences, and sense, too. This realization is why post-modern programming languages came into existence. Unfortunately, trying to have a single language that is everything to everyone ends up being a mess. However, there is still a lot of freedom within the context of any team's shared understanding and the boundaries of the programming language. That freedom is valuable: it is how each programmer on the team delivers their own maximal efficiency. So cherish the freedom to have a distinct style, and for others to have the same freedom.

This also opens up opportunities for experiencing new things. You should never, ever turn down the opportunity to be deeply exposed to a new way of doing things. Keep exposing yourself to it until it stops seeming freakishly strange, unnecessarily hard, or incomprehensibly silly. That is the point when you will have become a better programmer: you become better when you become broader.

Index

Get the eBook for only $10!

Now you can take the weightless companion with you anywhere, anytime. Your purchase of this book entitles you to 3 electronic versions for only $10.

This Apress title will prove so indispensible that you'll want to carry it with you everywhere, which is why we are offering the eBook in 3 formats for only $10 if you have already purchased the print book.

Convenient and fully searchable, the PDF version enables you to easily find and copy code—or perform examples by quickly toggling between instructions and applications. The MOBI format is ideal for your Kindle, while the ePUB can be utilized on a variety of mobile devices.

Go to www.apress.com/promo/tendollars to purchase your companion eBook.

All Apress eBooks are subject to copyright. All rights are reserved by the Publisher, whether the whole or part of the material is concerned, specifically the rights of translation, reprinting, reuse of illustrations, recitation, broadcasting, reproduction on microfilms or in any other physical way, and transmission or information storage and retrieval, electronic adaptation, computer software, or by similar or dissimilar methodology now known or hereafter developed. Exempted from this legal reservation are brief excerpts in connection with reviews or scholarly analysis or material supplied specifically for the purpose of being entered and executed on a computer system, for exclusive use by the purchaser of the work. Duplication of this publication or parts thereof is permitted only under the provisions of the Copyright Law of the Publisher's location, in its current version, and permission for use must always be obtained from Springer. Permissions for use may be obtained through RightsLink at the Copyright Clearance Center. Violations are liable to prosecution under the respective Copyright Law.

Get the eBook for only $10!

Now you can take the weightless companion with you
anywhere and everytime. Your purchase of this book
entitles you to 3 electronic versions for only $10.